Reason's Children

The Bucknell Studies in Eighteenth-Century Literature and Culture

The Bucknell Studies in Eighteenth-Century Literature and Culture aims to publish challenging, new eighteenth-century scholarship. Of particular interest is critical, historical, and interdisciplinary work that is interestingly and intelligently theorized, and that broadens and refines the conception of the field. At the same time, the series remains open to all theoretical perspectives and different kinds of scholarship. While the focus of the series is the literature, history, arts, and culture (including art, architecture, music, travel, and history of science, medicine, and law) of the long eighteenth century in Britain and Europe, the series is also interested in scholarship that establishes relationships with other geographies, literature, and cultures for the period 1660–1830.

Recent Titles in This Series

http://www.bucknell.edu/universitypress/

Reason's Children

Childhood in
Early Modern Philosophy

Anthony Krupp

Lewisburg
Bucknell University Press

Associated University Presses
2010 Eastpark Boulevard
Cranbury, NJ 08512

The paper used in this publication meets the requirements of the American National Standard for Permanence of Paper for Printed Library Materials Z39.48–1984.

Library of Congress Cataloging-in-Publication Data

Krupp, Anthony, 1968-
    Reason's children : childhood in early modern philosophy / Anthony Krupp.
      p. cm.
    Includes bibliographical references and index.
    ISBN 978-0-8387-5721-5 (alk. paper)
1. Children and philosophy. I. Title.

B105.C45K78 2009
305.2301—dc22

2008021403

PRINTED IN THE UNITED STATES OF AMERICA

For Sylvia Papazian Krupp,
whose infancy and toddlerhood passed as this book was written.

Contents

Acknowledgments

THANKS ARE DUE TO SEVERAL COLLEAGUES WHO GAVE ME SUBSTANTIAL feedback on one or more chapters: Traci Ardren, Adriana S. Benzaquén, Anne Cruz, Viviana Diaz-Balsera, Simon Evnine, John Fitzgerald, Ralph Heyndels, Horst Lange, Gema Perez-Sanchez, Elliott Schreiber, Maria Stampino, Frank Stringfellow, Amie Thomasson, Bridget West, Paul Wilson, and Barbara Woshinsky. Particular thanks are due to David Ellison, who read several versions of the manuscript and provided canny guidance throughout. I am indebted to John Lyon for inviting me to speak on "Damned Babies" in January 2006 at the University of Pittsburgh. I would also like to thank Risto Hilpinen for his conversational generosity in our accidental meetings and strolls. I am much obliged to Bucknell's anonymous reader, whose invaluable suggestions have improved this study.

My Bayle translation was polished according to the expert feedback of Karyn H. Anderson, David Ellison, and Barbara Woshinsky. Gabrielle Rapke assisted with Descartes's Latin, checking several quotations and translating part of a letter to Descartes. My translations from the early modern Latin of Zanchius and Baumgarten were improved by the kind assistance of Joshua Davies and Hugh Thomas. I regard my Baumgarten translation as functional, not graceful; I would like to hereby express the wish that someone well equipped to do so translate Baumgarten's *Aesthetica* into English soon.

A Max Orovitz Research Award provided financial support during the summer months of 2005. For permission to cross-list courses in the departments of History, Philosophy, and Religious Studies, and thereby test a number of ideas, I thank Guido Ruggerio, Steve Sapp, and Harvey Siegel.

A version of chapter 6 appeared as "Cultivation as Maturation," *Monatshefte* 98.4 (2006): 524–38. I would like to thank the University of Wisconsin Press for permission to reprint this material.

I am grateful for the sustained professional support of Hans Adler, Rebecca E. Biron, Rüdiger Campe, Dorothea von Mücke, Simon Richter, and above all David E. Wellbery. Their benefaction has helped sustain my scholarly sense of self.

My partner, Varsenik Papazian, provided uncountable forms of support, *sine qua non*; I owe her more than I can repay (though I will try). A small village (David and Nevart Kaminski; Maria, Maria del Carmen, and Oscar Papazian; Clara Garcia Vila; and Annik and Varsenik Wilson) assisted with child care, which allowed me to occasionally simulate the type of leisure Descartes claimed was necessary to research and write.

And thanks to Laura Mestayer Rogers for preparing the index.

Reason's Children

Introduction

WHAT ARE CHILDREN? WHAT CAN CHILDREN KNOW, AND HOW SHOULD they be taught? What do infants deserve, during and after this life, baptized or not? What obligations do children have? Can children's play count as genuinely aesthetic activity? My study considers answers to such questions in the works of five early modern philosophers: René Descartes, John Locke, Gottfried Wilhelm Leibniz, Christian Wolff, and Alexander Baumgarten. It bears emphasizing that the extent to which early modern (or any other) philosophers even considered such questions is only beginning to be uncovered. Recently, Susan M. Turner and Gareth B. Matthews edited a significant collection of papers on concepts of childhood in Socrates, Aristotle, the Stoics, Hobbes, Locke, Rousseau, Kant, Mill, Wittgenstein, Firestone, and Rawls.[1] Their opening remark eloquently expresses the concerns that motivate my own study:

> It is no overgeneralization to say that philosophers in the western tradition have not written about children in any systematic way. John Locke's *Some Thoughts on Education* and Jean-Jacques Rousseau's *Emile* are notable exceptions. Aristotle is also said to have produced a systematic work on childhood that is now long lost. But one would be hardpressed to think of anyone else. It is therefore no surprise that the attitudes philosophers in the tradition have had toward children and the various thoughts they have expressed about childhood here and there throughout their works have not been widely discussed or critically scrutinized. We aim, in this book, to begin to remedy this state of affairs.[2]

By including essays on Hobbes and Kant, this collection has augmented our understanding of early modern European philosophical discourse on childhood.[3] My study furthers this understanding by examining another four early modern philosophers neglected in the intellectual history of childhood, along with one (Locke) whose views have been distorted by omission.

When histories of childhood refer to the eighteenth century, they invariably focus on the importance of Locke and Rousseau.[4] The effect of Rousseau's 1762 *Émile* was indeed great; many of its readers came to feel that discussions of childhood before Rousseau (Locke excepted) were blind to the true nature and effective nurture of children. This gesture — the sweeping aside of all conceptions of childhood other than Locke's and Rousseau's — is repeated in many overviews of the history of childhood. But the Locke mentioned in these histories tends to be the one who wrote a pedagogical treatise and merely book one of his *Essay Concerning Human Understanding*, which amounts to less than 9 percent of that text. This is the Locke who said that the child's mind is like a blank slate upon which experience writes. But those who read beyond (and even in) book 1 can rapidly discover that many of Locke's statements on children have nothing to do with the blank slate thesis. The absence of Locke's actual views of children in the *Essay* from histories of childhood is a wrong that I have attempted here to redress. A good third of this study is devoted to the less well-known children of Locke's *Essay*. It should not occasion surprise that Locke occupies a significant portion of a study of early modern thinkers on childhood. What *should* surprise is that most of the children in Locke's *Essay* have been overlooked by histories of childhood.

In German literary criticism, several studies have identified the period "around 1800" as a turning point in the central European understanding of childhood.[5] It is fairly obvious that one could attribute such a turn to the reception of Rousseau's *Émile*, which sparked much discussion and reconsideration of children's nature and nurture. Whatever causal explanation one might give, it can be observed that the ways in which childhood was defined in central Europe changed markedly between the seventeenth and nineteenth centuries. A review of reference works spanning this period substantiates this claim nicely. In French and German encyclopedias and dictionaries from 1690 to 1775, childhood is defined as "the earliest years of man up until he has the use of reason,"[6] a period "when children have not yet attained their intellect,"[7] as an age "in which man lacks the perfect use of his bodily as well as mental powers. . . . because he has not yet come to his intellect,"[8] as "the time that transpires from birth until man has come to have the use of reason,"[9] and childish behavior refers to "the lack of intellect and reason . . . that is associated with childhood."[10] The higher cognitive faculties (namely, reason and intellect) define in all of these instances what it means to be fully human; since children lack these faculties and adults possess them, childhood per se is defined negatively, as a period of "lack," an age under the sign of "not yet." By contrast, nineteenth-century German lexica depict children as possessing qualities of their own, qualities that adults lack: "love . . . gratefulness . . . obedience . . . innocence . . . unaffectedness . . . sincerity," in an 1833 definition.[11] Such an attribution of opposed qualities can make the adult seem more deficient than the child. This and other nineteenth-century definitions suggest that within a century, the adult-centered prominence of reason in definitions of the human being had become problematic.

During the period we sometimes call the Age of Reason, children were defined as beings that have not yet attained the age of reason. For eighteenth-century lexicographers, childhood seems to be a category error. Research for this book began when I turned to rationalist philosophers as likely sources for this view of childhood. After repeatedly encountering variations on the same Locke-and-Rousseau paragraph in histories of childhood, I reflected that it makes sense that both would have developed an explicit philosophy of childhood, since both were empiricists. If one holds that knowledge is gained and formed through experience (as Locke and Rousseau did), then one's epistemology must necessarily consider infants and children, since experience begins at the latest with birth. I further hypothesized that the rationalists could not have written coherently or convincingly about childhood, and that studying what little they did write would certainly point to blind spots in their systems. I believed of early modern rationalism what Avital Ronell has posited for philosophy in general: that "in most cases [children] surpass or at least scramble the master codes of philosophical claims made on their behalf, and they elude the cognitive scanners that try to detect and classify them. Childhood constitutes a security risk for the house of philosophy. It crawls in, setting off a lot of noise."[12] According to this view, childhood is antithetical to philosophy itself. (Presumably, Ronell's view entails regarding reform efforts under the rubric of "philosophy for children" as misguided.)[13] My initial hypothesis pertained not to philosophy in general, but to rationalist philosophy in particular, which I believed would uniformly gloss over childhood mental development, about which Locke and Rousseau had so much to say. The results of my research show a more differentiated, nonuniform understanding of childhood than I expected to find in the early modern rationalists. Locke and Rousseau may have been (and will likely remain) the winners in this contest of ideas, but the losers are more interesting than one may have thought. Studying early modern rationalists on childhood allows one to better understand what was said about children in philosophy before Rousseau; it also allows us to better understand this philosophy. As intriguing as I find Ronell's claim that childhood forms a challenge for philosophy, I am also troubled by that claim's unhistorical, possibly essentialist view of both childhood and philosophy. The chapters I have written attempt to test the veracity of this claim with respect to a specific place (central and northern Europe) and time (1630–1750).

My study combines what Arthur Lovejoy, an early practitioner of intellectual history, argued should be kept separate: "In the historiography of ideas, it is the fortunes of distinct 'unit-ideas,' and their interrelations of congruity or opposition, that are to be exhibited, not the 'systems' of philosophers or schools, in which heterogeneous notions and reasonings on a variety of subjects are conjoined in a matter often determined chiefly by the peculiarities of the philosophers' temperaments."[14] My study makes the case that the unit-idea of childhood (broadly conceived, thus including infancy and adolescence) forms an integral part of the works (the systems, even) of the five philosophers I treat. Thus I share this premise with Turner and Matthews:

> If philosophers in the Western tradition had expressed no thoughts at all about childhood, then there would admittedly be nothing to remedy. But . . . it is hardly the case that these philosophers ignored childhood altogether. Remarks concerning the metaphysical, epistemological, and moral status of children, as well as the social and political status that should be accorded them, are scattered throughout their works. Such remarks might be of only sociological and historical interest if it were not for the fact that the views and attitudes they express often bear in interesting and important ways on their better known philosophical doctrines, theories, and arguments.[15]

My method in the following chapters might be described as treating such scattered remarks as archaeologists do pottery shards; careful examination of these parts can enable a conceptual reconstruction of the whole (the vase or the idea). And my findings support Turner and Matthews's claim that doing so can enrich our understanding of the more familiar aspects of these philosophers' systems. For example, one of Descartes's better known arguments is that philosophical method is designed to overcome prejudices. But it is not widely appreciated that prejudices are what they are precisely because they were formed in childhood. Although several Descartes scholars are cognizant of the general significance of childhood in his works, I believe I am the first to chart the evolution of Descartes's thinking on infants and children.

This study is devoted to bringing philosophers' ideas about children to the foreground. But it should be noted that my object of analysis is philosophy elaborated in Western Christendom. Thus, early modern theology forms a middleground concern of this study.[16] My discussion of Leibniz's 1710 *Theodicy* contrasts Jansenist and rationalist theology on the fate of infants dying unbaptized. I argue that although Leibniz was willing to explain many forms of evil as being consistent with God's optimal design of the universe, Leibniz treats the doctrine of infant damnation as an exceptional case: he rejects it as shocking to reason. But what Leibniz believed the fate of those infants to be (limbo or heaven?) remains a question: the answer I believe Leibniz had in mind differs from the answer proposed by the only other study of the subject of which I am aware. It is commonly known that many passages in Leibniz's text are responses to articles in Pierre Bayle's *Historical and Critical Dictionary*; I have found furthermore that two chapters of Bayle's *Reponse aux Questions d'un Provincial*, a text ignored in most anglophone scholarship, are crucial to Leibniz's arguments concerning infant innocence. In them, Bayle referees a debate between two major contemporary religious writers: Pierre Jurieu and Pierre Nicole. I have translated the two chapters into English to facilitate an assessment of this major intertext for Leibniz, and because they provide a glimpse into early modern theological discussions concerning infant innocence. The translation is provided as an appendix to this study.

The imbrication of philosophy and religion also informs my discussions of Locke on personal identity and species classification. Locke specialists have noted that Locke's philosophical theory of personhood is motivated by his religious beliefs concerning the Last Judgment and resurrection. But I submit that the curious role played by changelings in Locke has not been sufficiently recognized. Children in whom reason is absent, not only in infancy but beyond, seem to have troubled Locke's definition of the human being as rational in essence. Understanding one of the costs involved in his saving that definition results in a less familiar (perhaps even: less enlightened) Locke than has often been depicted.

The dualism that Descartes bequeathed to early modern rationalist philosophy entailed a view of infancy and childhood as a bodily limitation on an always already rational soul. Leibniz's monadology allowed him to explain the apparent lack of reason in childhood as resulting from a noncausal harmony of soul and body. Thus Leibniz could cheerfully regard the human soul as rational, even in cases where empirical evidence fails to support this view: in infants, the mentally impaired, changelings, and fetuses. The works of his student, Christian Wolff, generally reflect the contemporary lexicographical view of the child as "not yet" reasonable. Wolff's orientation is evident just from a review of the titles of his works: seven of them are called *Reasonable Thoughts on . . . .* Nevertheless, Wolff did attempt to explain the lack of rationality in childhood and depict the transition into rationality during maturation. Indeed, Wolff appears to be the first early modern rationalist to write extensively about educating children. However, his pedagogy largely amounts to encouragement to accelerate the maturation process. Wolff's particular rationalism places children in paradoxical positions. For example, young children lack the faculty that would allow them to display "childlike fear." Children should learn to "notice" things, but Wolff would have them learn this ability "without noticing." In fact, Wolff's statements on childhood not only intersect with central concerns of his philosophy (psychology, ethics, politics), they also form willy-nilly some of the most interesting passages in his oeuvre.

Descartes's dualism involved a hierarchy: mind over body, reason over sensation. In the German lands, Wolff did the most to systematically apply this hierarchy to discussions of maturation. Wolff's student, Baumgarten, may have intended to expand Wolffian rationalism, but in doing so he made the hierarchy questionable. Whereas one of reason's tasks (in Descartes and in Wolff) had been to turn away from, control, or suppress the senses, Baumgarten not only stated that reason should "regulate, but not tyrannize" the senses, he also treated sensation as a legitimate kind of knowing, rather than as a hindrance to knowing. Baumgarten's bestowal of philosophical dignity upon the formerly "inferior" faculties is a familiar footnote (if not chapter) in the history of philosophy. But it is not yet widely known that Baumgarten's reevaluation of rationalism begins with the identification of improvisation and play in infancy and childhood as a model for all aesthetic activity. Although Baumgarten uses the terminology of Wolff's rational psychology, his 1750 *Aesthetica* opens with a foray into a protodevelopmental psychology, which began to emerge as a discipline some thirty years later. In defining his field as the study of sensate cognition, viewed as the "analogue of reason," the father of philosophical aesthetics thereby drew attention to reason's childhood.

Anglophone students of the history of philosophy will want no justification for my presenting readings of Descartes, Locke, or Leibniz:

these are major figures whose works have been translated into English, and the first two are widely taught in college and university courses. My chapters on Wolff and Baumgarten will likely present new material to this readership. Thus it should be underscored that anyone with an interest in Kant can profit from learning about Wolff and Baumgarten. After all, German philosophical discourse before Kant's critical project began to appear was largely, if not totally, dominated by the Wolffian paradigm. And the simple fact that Baumgarten invented the noun form of the word *aesthetics* should justify the energy spent reading about him. But I believe these authors deserve attention in their own right, not only insofar as they do or do not anticipate Kant or Rousseau.

The twentieth century may not have been the century of the child, as Ellen Key had predicted, but its latter third saw the emergence and rapid development of a subfield of family history: the history of childhood. Although Philippe Ariès[17] was not the first scholar to regard childhood as an object of historical inquiry—Jan Hendrik van den Berg[18] published a sort of psychohistory of childhood in 1956, and Boas's 1966 study[19] grew out of his prior collaboration with Lovejoy—Ariès must be credited with inspiring social and then other sorts of historians to consider the depiction and treatment of children in the past. Classicists, medievalists, early modernists, modernists, and scholars of the contemporary world have all reacted to (and increasingly against) Ariès's claim that *le sentiment de l'enfance* (the idea or awareness of childhood) in the West is a rather recent, postmedieval invention.[20] I take as granted that this claim, so worded, is mistaken; medievalists in particular have demonstrated amply that Europe, and other locales, did very well have ideas about childhood. But as the best scholarship also demonstrates, ideas of childhood in past ages happen to differ significantly from contemporary ones.[21] How one evaluates this fact is another question. In some progressive narratives, past deviations from the truths held in the present to be self-evident must be regarded as errors. Lloyd de Mause, for example, regards the history of childhood as a nightmare from which we have just begun to awaken.[22] For de Mause, History evolves from worse to better; conversely, Ariès believed that history has devolved from better to worse, that children had more freedom in the medieval period than they have had since then, trapped as they now are in the prison of love that is the nuclear family. More careful scholars, such as James Schultz, observe the difference of past childhood concepts from those of the present, but refrain from interpreting this difference

through a truth/error distinction. These scholars hold that studying unfamiliar ideas can have the salutary effect of enabling one to question familiar dominant ideas. Engaging in intellectual history can entail becoming "an amateur philosopher."[23]

Like it or not, historians of concepts of childhood seem to orient their
narratives according to their philosophical commitments. In the inaugu-
ral volume of a new book series, *Ashgate Studies in Childhood, 1700 to the
Present*, Anja Müller casts "radical constructivism and historical essentialism" as the Scylla and Charybdis that threaten historical scholarship
on childhood.[24] As Müller depicts it, some scholars approach their task
with a preconceived idea of the truth of childhood, and thus fail to understand the coherence of past ways of viewing childhood. Other scholars regard childhood as a blank screen onto which adult fantasies, desires and needs can project almost anything. For the latter group, there
is no *truth* of childhood, except that it is a concept that is malleable for
various ideologies. Having identified these twin dangers, Müller offers
the only reasonable suggestion one can offer: to chart a middle path between them. But although Müller cites several studies that go wrong in
one or the other direction, it seems to me that neither premise poses a
necessary threat to historical knowledge; I would like to argue this point
by instancing both -isms in two historical studies I admire. When Turner
and Matthews speak of "false opinions"[25] about the potentialities of children, they imply that they possess true opinions about these potentialities, for example that children are capable of genuine philosophical
thinking. These opinions impel their activism on behalf of these children
who, unlike women and people of color, are not "in position to mount
any social or political resistance to the systematic misevaluation of their
potentialities and their worth."[26] Reasonable people will likely agree that
common beliefs can benefit from critical inquiry, but not all reasonable
people will agree that a minority of adults possesses the correct evaluation and the right opinions, in contradistinction to a society that systematically misevaluates the truth of childhood. While I believe that introducing philosophy into grade-school curricula sounds like a fine idea, I
am unsure whether I agree with Turner and Matthews on the essence of
children. My stance might be described as skeptical; what do *I* know
about children? But rather than trying to answer Montaigne's question
(also his motto: *Que scais-je?*), I have endeavored here to understand
what five philosophers believed they knew about childhood three centuries ago, just as the essays of Turner and Matthews's volume do. Such
an exercise brings with it, as a silent constant companion, the question:

what do *we* know about childhood? I agree with Schultz that examining what we have believed about childhood in the past might help us reflect on what we believe now.

Are children what we make of them? A social constructionist would likely answer this question affirmatively. Schultz eloquently describes how such a view of childhood can assist in the study of cultures. Schultz concedes to essentialism that there are some universal, biological facts, such as that children must be fed if they are to grow. But this nude fact never seems to find expression without cultural clothing. "In the Middle Ages nursing children were understood to imbibe the attributes of their nurse's character and lineage along with their milk."[27] Around 1900, Freud understood that infants derived a sensual satisfaction from nursing, and that later sexual experiences would depend upon this earlier one. Around 2000, Schultz notes, we are more likely to understand nursing in terms of forming trust between child and adult. It is because one could object—rightly, I believe—that the medievals were wrong about imbibing lineage that I used the verb "understand" rather than "know" in the previous sentences.[28] My scholarly interest lies here not with propositions, which are true or false, but rather with ideas, which simply are. In this respect, I follow Locke, who regards ideas as objects of understanding; knowledge is a separate question. To continue with Schultz: "The fact that children must be nursed acquires meaning in the context of a medieval belief that mothers' milk is a form of blood that transmits attributes, a turn-of-the-century theory of psycho-sexual development, and a contemporary American concern for the quality of personal attachments."[29] Studying claims about the *meaning* of feeding children (independent of nutritional *facts*) can instruct us about the persons or cultures that make these claims. In constructionist scholarship, "childhood" is treated not as a natural object to be described in terms of facts, propositions, and knowledge, but rather as a cultural object, a discursive regularity or meaningful idea that makes up a part of any human culture's self-understanding.

No particular prior belief about children's essence or social constructedness is required for the reader to profit from this study. If my book seems more congenial to constructionism than to essentialism, this is primarily because I have studied ideas about children, rather than actual children. I do not examine how families were organized, nor do I trace how the ideas of the luminaries I examine may have affected the care of children, including their own. (While writing this study, I have occasionally been asked about the "actual childhoods" and "actual children" of these philosophers. Regarding their childhoods, we have either their own words, which are quite sparing, or else possible reconstructions. Several remarks on these philosophers' children, while not directly relevant to my study, may be consulted by the curious at this note.)[30] Such an examination of the impact their ideas had on education would indeed be valuable, but it seems to me that a statement made nearly fifty years ago about American Studies rings true for a study of childhood in the early modern period: "To understand the encounter of ideas with action in a massive way, we need a systematic view of the ideas."[31] My study attempts to explore the importance of ideas of childhood in the works (even: systems) of early modern, mostly rationalist philosophers. Just as Schultz isolates a fact about children and food in order to then focus on how that fact is interpreted ("understood") in different times and places, I begin with what I shall hazard to call the fact—so often emphasized in eighteenth-century lexica—that young children do not display the use of rationality. The main subject of my book is how this fact is managed in several instances of early modern European philosophy.

Although the chapters are arranged in chronological order, the unity of this study is not to be found in an overarching narrative subtending the specific stories I tell. Such narratives are certainly available within childhood studies. For example, de Mause believes that all human history *is*, sadly, the history of child abuse. (Thus, he has argued that the Holocaust occurred due to Germans having been raised cruelly.)[32] But, happily, this history is also progressive. In de Mause's view, human history divides into six stages of increasingly better treatment of children. The final "helping" phase begins in the mid-twentieth century, roughly coinciding with the birth of de Mause's own son.[33] In my view, it is difficult not to view de Mause as belonging to the history of false messiahs. De Mause seems to believe that children have always been the same and have always had the same needs; historical change pertains only to the ways adults succeed or fail in meeting those needs. Against such crude teleology, Müller praises recent work in social history precisely for not falling prey to History: "The great narrative of childhood, with its implications of universal concepts, is gradually being replaced for a localized view which emphasizes the variety of childhood concepts depending on particular historical, social, cultural or economic contexts."[34] I agree with Müller on the imperative to localize, though I aim to analyze neither European culture nor its subcultures (Dutch, Prussian, etc.). Rather, I focus on philosophers (writing in British, Dutch, French, and

German lands in the languages of English, French, German, and Latin) whose ideas circulated (and in some cases still circulate) in European and other cultures. I would be glad if my readers found themselves in a better position to assess these cultures, their (mis)evaluations of childhood, and their claims about children's nature and nurture. But most immediately, this book aims to sensitize its readers to the systematic importance of childhood in early modern philosophy, even (especially) where this importance is expressed not through explicit thematization, but rather in a complication of discourse.

This study is a contribution to intellectual history, but I have avoided trying to write *a* history. Instead, I have several different, if connected, histories to tell: how Pierre Gassendi and Antoine Arnauld served as catalysts for Descartes to revise his prior ideas about childhood; how Locke populated his *Essay* with several kinds of children, thereby helping Leibniz become conscious of childhood as a philosophical issue; how Wolff attempted to think reasonable thoughts about unreasonable creatures; how Baumgarten unintentionally undermined Wolffian thought with his attention to childhood play and improvisation; and how the contributions of Leibniz and Baumgarten may have influenced German conceptualizations of childhood after Rousseau, from Kant to kindergarten.

1

Descartes:
Purging the Mind of Childish Ways

"When I was a child, I used to speak like a child, think
like a child, reason like a child; when I became a man,
I did away with [katērgika] childish things."
—Paul, 1 Corinthians 13:11 (New American Standard Bible)

PAUL SPEAKS OF HIS OWN MATURATION IN ORDER TO CONTRAST THE
mortal human state, where our knowledge is partial, with the afterlife,
where we will see God face to face and our knowledge will be complete.
Thus talking, thinking, and reasoning as a child signifies doing these
things defectively.[1] Becoming a man entails becoming free of the defects
of childhood. In rendering katērgika as "put away," "put aside," or "left
behind," several English renderings mischaracterize this action as something rather harmless (like putting away one's toys); the original Greek
term means "cause to be idle . . . make of no effect . . . mak[e] null . . .
cancel."[2] The Latin Vulgate translation of katērgika as evacuavi has even
more forceful connotations: "to weaken, to abolish, to destroy, to
annul,"[3] or "to purge, evacuate (the bowels)."[4] Descartes's understanding of childhood as a cognitive deficiency to be overcome may have
found inspiration in Augustine, as well as in Paul. In his study on the
Trinity, Augustine writes about the human mind, but expressly omits
consideration of the infant mind. After all, this age "cannot be questioned about what goes on within it, and which we ourselves have forgotten to a great extent."[5] The infant mind is a black box. Nonetheless,
Augustine asserts that the adult mind, which knows something, "shudders [exhorreat]" at the darkness of the infant's mind, "which is sub-
merged in vast ignorance."[6] Descartes seems to share Augustine's hor-
ror, and I suspect that he would have been more than happy to leave

24

infancy aside, had it not been for several interlocutors (Gassendi, Arnauld, and others) who insisted on asking him questions about infant cognition.

Henri Gouhier has drawn attention to parallels between Descartes and Christian writings on childhood.[7] According to the Cardinal of Bérulle, for example, Jesus humbled himself less through his death than through his birth: by appearing in the world as a mere infant. As Gouhier argues, Descartes transforms this Christian meditation on the incarnation of God as a child into a reflection on the incarnation of the human soul. It is of course a classic notion that the imprisonment of the soul (or mind) in the body is the scandal of the human condition, but "in Plato's view, it is that humanity is an exile of the soul; in Descartes's view, it is that the human being starts by being a child."[8] Descartes agrees with many Church fathers that infancy is "the most vile and abject state of human nature,"[9] but Descartes's focus is epistemological rather than moral: the survival of the child in the adult is the source of attachment to old opinions, an attachment that hinders one from accepting the claims of reason. For Descartes, childish sensualism is the principal obstacle to an accurate physics. The intellect can later begin to rectify the epistemological errors of youth, but because this faculty develops late, many false beliefs accumulate in the meantime. For this reason, a radical cure seems necessary to clear the ground for one's (now) pure reason to begin rebuilding a clear and distinct understanding of the world. In Gouhier's estimation, Descartes's method of radical doubt is analogous to a Pauline conversion experience, in which the old self (for Christians, the sinner; for Descartes, the child) is killed, replaced by a new self (for Christians, the convert; for Descartes, the adult). The Cartesian "therapy against infantilism"[10] requires a shock treatment: "we must precisely note the radical character of the cure: it is a matter of asphyxiating the infant who survived in the mature man; this is less a childbirth, according to Socratic metaphor, than an infanticide."[11] As should be clear by now, Gouhier's assessment of Descartes recalls Paul's sense of maturation as a purgation or a voiding of childish things.[12]

Daniel Garber's depiction of this therapy is less dramatic, and I believe ultimately more accurate, than Gouhier's.[13] Many scholars have regarded Descartes's method of radical doubt as intended to provide a corrective to skepticism. True though this be, Garber's study shows that another important target of Descartes's critique is Aristotelian science. It is specifically in Descartes's description of *common sense* that Garber discerns aspects of Aristotelianism. What Descartes presents as the individual faulty judgments of childhood amount, in fact, to judgments from what one might call the childhood of philosophy: "the common-sense worldview and the Scholastic metaphysics it gives rise to is a con-sequence of one of the universal afflictions of humankind: childhood."[14] But Garber argues that Descartes does not simply jettison common sense (or, in Gouhier's terms, kill the child). In the end, Descartes seeks to "find what is right in common sense and show how at least some of our youthful convictions can find their place in the Cartesian system."[15] That is, "the convictions of youth, unceremoniously shuffled out in med-itation 1, now [in meditation 6] return, properly tamed by reason."[16] Thus a bad (childish, Aristotelian) method may result in a good belief. But we cannot trust these beliefs until a good (adult, Cartesian) method is installed. The senses and imagination, which were dominant in child-hood, do remain part of a mature epistemology, but only when reason has attained its proper sovereign place. Thus the Cartesian project is a matter not of infanticide but rather of deposing the infant ruler in favor of mature reason: "it is this project, the dethroning of the senses that, from our earliest years, ruled the mind, and the elevation of reason, the rightful sovereign of the intellect, which must be undertaken, once in life."[17] As any reader of Descartes knows, the power vacuum that ensues when one begins to meditate is formidable. As I discuss in this chapter, it is first and foremost the sway of one's epistemological inner child that is made void when the mature (true) certainty of cognition replaces the former immature (false) certainty of sensation.

In most of Descartes's writings, infancy and childhood are discussed only in passing. This chapter brings these passages together in order to reconstruct Descartes's views on prematurity. As a way of gathering ev-idence, and in order to allow the reader to see the various contexts in which Descartes discusses childhood, I quote extensively from Descartes's writings: works he published; those he wrote in full or in part, but left unpublished; and letters he wrote to other philosophers. Although I cite English translations, I also insert original Latin or French terms (in italics and in brackets) when they make a difference to my discussion. To highlight one important issue, which I have not seen discussed in any of the scholarship on Descartes: reading translations into English, one may think that Descartes speaks now of "infancy," now of "childhood," but this difference is almost always a matter of translating from Latin vs. French texts. I submit that *infantia* and *enfance* usually denote the same age of life for Descartes. Context, rather than the original term, indicates (sometimes) whether we are dealing with a fetus, newborn, baby, toddler, or "child." I will thus occasionally use terms like "prematurity" where Descartes seems not to make such fine distinctions. Otherwise, I will use "childhood" as a blanket term to refer to pre-adult states.

Proceeding chronologically, I have discerned four stages of Descartes's thinking on infants and children. First, in his writings up to 1641, he dropped isolated comments connecting childhood to epistemological deficiency; the theory behind these comments was completely implicit. Second, in his *Replies* of 1641 and 1642 to various objections to his *Meditations*, Descartes explicated his views on infants' and children's cognition. Several contradictory explanations he provided indicate that Descartes was unsure whether the body, the mind, or their union best explained childhood cognitive deficiency. Third, the clarifications he made through these debates proved useful in his next publication, the 1644 *Principles of Philosophy*, which contains one of his most differentiated presentations of the premature judgments made by the immature mind. In this text, he identifies the immersion of the mind in the body during childhood as the primary source of epistemological error. It seems that *pre*judices and *pre*conceptions are defective precisely because they were formed *pre*maturely, in infancy or childhood. (This last sentence is intended not to be frivolous, but rather to alert the reader to the high frequency with which Descartes uses terms with the prefix *pre-* when he discusses infancy and childhood.) Correct judgments and good concepts can only be formed at a mature age, in adulthood. Attaining certain knowledge, which is the goal of Descartes's philosophy, must therefore presuppose overcoming childish habits of cognition. Fourth, in his late correspondence, Descartes returns to several unresolved issues concerning cognition in childhood, infancy, and in utero. In attempting to find the reasons for children's cognitive deficits, Descartes is ultimately unsure how much to blame the young brain, how much the young mind, how much their union. In the end, Descartes's dualism creates trouble for his philosophy of childhood.[18]

One problem with this chronological treatment deserves comment: the date of composition for Descartes's *The Search for Truth* is a matter of conjecture. This incomplete text, arranged as a conversation between three friends, displays clearly what I regard as a crucial tension in Descartes's thought, namely the tension between the imperative: "We *must* begin with the rational soul" (CSM 2:405; my emphasis) and the observation that we *actually* begin life as less than rational beings.[19] The "good man" whose intellectual progress Descartes charts in this text

"came into the world in ignorance, and since the knowledge which he
had as a child was based solely on the weak foundation of the senses and
the authority of his teachers, it was virtually inevitable that his imagination should be filled with innumerable false thoughts before reason
could guide his conduct" (CSM 2:400). The Aristotelian character, Epis-
temon, concurs that our early education is faulty, and compares

> the imagination of a child to a *tabula rasa* on which our ideas are to be
> traced. . . . Our senses, inclinations, teachers and intellect are the differ-
> ent artists who may work at this task, and among them the least compe-
> tent are the first to take part, namely our imperfect senses, blind instincts
> and foolish nurses. The most competent is the intellect, which comes last;
> and it must serve an apprenticeship of many years, following the exam-
> ple of its masters for a long time before daring to correct any of their er-
> rors. In my opinion, this is one of the chief causes of the difficulties we
> have in acquiring knowledge. For our senses see nothing beyond the
> more coarse and ordinary things and our natural inclinations are entirely
> corrupt; and as to our teachers, although undoubtedly you might find
> very perfect ones among them, they cannot force our judgement to ac-
> cept their reasonings until our intellect has done the work (which only it
> can do) of examining them. But the intellect is like an excellent painter
> who is called upon to put the finishing touches to a bad picture sketched
> out by a young apprentice. It would be futile for him to employ the rules
> of his art in correcting the picture little by little, a bit here and a bit there,
> and in adding with his own hand all that is lacking in it, if, despite his
> best efforts, he could never remove every major fault, since the drawing
> was badly sketched from the beginning, the figures badly placed, and the
> proportions badly observed. (CSM 2:406)

His interlocutor, Eudoxus, replies that the only true corrective measure
is to wipe the apprentice's picture away with a sponge, and have the
painter (the intellect) start over. In the same passage, Eudoxus switches
to the metaphor used in *Meditations*, that of the badly constructed house
that one should demolish and rebuild from scratch, once one is of sufficient maturity that intellect can lead the rebuilding.

The saying that "life begins at forty," if we lower the age to about
thirty-one, aptly expresses Descartes's ideas and ideals concerning the
life of the mind. Before this "life" begins, one is cluttered with prejudice
and dependent on conversation, books, and masters. And the younger
one is, the more the mind is dependent upon the body, trapped and immersed within it. Descartes's ideal of cognitive autonomy corresponds
precisely to his antipathy toward childhood, infancy, and life in utero.

An implicit theory of prematurity:
Rules, *The World*, *Discourse*, and *Meditations*

Early on, Descartes blames flawed knowledge on the defects of child-hood. Rule 13 of *Rules for the Direction of the Mind*, a project begun in or before 1628, contains a question concerning our knowledge of the mo-tion of the stars, along with this answer: "we must not freely assume, as the ancients did, that the earth is motionless and fixed at the center of the universe, just because from our infancy [*ab infantiâ*] that is how it appeared to us to be. That assumption should be called in doubt so that we may then consider what in the way of certainty our judgment may at-tain on this matter" (CSM 1:55, AT 10:436). In *The World*, written in 1629 but left unpublished during his lifetime, Descartes wants to exam-ine "why air, although it too is a body, cannot be perceived by the senses as well as other bodies. In this way we shall free ourselves from an error that has gripped all of us since our childhood [*dont nous avons tous esté préoccupez dés nostre enfance*], when we came to believe that there are no bodies around us except those capable of being perceived by the senses" (CSM 1:85, AT 11:17). According to these two quotes, we make erro-neous judgments either in childhood, or in adulthood but based on how things appeared to us in childhood. In either case, childhood is to blame for false beliefs, which we acquire through overreliance upon appear-ances and the senses. Because this childish overreliance will be tem-pered in a Cartesian adulthood, Descartes refers to the judgments made in childhood as "premature." Prejudices, a main target of the Enlighten-ment since Descartes, are possible because we once judged as children. By calling our assumptions into doubt, mistrusting appearances, and turning away from the senses, we can attempt to "free ourselves" (ibid.) from captivity, that is, from the deficient knowledge of infancy and childhood.

The 1637 *Discourse on the Method*, which narrates such a self-libera-tion, names two further sources of faulty knowledge: knowledge via au-thority and custom. "From my childhood [*dés mon enfance*] I was nour-ished upon letters" (CSM 1:112, AT 6:4). Descartes had been led to believe he could find certain knowledge through erudition, but the more he learned, the more he felt that his epistemological foundations were shaky. Thus he abandoned his books "as soon as I was old enough [*sitost que l'aage me permit*] to emerge from the control of my teachers" (CSM 1:115, AT 6:9). This gesture of adolescent protest took him out of the study and into the world, where he spent "the rest of [his] youth [*je-*

unesse] traveling" (CSM 1:115, AT 6:9) and conversing. But the multitude of customs he observed ultimately left him feeling no more secure about laying foundations for certain knowledge; conversations with men of the world, while a practical corrective to the scholastic lifestyle, finally seemed insufficient: "I resolved one day to undertake studies within myself too" (CSM 1:116). By turning away from the books of his childhood and by turning away from customs (both those of his own country and those encountered during the travels of his youth), Descartes could at least avoid further sources of faulty knowledge. As will become clear in *Meditations*, the "studies within oneself" would provide the only means of gaining certain knowledge.

But at age twenty-three, Descartes was not yet mature enough to meditate. Nonetheless, his studies within himself commenced during his youth, on November 10, 1619, when Descartes found himself "alone [*seul*]" (CSM 1:116, AT 6:11) in a stove-heated room, either near Ulm or in the principality of Neuburg.[20] What began in that room might be described as the initial recognition that his knowledge was "cluttered." Nine years later, at the end of his youth, he could begin the actual "demolition work" prerequisite to laying a new, firm foundation and reconstructing his "house," that is to say, his way of thinking. But he had to generate a construction plan before engaging in such demolition. Descartes expresses three related preferences, namely for (1) houses constructed according to the viewpoint of "a single architect [*un seul*]" (CSM 1:116, AT 6:11), vs. those planned by multiple craftsmen, (2) cities laid out on level ground by planners, vs. those which evolved from villages to towns, and (3) law codes drafted at once by a wise legislator, vs. those cobbled together by a group as it slowly becomes civilized. In each case, Descartes prefers methodical, rational order to accidental, historical accumulation. Clearly, he regards his own education as just such an accumulation: the erudition of his childhood is like a jumbled city, or a badly built house, put together by his various teachers. As a twenty-three-year old youth, Descartes was able to recognize the jumble, but he was limited in his ability to begin cleaning it up; he had not yet become that ideal solitary architect of "a more mature [*bien plus meur*] age" (CSM 1:122, AT 6:22), one who could rationally rebuild.[21] Of all the sciences, it seemed that only mathematics could offer him some certainty, so he spent several months solving algebraic problems, in order to exercise his mental powers. Near the conclusion of part 2, Descartes uncharacteristically uses a child to exemplify epistemic success: "if a child [*un enfant*] who has been taught arithmetic does a sum following the rules, he can be sure of having found everything the human mind can discover regarding the sum he was considering" (CSM 1:121, AT 6:21). Descartes is not celebrating childhood cognition here; he is trying to show that mathematics must be the most secure basis for a philosophical method, if it can lead *even* a child into certain knowledge. But this is a highly preliminary stage of certainty. In the next paragraph, which concludes part 2, Descartes recognizes that he should establish certain principles in philosophy, but also that he was not yet mature enough to do so. This youth was no longer the child with a basic math problem, but nor was he yet the adult architect.

During the nine years between the epiphany in Ulm or Neuburg and the meditations in Holland, Descartes still believed he might be able to uproot his wrong opinions by conversing with people during his travels. In part 3 of the *Discourse*, he reports having had limited success with this method, but he also insists that his philosophical maturity truly began with the meditations described in part 4, meditations that were possible only at age thirty-one in Holland, where he was able to lead a life "as solitary and withdrawn as if I were in the most remote desert" (CSM 1:126).[22] The end of his gregarious travels (also the end of his youth) mark the beginning of maturity.[23]

Meditation appears to be the only sure way of ridding oneself of the prejudices and false opinions acquired since childhood. In the 1641 *Meditations*, Descartes only mentions childhood twice, in both instances reiterating beliefs previously expressed in the texts discussed above. The very first sentence of *Meditations* (rendered as three sentences in this English translation) highlights Descartes's assessment of childhood as the source of uncertainty:

> Some years ago I was struck by the large number of falsehoods that I had accepted as true in my childhood [*ineunte ætate*], and by the highly doubtful nature of the whole edifice that I had subsequently based on them. I realized that it was necessary, once in the course of my life, to demolish everything completely and start again right from the foundations if I wanted to establish anything at all in the sciences that was stable and likely to last. But the task looked an enormous one, and I began to wait until I should reach a mature enough age [*eamque ætatem expectabam, quæ foret tam matura*] to ensure that no subsequent time of life would be more suitable for tackling such inquiries. (CSM 2:12, AT 7:17)

Descartes's "skeptical therapy"[24] begins with his holding suspect all knowledge gained from the senses, which predominated his apprehension of truths in his childhood and youth. This immature (or premature) manner of acquiring knowledge is to be replaced, starting "today" (CSM 2:12), with a method that has a better foundation. But the way to laying this foundation must begin by wrecking the old, badly constructed house. This means that one must return to one's opinions, acquired since childhood, in order to review them with one's erstwhile mature mind. The more Descartes can then get used to "leading [his] mind away from the senses" (CSM 2:37), the more he can develop a rational foundation for the search for certain truth. This new habit leads Descartes away from his childhood cognitive habits, so much so that childhood is mentioned again only in the sixth and final meditation: "I have simply made this judgement from childhood onwards [*ab ineunte ætate*] without any rational basis" (CSM 2:57, AT 7:83). In *Meditations*, childhood signifies above all the lack of rational basis, the absence of reason. No wonder, then, that this rationalist philosopher had so little to say about childhood thus far.

With so few words dropped on the subject in *Meditations*, one might be surprised to learn that infancy and childhood became a topic of debate in the *Objections* of various thinkers and in Descartes's *Replies*. (Six sets of each were published along with the text of *Meditations* in 1641; the 1642 edition included a seventh set.) Since much of this controversy centered on the third meditation, a summary thereof seems warranted: although it is entitled "the existence of God" (CSM 2:24), it could just as well have been entitled "concerning ideas." Early on, Descartes makes a distinction that has been part of "nature vs. nurture" debates ever since: "Among my ideas, some appear to be innate, some to be adventitious, and others to have been invented by me" (CSM 2:26). After considering the nature of ideas over fifteen paragraphs (in which we learn that the cause of ideas is not from physical things existing outside of us, as we had thought since infancy; that ideas appear to come from within, but are not controlled by our wills; that the idea of God must, though, have derived only from within us; that God therefore exists, and thus we are not alone in the world), Descartes turns to the idea of substance, his own in particular, and considers several candidates for the first cause of his substance: himself, his parents, God, and other causes less perfect than God. The last suggestion is quickly refuted, for there cannot be less reality in the cause than in the effect, he argues. He asks whether he could maintain his existence on his own, or whether his parents conserve his existence. Both suggestions are refuted: he is not a self-causing agent, and his parents not only did not make his mind, they also did not shape it through any sort of instruction. Rather, they did nothing more than place "certain dispositions in the matter which I have always regarded as containing me, or rather my mind, for that is all I now take myself to be" (CSM 2:35).[25] Descartes may owe something of his body to his parents, but his mind is completely independent of biological parent-child relations: his mind owes its existence and conservation solely to God. The idea of God, he continues, cannot have come from the senses, and cannot have been fashioned only by himself, so he concludes that his idea of God is innate in him, as is his idea of himself. When several of his first readers contested the notion of innate ideas or asked for further clarification, Descartes began to write more extensively about the infant's mind than he ever had previously.

EXPLICATING THE THEORY:
OBJECTIONS AND *REPLIES*

Antoine Arnauld was the first to argue with Descartes about the premature mind. In the fourth set of objections, Arnauld noted: "The power of thought appears to be attached to bodily organs, since it can be regarded as dormant in infants [*in infantibus sopita*] and extinguished in the case of madmen. And this is an objection strongly pressed by those impious people who try to do away with the soul" (CSM 2:143, AT 7:204). Descartes, who arguably tries to do no such thing, makes a distinction that detaches thought from the body: "The fact that thought is often impeded by bodily organs, as we know from our own frequent experience, does not at all entail that it is produced by those organs" (CSM 2:160).[26] In the *Replies*, as I show below, Descartes comes to articulate a coherent view of infancy and childhood as precisely a physical impediment to the essentially unphysical activity of thought.

In order to argue that the mind may not be aware of all of its contents, Arnauld considers the mental life of a fetus:

> The author lays it down as certain that there can be nothing in him, in so far as he is a thinking thing [*res cogitans*], of which he is not aware [*conscius*], but it seems to me that this is false. For by 'himself, in so far as he is a thinking thing', he means simply his mind [*mentem suam*], in so far as it is distinct from the body. But all of us can surely see that there may be many things in our mind of which the mind is not aware [*mens conscia non sit*]. The mind of an infant in its mother's womb has the power of thought, but is not aware of it. [*Mens infantis in matris utero habet vim cogitandi; at ejus conscia non est.*] (CSM 2:150, AT 7:214)

In rebutting Arnauld, Descartes had to give a counter-explanation of fetal mental life. To rescue the tight fit he had posited between cognition and awareness, Descartes had to bring in a third term, namely memory: "I do not doubt that the mind begins to think as soon as it is implanted in the body of an infant [*statim atque infantis corpori infusa est*], and that it is immediately aware of its thoughts, even though it does not remember this afterwards because the impressions [*species*] of these thoughts do not remain in the memory" (CSM 2:171–72, AT 7:246). Neither cognition nor awareness is lacking in the unborn infant's mind; only memory can be blamed if this awareness is not evident. In the next set of objections and replies, Descartes will explain that this failure of memory is due to a purely physical cause; the mind per se requires no development to become rational. Rather, the mind is always already rational, even when it least appears to be so: in utero.

Through his long-winded fifth set of objections, Pierre Gassendi occasioned Descartes to clarify his tenet that physical development does not entail mental development. (Gassendi's sense that Descartes ascribed too much autonomy to the mental realm led him to address Descartes as *Mens*, Mind. Descartes returned the favor by addressing Gassendi as *Caro*, Flesh.) Gassendi asked: "When the body . . . is growing, are not you growing also? And when the body is weak, are not you weak too? [*Et nonne, illo corpore, cujus eæ sunt partes, adolescente, ipsa adolescis? & dum illud debilitatur, debilitaris quoque ipsa?*]" (CSM 2:182, AT 7:261). Gassendi cited this synchronicity in order to suggest a causal relationship: that the state of the body determines the state of the mind. Descartes could never accept such a causal explanation; perhaps this is why he rejected Gassendi's account of the synchronous development of mind and body. In doing so, he provided this alternative explanation:

> I do not accept your statement that the mind grows and becomes weak along with the body. . . . It is true that the mind does not work so perfectly when it is in the body of an infant as it does when in an adult's body [*in corpore infantis quàm adulti*], and that its actions can often be slowed down by wine and other corporeal things. But all that follows from this is that the mind, so long as it is joined to the body, uses it like an instrument to perform the operations which take up most of its time. It does not follow that it is made more or less perfect by the body. Your inference here is no more valid than if you were to infer from the fact that a craftsman works badly whenever he uses a faulty tool that the good condition of his tools is the source of his knowledge of his craft. (CSM 2:245, AT 7:354)

For Descartes—at least until the sixth set of *Replies*—the mind is a clever craftsman, one who apparently never needed an apprenticeship to perfect his craft. Only his tool, the body, demonstrates progress: faulty in infancy and childhood, the body achieves its optimal condition during maturity (as long as one is sober). The mind, by contrast, always seems to already be an adult.

But Gassendi has difficulty viewing the mind as fully capable of thought during unconscious states, such as he takes sleep and prenatal life to be:

> I want to stop here and ask whether, in saying that thought cannot be separated from you, you mean that you continue to think indefinitely, so long as you exist. . . . [This] will hardly convince those who do not see how you are able to think during deep sleep or indeed in the womb [*per soporem lethargicum, aut in utero etiam, cogitare*]. And here I pause again and ask whether you think that you were infused into the body, or one of its parts, while still in the womb or at birth. But I do not want to press the point too insistently and ask whether you remember what you thought about in the womb or in the first few days or months or even years after you were born; nor, if you answer that you have forgotten, shall I ask why this is so. I do suggest, however, that you should bear in mind how obscure, meagre and virtually non-existent your thought must have been during those early periods of your life. (CSM 2:184, AT 7:264)

Descartes and Gassendi both accept the fact that we cannot recall early childhood. But whereas Gassendi concludes that no cognition takes place in utero and thus ascribes deficiency to the immature mind, Descartes blames only the physical apparatus of memory and thus shields the incorporeal mind from the charge of deficiency:

> But why should [the soul] not always think, since it is a thinking substance? It is no surprise that we do not remember the thoughts that the soul had when in the womb or in a deep sleep, since there are many other thoughts that we equally do not remember, although we know we had them when grown up [*adulti*], healthy and wide-awake. So long as the mind is joined to the body, then in order for it to remember thoughts which it had in the past, it is necessary for some traces of them to be imprinted on the brain; it is by turning to these, or applying itself to them, that the mind remembers. So is it really surprising if the brain of an infant [*cerebrum infantis*], or a man in a deep sleep, is unsuited [*ineptum*] to receive these traces? (CSM 2:246–47, AT 7:356–57)

For Gassendi, infant mental life per se is impoverished; for Descartes, only the infant's brain is defective, such that a rich mental life cannot be recorded for later recall.

By the time he came to respond to the sixth set of objections (of unknown multiple authorship, compiled by Marin Mersenne), it seems to me that Descartes had been reflecting further on the questions put to him by Arnauld and Gassendi. These latest objections listed nine difficulties, the final one being Descartes's "assertion that we ought to mistrust the operations of the senses and that the reliability of the intellect is much greater than that of the senses. But how," the objection went, "can the intellect enjoy any certainty unless it has previously derived it from the senses when they are working as they should?" (CSM 2:281–82) This question was succinct enough; Descartes's reply, almost five times longer, complicates the opening gesture of *Meditations*, which stated generally that "the senses deceive" (CSM 2:17). In place of that blanket statement, Descartes now distinguishes three "grades" of sensory response. The first grade designates the immediate stimulation of bodily organs by external objects. The second grade designates the immediate effects produced in the mind as a result of being united with a bodily organ; here he refers to what he later calls "the passions." The third grade designates all the judgments about external things we have been accustomed to make "from our earliest years [*a primâ ætate*]" (CSM 2:295, AT 7:438). Interestingly, Descartes concludes that there is no uncertainty about the first and second grades of sensory response: the organs themselves and the passions do not err. Only the third grade of sensory response, which depends upon intellect, is susceptible to error. He now qualifies his earlier claim that the reliability of the intellect is much greater than that of the senses: "this means merely that when we are grown up [*jam provectâ ætate*] the judgements which we make as a result of various new observations are more reliable than those which we formed without any reflection in our early childhood [*a primâ infantiâ et absque ullâ consideratione*]" (CSM 2:295, AT 7:438). What to a mature adult is a mere appearance (a stick in water appears to be bent) is to a child a judgment (the stick is bent). And we (adults) might even form that same faulty judgment, if we follow "the preconceived opinions [*præjudicia*] which we have become accustomed to accept from our earliest years [*ab ineunte ætate*]" (CSM 2:296, AT 7:438–39). In order to judge correctly, we adults must break the habit of relying on these prejudices.[27]

What is lacking such that young children unavoidably make false judgments? Descartes specifies here that children lack reflection [*consideration*] and reason, faculties adults presumably possess: "we did not have this power of reasoning in our infancy [*ratio, cùm in nobis ab infantiâ non fuerit*]" (CSM 2:296, AT 7:439). At this point, Descartes does not explain why reason was absent in infancy, but he goes on to suggest that the mind-body relationship in infancy may explain these defects. In his final replies to the sixth set of objections, Descartes recapitulates his autobiography once more: he tells us that after establishing through logical reasoning that mind and body are separate, he went on to consider physical things according to his newly won wisdom. Thus he came to see that gravity is to be explained by motion, not by an inclination to attract inherent in bodies (which common sense appears to tell us). He recognized that this and other new opinions differed completely from those he had previously held. He began to consider the explanation for this divergence, and found the following principal cause:

> From infancy [*ab infantiâ*] I had made a variety of judgements about physical things in so far as they contributed to preserving the life which I was embarking on; and subsequently I retained the same opinions I had originally formed [*præconceperam*] of these things. But at that age the mind employed the bodily organs less correctly than it now does, and was more firmly attached to them; hence it had no thoughts apart from them and perceived things only in a confused manner. Although it was aware of its own nature and had within itself an idea of thought as well as an idea of extension, it never exercised its intellect on anything without at the same time picturing something in the imagination. (CSM 2:297, AT 7:441)

Descartes here revises the reply he had made to Gassendi (that the tool, not the craftsman, is at fault). Now, Descartes says that children make false judgments because they are not yet master craftsmen—their intellects are overly attached to their "tool," the body. The mind's detachment from body ensures that judgments will not be compromised by the senses or by the imagination, but this detachment becomes possible only in adulthood. The process of detachment amounts to freeing oneself from preconceived opinions. Only thus can one graduate from confused to distinct cognition.

In July 1641, Descartes received an anonymous letter (AT 3:397–412), likely from a supporter of Gassendi, with objections to both *Medi-*

tations and *Replies*. This letter's second objection concerned Descartes's assertion that the mind does not grow and decline along with the body, as Gassendi had stated. Descartes had conceded to Gassendi that the mind works less perfectly in an infant than in an adult, but he had insisted that it does not follow that the mind is made more or less perfect *by* the body. The anonymous correspondent now objected that it does not follow that the mind is *not* made more or less perfect by the body, that Descartes had weakened his argument by failing to make a clear statement about the influence of body upon mind. In a reply letter of August 1641, addressed to Gassendi's champion (Descartes names him "Hyperaspistes"), Descartes elaborates on the body-soul connection in infancy and in utero:

> [If one may conjecture on such an unexplored topic:][28] we know by experience that our minds are so closely joined to our bodies as to be almost always acted upon by them; and although when thriving in an adult and healthy body the mind enjoys some liberty to think of other things than those presented by the senses, we know there is not the same liberty in those who are sick or asleep or very young [*in pueris*]; and the younger [*minorem*] they are, the less liberty they have. It seems most reasonable [*nihil magis rationi consentaneum est*] to think that a mind newly united to an infant's body [*corpori infantis*] is wholly occupied in perceiving in a confused way or feeling the ideas of pain, pleasure, heat, cold and other similar ideas which arise from its union and, as it were, intermingling with the body. None the less, it has in itself the ideas of God, of itself, and of all such truths as are called self-evident, in the same way as adult human beings have these ideas when they are not attending to them; for it does not acquire these ideas later on, as it grows older [*crescente ætate*]. I have no doubt that if it were released from the prison of the body, it would find them within itself. (CSMK 3:190, AT 3:423–24)

For reasons unknown, Descartes published neither the letter nor the reply in the second edition of *Meditations*, as he had indicated he would do. Nonetheless, this reply represents one of Descartes's clearest explanations for the infant's apparent nonrationality. That the body is prison to the soul is of course a classic notion of philosophy and theology, but in Descartes, the prison is much less restrictive in maturity, when the mind enjoys relative liberty, and can thus reflect.[29]

In replying to his critics, Descartes explores three positions on the mind-body connection in infancy and childhood. The fifth replies blame the "tool," i.e., the body, for deficient cognition, while exonerating the "craftsman," i.e., the mind. The sixth replies give the opposite explanation: the senses do not themselves deceive, which means that the tool is in good working order. Rather, the intellect is not operating correctly with the tools. Thus, it is now the craftsman whose operations are deficient. Following on this vacillation, Descartes's letter of 1641 chooses not to decide between the mind and the body, but rather to blame the defects of childhood cognition on precisely the union of mind and body. In a philosophical system that generally operates by presuming a duality of mind and body, I submit, reflection on states that highlight the unity of mind and body (such as infancy and childhood) must create particular trouble. Although Descartes's indecision in naming the cause of childhood cognitive deficiency (is it the body, the mind, or the union thereof?) is evident in 1641, a publication of the following year shows that Descartes did not waver in viewing childhood as an age of cognitive deficiency.

Descartes's rather testy debate with Pierre Bourdin (in the seventh set of objections and replies, published in 1642 with the second edition of *Meditations, Objections* and *Replies*) resulted in a novel illustration of Cartesian method: since we store up many false judgments since childhood, the only way to philosophize is to dump out all opinions, then judge them one by one for their soundness: "Suppose [my critic] had a basket full of apples and, being worried that some of the apples were rotten, wanted to take out the rotten ones to prevent the rot spreading. How would he proceed? Would he not begin by tipping [*effundenda*] the whole lot out of the basket [*ex corbe rejiceret*]?" (CSM 2:324, AT 7:481; see also CSM 2:349, AT 7:512). Descartes does not name the mental equivalent of the "spread" of "rot." Perhaps it is the inferring of new beliefs from old (rotten) ones. In any case, Descartes insists on the potential for conceptual contagion: "those who do not abandon their preconceived opinions [*præjudicia*] will find it hard to acquire a clear and distinct concept of anything; for it is obvious that the concepts which we had in our childhood [*in pueritiâ*] were not clear and distinct, and hence, if not set aside [*depositi*] they will affect any other concepts which we acquire later and make them obscure and confused" (CSM 2:352–53, AT 7:518). Although the model proffered at the outset of *Meditations* (demolishing the foundation of a house) evokes more anxiety than does this model (overturning a basket of apples), they are otherwise quite similar.[30] Both target the same problem: prejudices from childhood.

The theory systematized:
Principles of Philosophy

Descartes's next major publication, *Principles of Philosophy* (1644 in Latin, 1647 in French) was meant to be a standard textbook on Cartesian thought, for use at the universities. Because he eschewed the first-person approach taken in *Discourse* and *Meditations*, he had no occasion to refer to his own childhood. Nevertheless, Descartes presented in this text the most elaborate theory of childhood he would ever publish. I shall focus on the first of four parts. (Suffice it to say that parts 2 and 3 contain several references to childhood errors; these illustrate the common-sense way of imagining stars, vacuums, and motion, as opposed to the Cartesian physics there advanced.) Part 1 is subtitled "The Principles of *Human* Knowledge" (my emphasis), but Descartes takes pains to distinguish between children's and adults' ways of knowing.

Principle 1 recalls the opening statement of *Meditations*, but also incorporates a specification elaborated in the sixth set of *Replies:* "Since we began life as infants [*infantes nati sumus*], and made various judgements [*judicia*] concerning the things that can be perceived by the senses before we had the full use of our reason [*prius . . . quàm integrum nostræ rationis usum haberemus*], there are many preconceived opinions [*præjudiciis*] that keep us from knowledge of the truth. It seems that the only way of freeing ourselves from these opinions is to make the effort, once in the course of our life, to doubt everything which we find to contain even the smallest suspicion of uncertainty" (CSM 1:193, AT 8.1:5). Much more than in *Meditations*, Descartes emphasizes that infancy is to blame for our epistemological problems. We cannot, of course, avoid having been infants, but we can consider how we can correct "the preconceived opinions of our early childhood [*primæ ætatis præjudicia*]" (CSM 1:208, AT 8.1:22).[31] But in this part 1, Descartes devotes most of his energy to describing the difficulty of correcting prejudice. Principle 47 focuses on the anthropological necessity for the mind's preoccupation in our earliest years:

> In our childhood [*in primâ ætate*] the mind was so immersed in the body that although there was much that it perceived clearly, it never perceived anything distinctly. But in spite of this the mind made judgements [*judicârit*] about many things, and this is the origin of the many preconceived opinions [*præjudicia*] which most of us never subsequently abandon. (CSM 1:208, AT 8.1:22)

To judge during prematurity is to prejudge.[32] The mind's immersion in the young body is to blame for the indistinctness of judgments made during the most inferior age of life. Principle 66 distinguishes superior acts of mind (such as judgment) from inferior ones (sensations, emotions, appetites); the latter are inferior because they are tied to the body. We may perceive sensations clearly, but our judgments concerning them may be mistaken, especially so in childhood. Descartes exhorts us to be careful concerning our judgments, but again he underscores how difficult the application of this rule can be: "For all of us have, from our early childhood [*ab ineunte ætate*], judged that all the objects of our sense-perception are things existing outside our minds and closely resembling our sensations" (CSM 1:216, AT 8.1:32). Having once made this premature (Aristotelian) judgment, one needs to experience an epistemological conversion to begin making mature (Cartesian) judgments.

The concluding principles of part 1 clearly mark childhood and infancy as the source of our troubles. Principle 71 reads: "The chief cause of error arises from our preconceived opinions of childhood [*Præcipuam errorum causam à præjudiciis infantiæ procedere*]" (CSM 1:218, AT 8.1:35). Descartes's commentary on this principle deserves lengthy quotation:

> In our early childhood [*in primâ ætate*] the mind was so closely tied to the body that it had no leisure for any thoughts except those by means of which it had sensory awareness of what was happening to the body. It did not refer these thoughts to anything outside itself, but merely felt pain when something harmful was happening to the body and felt pleasure when something beneficial occurred. . . . The next stage arose when the mechanism of the body . . . twisted around aimlessly in all directions in its random attempts to pursue the beneficial and avoid the harmful; at this point the mind that was attached to the body began to notice that the objects of this pursuit or avoidance had an existence outside itself. . . . Since the mind judged everything in terms of its utility to the body in which it was immersed, it assessed the amount of reality in each object by the extent to which it was affected by it. . . . Right from infancy [*à primâ infantiâ*] our mind was swamped with a thousand such preconceived opinions [*præjudiciis*]; and in later childhood [*deinde in pueritiâ*], forgetting that they were adopted without sufficient examination, it regarded them as known by the senses or implanted by nature, and accepted them as utterly true and evident. (CSM 1:218–19, AT 8.1: 36)

We cannot remember having made judgments in infancy. This particular amnesia results in the false belief that we acquire some of our knowledge as Aristotelians and empiricists would have it, namely through the senses. Descartes's rationalist explanation reconstructs what lies beyond this amnesia: reason is present and is active even in infancy. But it is equally important to note that the reasonable mind's acts are compromised in infancy by its strong connection to (or: immersion in) the body. Even in adulthood, when the mind has, as it were, *emerged* at least somewhat from bodily immersion, the judgments made during earlier times still retain their force. Principle 72 examines this second cause of error: "In later years [*quamvis jam maturis annis*] the mind is no longer a total slave to the body, and does not refer everything to it. . . . But despite this, it is not easy for the mind to erase these false judgements from its memory. . . . For example, in our early childhood [*à primâ ætate*] we imagined the stars as being very small . . . . Our preconceived opinion is still strong enough to make it very hard for us to imagine them differently from the way we did before" (CSM 1:219–20, AT 8.1:36–37). The third cause of error, named in principle 73, is simply the fact that abstract thought is exhausting. Specifically, it is tiring to think without reference to the senses, and so in many cases we naturally rely on the testimony of the senses, which is to say: we rely on our prejudices. Descartes speculates that "this may be due to the very nature that the mind has as a result of being joined to the body; or it may be because it was exclusively occupied [*occuparetur*] with the objects of sense and imagination in its earliest years [*in primis annis*]" (CSM 1:220, AT 8.1:37). (I highlight the verb *occuparetur* because it recalls Descartes's statement of 1629 concerning "an error that has gripped [*préoccupez*] all of us since our childhood" [CSM 1:85, AT 9:17].) Descartes's speculation considers significant alternatives: error may be due either to the *nature* or the *history* of the embodied mind. According to the one view, the body per se contaminates the mind's activity; according to the other, the *infant* body has contaminated the mind's activity, such that a decontamination proves necessary once in life, in maturity. As far as I have seen, Descartes usually gives the latter explanation. To this extent, I can concur with Gouhier: "The Cartesian critique opposes the reasonable nature of man and his historical condition, man in his essence and the individual, whose existence begins with childhood."[33]

Given the serious impediments discussed above, it would seem that philosophizing correctly is almost impossible. Nonetheless, the penultimate principle of part 1 (principle 75) summarizes the rules to be observed in order to philosophize correctly, and they are consonant with those listed in the *Discourse*. Difficult though this may be, "we must first

of all lay aside [*deponenda*] all our preconceived opinions [*præjudicia*]"
(CSM 1:221, AT 8.1:38). (Recall the seventh replies, where Descartes
explained that the prejudices to be "set aside" [*depositi*] are concepts from
childhood.) The final principle of part 1 (principle 76) is double-tongued.
It states on the one hand, perhaps to appease the censors, that whatever
God has revealed to us must be taken to be more certain than anything
else.[34] But it goes on to say that in matters where God does not instruct
us, we must be Cartesians. That is, we must not accept anything as true
that we have not ourselves thoroughly scrutinized. This statement, which
encapsulates the self-reliance of "modernity" and lends support to considering Descartes the "father of modern thought," is only the first half of
the final sentence of part 1. The second half of that sentence introduces a
theme less often considered in summaries of Descartes's philosophy:
"and [a philosopher] should never rely on the senses, that is, on the ill-
considered judgements of his childhood [*inconsideratis infantiæ suæ judiciis*]
in preference to his mature powers of reason [*maturæ rationi*]" (CSM
1:222, AT 8.1:39). It is accurate to conclude that Descartes's philosophy
"distrusts the senses" only if one takes *the senses* to be a shorthand description for *judgments made prematurely, during infancy and childhood*, judgments stored in memory as sensations rather than as judgments. The famous Cartesian turn away from the senses is equivalent to a turn away
from childhood.

INFANT OBLIVION, CHILDHOOD MEMORY, ADULT METHOD

To maintain his argument that thought is the essence of mind, Descartes
must explain a specific failure of memory: why we cannot recall having
thoughts in early childhood, in infancy, and in utero. In a letter to Arnauld of June 4, 1648, Descartes again contrasts the history of the embodied mind, in which clarity of cognition is initially absent, with the nature of mind, which demands that potentially clear cognition be present:

> I am convinced that in the mind of an infant there have never been any
> pure acts of understanding, but only confused sensations. Although
> these confused sensations leave some traces [*vestigia*] in the brain, which
> remain there for life, that does not suffice to enable us to remember
> [*aduertamus*] them. For that we would have to observe that the sensa-
> tions which come to us [*adueniunt*] as adults are like those which we had
> [*recordemur*] in our mother's womb; and that in turn would require a cer-
> tain reflective act of the intellect, or intellectual memory, which was not

in use in the womb. Nevertheless it seems necessary that the mind should always be actually engaged in thinking; because thought constitutes its essence. (CSMK 354–55; AT 5:192)

Recall that in the fourth replies, Descartes had asserted that "the impressions [*species*] of these thoughts do not remain in the memory" (CSM 2:171–72, AT 7:246).[35] In his further correspondence with Arnauld, he comes to blame this defect on the immature brain. Descartes's letter to Arnauld of July 29, 1648 clarifies why infants' and children's brains are unsuited to receive traces of cognition:

> It seems to me very true that, as long as the mind is united to the body, it cannot withdraw itself from the senses whenever it is stimulated with great force by external or internal objects. I concede further that it cannot withdraw itself whenever it is attached to a brain which is too soft or damp, as in children [*alligata est cerebro nimis humido & molli, quale est in infantibus*], or otherwise in poor condition, as in those who are lethargic, apoplectic or frenetic, or as in all of us when we are deeply asleep. . . . If ever I wrote that the thoughts of children leave no traces [*vestigia*] in their brain, I meant traces sufficient for memory, that is, traces which at the time of their impression are observed by pure intellect to be new. In a similar way we say that there are no human tracks [*vestigia*] in the sand if we cannot find any impressions shaped like a human foot, though perhaps there may be many unevennesses made by human feet, which can therefore in another sense be called human tracks. Finally, we make a distinction between direct and reflective thoughts [*visionem*]. . . . I call the first and simple thoughts of infants [*primas & simplices infantum cogitationes*] *direct* and not reflective. . . . But when an adult feels something, and simultaneously perceives that he has not felt it before, I call this second perception *reflection*, and attribute it to the intellect alone, in spite of its being so linked to sensation that the two occur together and appear to be indistinguishable from each other. (CSMK 356–57, AT 5:219–21)

Infancy is a black box. Thoughts occur in the infant mind, but they cannot be recalled under any conditions. These thoughts even leave traces, but untraceable ones: they are like human tracks "in another sense" (ibid.), that is, human tracks we are unlikely to recognize as human.[36] In this first phase of life, infancy, rationality is present but not self-aware, thus not properly rational.

Traces of our earliest cognition fail to be physically stored in memory. But at some point in childhood, cognition does begin to leave traces upon the brain that can be later recalled; unfortunately, it is prejudices that are henceforth stored in memory. Given that Descartes's metaphors of eliminating prejudices (destroying bad foundations, dumping out apples, wiping a painting clean) seem to suggest that these bad judgments can be obliterated, it makes sense that Descartes's opponents, including Gassendi and Voetius, would draw attention to the permanence of these traces and insist that the attempt to forget them must be doomed to failure. But these opponents misunderstood Descartes. In a letter to Voetius of May 1643, Descartes accuses him of being a bad reader: "in all the passages you cite there is no word of 'forgetting' but only of removing preconceived opinions" (CSMK 221). According to Descartes, one is not supposed to forget prejudices; rather, one should attempt to make them ineffective—recall the Pauline term *katērgika*—by relying on mature method.[37] That is, if one believes prejudicially that one possesses hands and a body, the only way to attain a certain belief is to counter the prejudice. By meditating, which begins with radical doubt, one can impress into the mind the opposite prejudice, namely that one is nothing more than mind, that one lacks hands and a body. By opposing one prejudice with a counter-prejudice, Descartes suggests, prejudice itself will lose its force of conviction. By following Descartes's method, prejudices can be neutralized (if not forgotten), and one will henceforth be swayed only by reasons.

When the newly rationalized adult relies on method, his or her mind may well remain cluttered with memories and prejudices. But Cartesian method allows him or her to write on clean paper, never mind the historical accretions (traces in the brain, imprints on the "wax") of the individual mind.[38] In Timothy Reiss's view, method is a form of writing designed to "get around memory and to find new ways to jump over it. . . . Method had nothing to do with memory. . . . Method was the opposite of memory."[39] And yet, Descartes continues to rely upon memory for method to function. The end of the fifth meditation displays this ambivalence. On the one hand, memory threatens clear and distinct cognition: "so long as I perceive something very clearly and distinctly I cannot but believe it to be true. But my nature is also such that I cannot fix my mental vision continually on the same thing, so as to keep perceiving it clearly; and often the memory of a previously made judgement may come back" (CSM 2:48). But on the other hand, memory also supports clear and distinct cognition: "even if I am no longer attending to the arguments which led me to judge that this is true, as long as I remember that I clearly and distinctly perceived it, there are no counter-arguments. . . . I have true and certain knowledge of it" (ibid.). The move to mature method involves a move from bad memories (those of premature judgments of childhood) to good ones (those of clear, distinct perceptions). Notably, Descartes omits memory from the list of mental faculties in *Principles*.[40]

Descartes never resolves his ambivalence concerning memory: his correspondence alternately presents memory as partly physical and as purely mental. In a discussion of the pineal gland, in a letter to Lazare Meyssonnier of January 29, 1640, Descartes noted: "as for the impressions [*especes*] preserved in the memory, I imagine they are not unlike the folds which remain in the paper after it has once been folded" (CSMK 143, AT 3:20). Later that year, Descartes complicated this model in a letter to Mersenne of June 11: "there is no doubt that the folds of the memory get in each other's way, and that there cannot be an infinite number of such folds in the brain; but there are still quite a number of them there. Moreover, the intellectual memory has its own separate impressions [*especes*], which do not depend in any way on these folds" (CSMK 148, AT 3:84). Now, it seems that the mind has its own pure memory separate from the brain with its physical, finite folds. Although Descartes made this distinction between intellectual and physical memory, he unfortunately did not explicate it further.[41] Eight years later, in a discussion between Descartes and Frans Burman, the distinction reemerges: Burman placed great hopes in the distinction between physical and intellectual memory. The latter, he argued, should allow for the possibility of our reclaiming our earliest thoughts. He noted that even if no physical traces were left on the immature brain, still "this intellectual memory ought to enable the mind to remember its thoughts" (CSMK 336). But Descartes was evasive, pointing out that "this intellectual memory has universals rather than particulars as its objects, and so it cannot enable us to recall every single thing we have done" (CSMK 337). Although he cannot finally explain the amnesia of intellectual memory, the fact that he posits the existence of an incorporeal faculty of memory does seem to indicate that despite his exploration into the substantial connection of body and mind, Descartes finally did regard the body as the mind's tool. At least in the conversation with Burman, Descartes repeats one of his views on that tool being the cause of cognitive deficiency in childhood: "in infancy [*in infantiâ*] the mind is so swamped [*immersa*] inside the body. . . . The body has an obstructive effect on the soul. . . . The body is always a hindrance to [*impedit*] the mind in its thinking, and this was especially true in youth [*sic illud maxime fecit in juventute*]" (CSMK 336, AT 5:150). But this discussion with Burman does not address Descartes's previously articulated opposite view: that the body as tool was in order, but the mind as craftsman used it badly. In the end, Descartes did not settle on whether to blame the cognitive deficiency of childhood on the mind, the body, or their unity. It is no wonder that in his late correspondence, Descartes continuously returned to discussions of corporeal and incorporeal memory.

Plato believed that infants come into the world with innate ideas that have been forgotten and that must be recollected with the help of a Socratic midwife.[42] Descartes's explanation of the lack of access to innate ideas follows a different track: it is not that the mind has forgotten its (universal) innate ideas, but rather the mind in infancy and childhood is too swamped with bodily stimuli to form any (particular) ideas beyond the way the body is being affected.[43] The infant cannot reflect on anything, and most adults are pre-occupied with pre-conceived pre-judices based on "the senses," that is, based on deficient judgments of sensory data made during infancy and childhood. These premature judgments are no longer recalled as judgments, but rather are taken to be simple sense perceptions. According to Descartes, what we have forgotten is not the innate ideas; we have forgotten that we have made judgments in the womb, in infancy, and in childhood. Thus, unlike in Plato, anamnesis is not Descartes's path toward accessing innate ideas. Indeed, attempting to recover early memories seems a futile project, since accessible memory traces are not left on the soft, humid brains of infants. It seems to me that this is why Descartes bases his method not on Socratic dialogue, which seeks to remind one of the innate ideas one has forgotten, but rather on radical doubt, which dumps out the basket of apples or demolishes the house, so that one can then rationally reconstruct one's world view. The access one thereby gains to innate ideas does not take the form of remembrance. As Ralph Heyndels notes, "memory is radically incompatible with the *achronical* light—at once instantaneous and eternal—of intuitive evidence."[44] One might also say that the transparency of Descartes's natural light is located in a punctual *now* that the *Meditations* explore. But this present tense, I would like to underscore, only affords such transparency in one's mature years.

What, then, is the role of education in childhood? For Descartes, it would seem, it cannot matter much what one learns as a child, since one's method of gaining knowledge would necessarily be flawed, leading only to the acquisition of prejudices. It would seem that Descartes is an epistemological anabaptist—one must be an adult before one can reform one's cognitive ways, by submerging oneself into radical doubt.[45] Whereas Locke would later famously argue that children's minds are like blank slates, onto which knowledge is written through experience, Descartes argues that one must wipe one's own slate clean, once in life, say at age thirty-one. Childhood seems to be little more than a period of waiting for this rebirth.

But lest we overemphasize (with Gouhier) the born-again status of reason, let us recall (with Garber) that one emerges from mature meditation not completely different from before. We do get to trust our senses, after all, at least with regard to middle-sized objects. But this is so because we now have a good reason to trust our senses, a reason we lacked in childhood. Experiential learning is possible in Descartes, both in childhood and in adulthood. But if one wishes to gain certain knowledge, and thus engage in science, then the beliefs acquired during childhood must be cast out, once in one's life, and readmitted insofar as they are certified to be good beliefs.[46] The mature mind, following a secure method, certifies these beliefs as either good or bad. Thus, Cartesian method does not kill the child; it purges childish ways.

2

Locke and Leibniz: Understanding Children

A CURSORY GLANCE AT HISTORIES OF PHILOSOPHY AND HISTORIES OF concepts of childhood can lead one to believe that John Locke was the only early modern philosopher to have given children and childhood more than a passing thought. Much has been written about Locke's contribution to, even inauguration of, philosophical reflection about children. But although Locke is the most studied of early modern (or any other) philosophers in histories of ideas of childhood, references to his *Essay Concerning Human Understanding* in these histories tend to be restricted to book 1, which makes up less than a tenth of the *Essay*.[1] Cleverley and Phillips refer to Locke's denial of innate ideas as a source of inspiration for the thought of Helvétius, Rousseau, and eventually Piaget. Locke's importance in this respect is undeniable. But in his *Essay*, Locke wrote much more about children than merely to deny them innate ideas. He also discussed cultures that practice infanticide, enumerated the intellectual deficits of children, insulted other philosophers by saying that they talked like children, explored children's language acquisition in ancient and modern times, and reflected on the physical and moral status of changelings, beings once thought to have been switched with human children, at birth or in early infancy, by demons or fairies. As this short list should already indicate, what Locke actually wrote about children in the *Essay* is not well represented by the summary discussions of the *Essay* in histories of childhood. Not surprisingly, Locke scholarship more accurately observes the multiple valences of childhood in Locke's works. But even in Yolton's *A Locke Dictionary*, to give a prominent example, Locke is depicted primarily as a friend to children, one who wanted to "understand [their] minds and passions."[2] This characterization is incomplete in that it overlooks the role of children in Locke's discussions of language, substance, and classification.

To present a more balanced assessment of childhood in Locke's *Essay*, this chapter and the one following examine all four of its books. The point of this exercise is not only to improve our understanding of the history of childhood by disclosing what one of its major figures actually wrote about childhood, but also to improve our understanding of Locke. I submit that childhood is significantly involved in many of Locke's philosophical concerns, including epistemology, morality, personal identity, linguistics, and anthropology. Demonstrating this importance necessitates entering into these multiple concerns of the *Essay*, and may entail the risk of mimicking its sprawling feel. I have attempted to combat this sprawl by subdividing my chapters into named sections. Further orientation may derive from my generally following the order of the *Essay*'s chapters.

Locke is less of a child-centered philosopher and more of a rationalist than he has been sometimes depicted. Some of Locke's ostensible notes on children are really about mature human beings. A case in point: he imagines an experiment of placing "a Colony of young Children" upon an island (1.4.11) and depriving them of fire. They would never develop any such notion, Locke asserts. Nor would they develop a notion of God, until one of the colonists meditated in a manner similar to Descartes, i.e., "imployed his Thoughts, to enquire into the Constitution and Causes of things" (ibid.), then teaching others of God, such that "Reason" (ibid.) would ensure the further propagation of this idea. But according to the developmental psychology of the *Essay*, as I demonstrate shortly, the first "child" to do this would have to have matured first. In this thought experiment, childhood stands for nothing more than a lack of access to received opinion or doctrine. The intellectual operations needed to develop ideas of God cannot be performed by children. Man is still the measure, for Locke just as well as for any other early modern philosopher. "So that to me it seems, that *the constant and regular Succession of Ideas* in a waking Man, *is* as it were, *the Measure* and Standard *of all other Successions*" (2.14.12). It is against this standard that Locke measures children, and they are often found wanting. Although Locke does not demonstrate Descartes's aversion to childhood cognition, there are significant points in common between them, as I discuss below. But examining the Descartes-Locke relation is a tertiary concern of this chapter.[3] Its secondary concern involves a different rationalist, Gottfried Wilhelm Leibniz.

The primary concern of this chapter (and the one following) is to consider the children in Locke's *Essay* who have been overlooked in summary and even in extensive discussions of this text. The first half of this chapter treats Locke's famous denial of innate principles, both speculative and practical; after reviewing this more familiar territory in a perhaps less familiar light, I turn to what might be anachronistically called Locke's developmental psychology and conclude with a discussion of personal identity. Locke's theological motivation for elaborating his theory of personhood, while often overlooked by subsequent personal identity philosophers, has been recognized by Locke scholars. Yet I have not found a scholarly treatment that considers how Locke's infants, who are not yet persons, are supposed to fare on Judgment Day.[4] Histories of childhood have noted Locke's use of children in epistemology; I show the relevance of children for Locke's moral and religious philosophy as well.

Leibniz's book-length reply to Locke, the *Nouveaux Essais sur l'Entendement Humaine*, contains the most that Leibniz ever wrote about children. Written in 1704–5, this text attempted to simulate the dialogue with Locke that Leibniz eagerly but unsuccessfully sought. (Since Locke's death put an end to Leibniz's hopes for discussion, he set the manuscript aside; it was not published until 1765.)[5] Placing Locke's thoughts and words in the mouth of Philalethes, and his own thoughts in the mouth of Theophilus, Leibniz wrote a point-by-point discussion of Locke's *Essay*. Its style is awkward, and its contents have been controversial at least since Bertrand Russell concluded that this book does not comport with the rest of Leibniz's philosophy.[6] Be this as it may: in my view, this reply to Locke occasioned Leibniz to cease regarding children as belonging to the category of the obvious, and to begin considering childhood as relevant to explicit philosophical concerns.[7] Indeed, Leibniz sometimes regards children as capable of more than Locke would have allowed. One example contrasts well with Locke's thought experiment discussed above: Leibniz agrees that nature can teach "men" of God, and he instances a "*child* deaf and dumb since birth [who] has been seen to worship the full moon" (*NE* 76, my emphasis). In this chapter, I begin to explicate Leibniz's counter-philosophy of childhood, developed in his responses to books 1 and 2 of Locke's *Essay*. Because a thorough point-by-point oscillation between Locke and Leibniz would quickly prove tiresome, I incorporate only those of Leibniz's responses that are of immediate relevance to concepts of infancy and childhood. Leibniz's *New Essays* certainly deserve a focused study in the context of ideas of childhood, but in the present chapter its role is to provide counterpoint to Locke's cantus firmus.

Several major philosophical differences between Locke and Leibniz are expressed in terms of infants and children. In a chapter on relation, for example, Locke states that one can have a clear relational concept (brotherhood) even if the substance to which the elements of the relationship belong (humanity) is not clearly understood (2.25.8). A later chapter gives this instance:

> If I know what it is for one Man to be born of a Woman, *viz. Sempronia*, I know what it is for another Man to be born of the same Woman, *Sempronia*; and so have as clear a Notion of Brothers, as of Births, and, perhaps, clearer. For if I believed, that *Sempronia* digged *Titus* out of the Parsley-Bed, (as they use to tell Children) and thereby became his Mother; and that afterwards in the same manner, she digged *Cajus* out of the Parsley-Bed, I had as clear a Notion of the Relation of Brothers between them, as if I had all the Skill of a Midwife; the Notion that the same Woman contributed, as Mother, equally to their Births, (though I were ignorant or mistaken in the manner of it,) being that on which I grounded the Relation; and that they agreed in that Circumstance of Birth, let it be what it will. (2.28.19)

To this Leibniz objects that "if the very form of the relation involved knowledge of what is obscure in the subject, the relation would share in this obscurity" (*NE* 227). Leibniz's response to Locke's parsley-bed birth not only illustrates his objection but also indicates one element of a counter-theory of motherhood: "Yet one time when a child was told that his new-born brother had been drawn from a well (which is how the Germans satisfy children who are curious about this matter), the child replied that he was surprised they did not throw the baby back into the same well when it troubled his mother by crying so much. The point is that the account gave him no explanation for the love the mother showed towards the baby. It can be said, then, that if someone does not know the foundation of a relation, his thoughts about it are [of the kind I call partly deaf]"(*NE* 254).[8] The epistemological issue here is what children do or do not adequately know about the mother-child relation, given the lies adults tell them. Before we examine the famous discussion about innate ideas, which concerns what infants do or do not know at birth, we should note that both Locke and Leibniz allude to a general epistemological issue—what human beings can or cannot know—from the outset of both texts. In Locke's case, this involves yet another child.

LOCKE'S INSCRUTABLE UTERUS
AND LEIBNIZ'S LEGIBLE HEART

The first child of Locke's *Essay* comes before the beginning.[9] Since the fourth edition (1699), the title page has had two epigraphs, one classical and one biblical: "As thou knowest not what is in the way of the Spirit, nor how the bones do grow in the Womb of her that is with Child: even so thou knowest not the works of God, who maketh all things" (Eccles 11:5).[10] Later in the *Essay*, Locke's child will be a blank slate, but here it is an unknown quantity in the black box of its mother's womb. Stephen Buckle states correctly that "the passage insists that human beings do not have knowledge of the realm of spirit, nor of the realm of matter."[11] Buckle then incorrectly concludes that the epigraph signals a general skepticism: "since these two realms jointly comprise all that there is, human beings are therefore shown not to have knowledge of what there is."[12] I submit that a careful reading of Locke shows that these two realms are not all that there is. As I show in the final section of this chapter, Locke expresses skepticism about our ability to know material and spiritual substance, yet claims that we can nevertheless know what makes a person. But I would still emphasize that, since the fourth edition, the first child of Locke's *Essay* serves to mark what we cannot know.[13]

Since Leibniz read Locke in a French translation of the fourth edition, it seems plausible that he would have wanted to counter the semiskeptical position suggested by Locke's epigraph. Early in his preface, Leibniz refers to Romans 2:15, where Paul says that God's law is written in our hearts. Here Leibniz follows natural law theorists, every one of whom since Aquinas had cited this passage to argue for innate morality.[14] Certainly, Leibniz is not arguing for immediate transparency. He admits that one cannot "easily read these eternal laws of reason in the soul, as the Praetor's edict can be read on his notice-board, without effort or inquiry; but it is enough that they can be discovered within us by dint of attention" (*NE* 50). In citing Paul, Leibniz suggests that the heart is not unknowable; by replacing the inscrutable uterus with the scripted and legible heart as a symbol of human interiority, Leibniz counters Locke's "Thou knowest not."[15]

It is not that Locke favors mystery or obscurity; quite the contrary. Within the realm of things that can be known, Locke wants things to be known clearly and distinctly. Of his own *Essay Concerning Human Understanding*, he asserts: "*I desire it should be understood*" (*Essay*, 9). And for

Locke, understanding is binary: whereas Leibniz observes gradations of consciousness, Locke holds that one either has an idea or one does not. This may be why Locke replaces the terms "clear *and* distinct" with "determinate *or* determined" (*Essay*, 13); doing so allows him to avoid the Cartesian association of light's gradational quality with ideas and knowledge. In Locke, one has *either* "clear or distinct Ideas" *or* "obscurity and confusion" (ibid.). Leibniz's best rejoinder to Locke, or at least his most cited one, is his insistence on intermediate states of knowing,[16] especially the "clear and confused" ideas that would later form the basis for philosophical aesthetics in the work of Alexander Baumgarten. (See my chapter 6.) Although Locke was no friend of obscurity or confusion, he holds that there are aspects of reality (such as the nature of substances) beyond the limit of what human beings can know. His agnostic stance concerning spiritual substance in particular drew the ire of orthodox theologians as well as the critical attention of rationalist philosophers.[17] Locke's call for epistemological modesty reveals enlightenment to be a limited affair: we operate "by Candle-light," not in "broad Sun-shine" (1.1.5). We can certainly trust the candlelight, but we can only know what it illumines.[18] Knowing "the Bounds between the enlightened and dark Parts of Things" (1.1.7) is paramount, and complaining about the limitations of human understanding would be "Childish Peevishness" (1.1.5). Leibniz disagrees on the bounds and even on the idea of a distinct border between two discrete realms: *either* enlightened *or* dark. Nature makes no leaps, and based on this dictum, Alexander Baumgarten would later recall that dawn is located between darkness and midday. Epistemologically speaking, clear and confused cognition is located between obscure and distinct cognition. Subtending all conscious thought are what Leibniz calls minute perceptions [*petites perceptions*]. What for Locke is not *in* the mind, that is, within the candlelight of consciousness, must be outside the mind; for Leibniz, whatever is not in clear view is nevertheless in the mind, just not in clarity and distinctness. Necessary truths (if not contingent ones) are all potentially knowable, waiting for us to search within to see them (see *NE* 79).

When Locke proposes to explore how ideas "come into" (1.1.8) the mind, simple ideas seem to be his model: what gives rise to them was previously "without," in the world, in the objects we apprehend first and foremost through the senses. (Complex ideas and mixed modes are created in the mind, by the mind.) Though he does not use this term, Leibniz presumes that ideas come into the conscious mind from the *preconscious* mind. Even if the first ideas are apprehended through the senses, this chronological *firstness* is insignificant.[19] The principle of noncontradiction—an idea Locke would say is had very late, if ever—lies implicit within the baby's judgment that its mother is different from its neighbor. According to Leibniz's explanation, certain principles are innate, if innateness is so understood. They function whether or not they are made explicit.

This basic disagreement on the bounds of the mind, it seems to me, determines many specific disagreements between Locke and Leibniz on innate ideas. Locke denies that truths can be found within oneself; according to Leibniz's monadology, there *is*, strictly speaking, only a "within oneself." There is no outside from which sense impressions could enter the mind and thus spark ideas. Each monad, rather, represents (one might say: contains) the entire universe.[20] Monads are, in Nicholas Jolley's nice formulation, confusedly omniscient.[21] All learning is a matter of retrieving knowledge from one's depths. Referring to Plato's *Meno*, Leibniz claims that "the whole of arithmetic and of geometry should be regarded as innate, and contained within us in an implicit way. . . . Plato showed this, in a dialogue where he had Socrates leading a child to abstruse truths just by asking questions and without teaching him anything" (*NE* 77). Leibniz also references a more contemporary example, a Swedish boy who could perform complex calculations in his mind. Leibniz submits this boy as evidence that the mind can obtain "necessary truths from within itself" (ibid.). He certainly does not say that it is easy to do so, just that it is possible to discover these truths without the help of the senses. It seems to follow from Leibniz's argumentation that *all* knowledge (not just knowledge of necessary truths) is innate.[22] Locke anticipates just this sort of claim: "If Truths can be imprinted on the Understanding without being perceived, I can see no difference there can be, between any Truths the Mind is capable of knowing in respect of their Original: They must all be innate, or all adventitious: In vain shall a Man go about to distinguish them" (1.2.5). Locke thus poses a challenge for a theorist of innate ideas to produce a nonuniversal (and thus nontrivial) claim. Likely in response to Locke's challenge, Leibniz does sometimes seem to want to limit the number of innate ideas to necessary truths, which "are proved by what lies within, and cannot be established by experience as truths of fact are" (*NE* 79). Since this limitation does not comport with the monadology, the price of Leibniz's concession may have been philosophical inconsistency.

Be this as it may: Leibniz's capacious notion of consciousness allows us to distinguish between the *thoughts* of infancy and childhood and the (minute) *perceptions* thereof. If innate ideas are located in the latter, rather than the former, then Locke's conclusion (that there are no innate ideas, because the ideas touted as innate are absent from the thoughts of infancy and childhood) fails. But Leibniz's rebuttals, cogent though they may be, have not discouraged many nineteenth- and twentieth-century readers from turning to Locke for guidance. Especially since the advent of developmental psychology, many have read Locke for an explanation of the observable progress made in the thoughts of childhood. However, I am not suggesting here that "empiricism" beat "rationalism" in this contest over the contents of children's minds.[23] As the present study aims to show, not all rationalisms are created alike: Descartes before and Christian Wolff after tend to minimize discussion of infancy and childhood, whereas Leibniz was willing and able to at least attempt an alternative to Locke's ideas of prematurity. In particular, Leibniz's theory of perception, specifically of minute perceptions, allows for cognitions in infancy and childhood that Locke barred from possibility. Both Locke and Descartes were all-or-nothing in their theories of consciousness (either one has a clear idea or one does not); Leibniz's "discovery of the unconscious" was arguably as important to future thinking on children, though in a different manner, as was Locke's depiction of "the progress whereby their Minds attain the knowledge they have" (1.4.13). If Locke's progressive psychology helped lead to Piaget, then Leibniz's psychology of minute perceptions may have helped lead to Freud.[24]

UNDERSTANDING CHILDREN'S UNDERSTANDING

Locke's essay on *human* understanding begins by reflecting upon *children's* understanding. Even more precisely, it begins by reflecting upon children's *not* understanding. In refuting the notion of innate ideas, Locke submits that children do not have the speculative principles (that whatever is, is; and that something cannot both be and not be) that have been touted as innate.[25] Through most of the chapter "No innate speculative Principles," children consistently illustrate this negation. But Locke also makes positive statements about what children do perceive and understand, and in the final paragraphs, his emphasis shifts markedly. Compared to his initial presentation of children's intellectual deficits, Locke's final statements in this chapter sound almost Romantic in their praise of children's sincerity. *Almost* Romantic: Locke may begin with children's ideas, but his essay's telos (in book 4) is adults' knowledge. But that Locke does not ultimately promote a cult of childhood[26] should not obscure his novel gesture of beginning a philosophy of mind with sustained consideration of children's cognitive capacities. Indeed, significant portions of the *Essay* can be regarded as an attempt to understand children's understanding.

Locke's first objection against innate ideas states that universal consent is not given to them (and even if it were, that would still not prove them innate). His first evidence against universal consent: "*Children* and *Ideots*" (1.2.5) have no thought of supposedly innate principles.[27] Locke expands this list to include savages and illiterate people, concluding that probably half of humankind has never even heard of these principles. "But were the Number far less, it would be enough to destroy universal assent, and thereby shew these Propositions not to be innate, if Children alone were ignorant of them" (1.2.24). Children disprove general assent because while they lack these general speculative principles, children do have thoughts. If these principles are convincing, once brought to one's attention, this proves their self-evidence but fails to prove their innateness. Locke regards these principles as the fruit of advanced mental labor. Rather than being common property, Locke says that only few sages can "light at first on these Observations" and then propose them, such that "unobserving Men, when they are propos'd to them, cannot refuse their assent to" (1.2.21). But children are in a class below that of unobserving men. Although "Men grown up" (1.2.26) may assent to them as soon as they are proposed, still "those of tender Years" (ibid.) do not think of them and cannot assent to them, since children often learn the words of the proposition before they understand the significations of the words; thus children cannot assent at first hearing to propositions containing words they do not understand. Therefore, these supposedly innate ideas "cannot pretend to universal assent of intelligent Persons" (ibid.). I would underscore that Locke here includes children, despite their being poor observers, in the category of intelligent persons. This is generally notable because he does so in spite of a contemporary consensus about children's lack of intelligence.[28] And it is specifically notable in the context of the *Essay*: as I explore at the end of this chapter, it is unclear, according to Locke, when children may be regarded as persons, much less as intelligent persons.

Throughout the first half of his chapter on innate speculative ideas, Locke's children are cited exclusively as nonperceivers, nonunderstanders. Along with savages, illiterates, and idiots, children have a soul which "perceives or understands not" (1.2.5) these ideas. This rigid distinction between normal children and literate, civilized, normal adults relaxes in the second half of the chapter, where Locke begins to indicate what children do perceive and understand. "Whether we can determine it or no, it matters not, there is certainly a time, when Children begin to think, and their Words and Actions do assure us, that they do so" (1.2.25). We have already seen from the title page that the fetus represents mystery to Locke. Although he states that he will not argue from the "thoughts of Infants," which are "unknown to us" (1.2.25), he does seem to believe that the thoughts of children *can* be known to us, at least as soon as they are able to speak.[29]

But infancy is not so mysterious as to prevent Locke from maintaining this item of certain knowledge: the mind is initially contentless. Famously, Locke argues that ideas are acquired through experience, not innate (imprinted on the soul by God). Whereas Descartes viewed the senses as a potentially muddying medium that disturbs the view of these innate ideas, Locke held that the senses provide (rather than obscure) the basic materials of knowledge. Locke could agree with Descartes that infants and children are directed by the senses, but this tenet has different consequences for the two philosophers. For Locke, children represent the beginnings of knowledge. As beginners, children may be deficient thinkers and observers, but they are not defective.[30]

Locke's several lists of what "a child knows" (1.2.15) and what "a Child knows not" (1.2.16) indicate that children's knowledge is initially restricted to particular ideas. For example, an infant knows that sweet is not bitter; afterward, when able to speak, the child it has become knows that a sugar-plum is not worm-wood. But that child does not know that 3+4=7 until it can both count to seven and "has got the Name and *Idea* of Equality" (ibid.).[31] A child also knows that an apple is not fire (1.2.23), and that "the *Nurse* that feeds it, is neither the *Cat* it plays with, nor the *Blackmoor* it is afraid of; That the *Wormseed* or *Mustard* it refuses, is not the *Apple* or *Sugar* it cries for" (1.2.25). Whereas in the first half of chapter 1.2, children served to illustrate not understanding certain general ideas, it becomes clear in the second half that children do understand a host of particular ideas. From an initially contentless infant mind, the child acquires more and more particular ideas, gained from the senses, until upon sufficient subsequent reflection, it is able to abstract from these particulars to form general ideas. This process of abstraction involves subtracting features from particular ideas, which discloses resemblances between them, thereby forming a general idea. For example, a child is initially acquainted with specific people: its mother, nursemaid, and neighbors. In the course of abstraction, the particularities become effaced as the child forms a general concept of Man. Young children are total empirics, and most adults content themselves with empirically gained knowledge even after attaining the age of reason. What distinguishes Locke from rationalists like Descartes or Leibniz is his belief that epistemological inquiry should focus not on general speculative truths supposedly held in common and supposedly the foundation of knowledge, but rather on the "Steps and Ways Knowledge comes into our Minds" (1.2.23). What all humans share is not a set of implanted rational principles, as Locke's opponents (Aristotelian scholastics, Cartesians, and certain theologians) believed, but rather a sensual education that yields simple ideas.

It is well known that Locke provided impulses for the emergence of developmental psychology in the late eighteenth century; this new field took up Locke's suggestion: "If we will attentively consider new born *Children* . . . one may perceive how, by degrees, afterwards, *Ideas* come into their Minds" (1.4.2).[32] Locke's brief sketch (in book 1) and more extensive portrayal (in book 2) of mental development rests on this presupposition: that Locke could indeed observe what goes on in children's minds. Although he had conceded that infants' minds were inscrutable — which did not stop him from making certain claims about particular ideas they do have, namely those of their mothers and nurses, as well as of sweet and bitter — Locke never seemed to doubt that children's minds were open to observation. Toward the end of chapter 1.2, Locke has a new role for children: they now illustrate a sincerity and truth that adults, or at least certain overeducated rationalists, lack. To the extent that we can know the thoughts of children, we know they concern sense objects (mustard is not sugar) rather than propositions (the same thing cannot both be and not be). Locke scorns anyone who would say that "Children join these general abstract speculations with their sucking bottles, and their Rattles" (1.2.25). Such proponents of innate ideas "may, perhaps, with Justice be thought to have more Passion and Zeal for his Opinion; but less Sincerity and Truth, than one of that Age" (1.2.25). Locke here emphasizes the transparency of children's minds; he regards them as *specula naturae*.[33] The widespread acceptance of this concept explains why Locke can presume to be well understood when he protests that innate ideas should be clearest in those beings who are most transparent, i.e., "Children, Ideots, Savages, and illiterate People, being of all others the least corrupted by Custom, or borrowed Opinions. One might reasonably imagine, that in their Minds these innate Notions should lie open fairly to every one's view, as 'tis certain the thoughts of children do" (1.2.27).[34] If children's minds are transparent, and we cannot view speculative principles in those minds, then one must conclude that these principles are absent, thus not innate. Until this point of the *Essay*, Locke has depicted children (along with savages, the illiterate, and idiots/naturals) as ignorant. But now, in his chapter summary, Locke praises the ignorant as sincere, if simple, minds uncorrupted by scholastic niceties.

Against Locke's sudden upsurge of primitivism, Leibniz objects:

> Innate maxims make their appearance only through the attention one gives to them; but [children, idiots, and savages] have almost no attention to give, or have it only for something quite different. They think about little except their bodily needs; and it is appropriate that pure and disinterested thoughts should be the reward for having nobler concerns. It is true that the minds of children and savages are less "spoiled by customs," but they are also less improved by the teaching which makes one attentive. It would be very unjust if the brightest lights had to shine better in minds which are less worthy of them and are wrapped in the thickest clouds. (*NE* 87)

Around 1800, Wordsworth wrote in his poem "Intimations of Immortality" that children come into the world trailing clouds of glory; a century earlier, Leibniz effectively stated that there are more clouds than glory. Though the minds of children are inherently rational, they are more immersed in their bodies than are the minds of (educated, civilized) adults. As Leibniz continues, he contrasts Locke's implicit primitivism to the ideal of rational civilization: "People as learned and clever as you, Philalethes, or your excellent author, should not flatter ignorance and barbarism; for that would be to disparage the gifts of God. . . . In so far as one is capable of knowledge, it is a sin to neglect to acquire it, and the less instruction one has had the easier it is to fall into this" (*NE* 87–88). But Locke is not consistently primitivist. As I outline further below, many passages in book 2 depict adults as epistemologically superior to children. But much more troubling to Leibniz than Locke's brief praise of the ignorant was Locke's apparently relativist view of cultural differences regarding the treatment of children and infants.

Destroying and Principling Children

In Locke's chapter "No innate practical Principles," children tend to be objects of handling and especially mishandling, rather than the cognitive subjects they are in much of the *Essay*. To contest the notion of innate practical (today we would say moral or ethical) principles, Locke instances cultures that expose, geld and eat, bury alive, or otherwise dispatch of their children (1.4.9; see also 1.4.19, which adds abortion to this list of atrocities). Aberrant individuals who commit heinous acts could be seen as exceptions that prove the rule of innate morality, but Locke refers here to practical rules that are "universally, and with publick Approbation, or Allowance, transgressed" (1.4.11) in order to thereby dispute their innateness. And if any rule *could* reasonably be thought to be innate, Locke says it would be this one: "*Parents, preserve and cherish your Children*" (1.4.12). But the examples he cites to the contrary controvert the universality, and thus the innateness, of such a rule. Furthermore, its being a command entails that several other notions would also have to be innate for it to be understood: duty, and therefore a lawmaker, and therefore reward and punishment. In short, for this one command to be innate, God and the afterlife would have to be innate ideas as well. Leibniz cheerfully welcomes the innateness of all of these ideas, but he then has to explain why any individuals or cultures could deviate from them:

> Since demonstrations do not spring into view straight away, it is no great wonder if men are not always aware straight away of everything they have within them, and are not very quick to read the characters of the natural law which, according to St. Paul, God has engraved in their minds. However, since morality is more important than arithmetic, God has given to man instincts which lead, straight away and without reasoning, to part of what reason commands. . . . *The largest and soundest part* of the human race bears witness to them. . . . One would have to be as brutalized as the American savages to approve of their customs which are full of a cruelty surpassing even that of the beasts. (*NE* 92–93, my emphasis)

Leibniz's belief in the natural light within us is confronted by the fact of cultural difference around us. At this point, Leibniz's own essays on human understanding have the burden of showing that they are not really essays on European understanding. This is the robust part of Locke's challenge: "Men presuming themselves to be the only Masters of right Reason, cast by the Voices and Opinions of the rest of Mankind, as not worthy the reckoning" (1.3.20). As we see in the preceding quote from Leibniz, one way to explain the American savages' apparent lack of *human* understanding of morality is to refer to their *brutishness*. Leibniz's conceptual gain comes at the price of cultural insensitivity, to put it mildly. But Leibniz is by no means a pure Eurocentrist; he continues: "However, these same savages have a good sense of what justice is in other situations" (*NE* 93). And Leibniz later insists that reason "is present in all men" (*NE* 326), whether Negro, Chinese, American Indian, or European.[35] As I discuss in chapter 4, Leibniz later raises the charge of (theological) cruelty to children against several of his European contemporaries, the Jansenist theologians. I will thus hazard the thesis that in this respect, Leibniz is not eurocentric: he is against child abuse wherever it appears.

Against Locke's insistence on *universal* consent as necessary for verifying the innateness of an idea, Leibniz points to *majority* consent: "although there may be no wicked custom which is not permitted somewhere and in some circumstances, nonetheless most of them are condemned most of the time and by the great majority of mankind" (*NE* 93). Most cultures, the best ones, do follow the innate practical principle, according to which children should be preserved and cherished. The majority agreement tells Leibniz that most people in most cultures do follow natural instincts. And "in addition to this general social instinct, which can be called 'philanthropy' in man, there are more particular ones such as the affection between male and female, the love of fathers and mothers for their offspring, which the Greeks called *storge*, and other similar inclinations" (ibid.). These instincts make up natural law. It is true that not all individuals and not all cultures actually read these engraved characters correctly. But the more one cultivates reason, the better guides one will have, and one will be better able to apprehend universal practical principles.[36]

According to Leibniz's arguments, aberrant cultures that harm their children do so because they have not cultivated reason, and thus fail to read what God has written on all of our hearts. In a word, the members of such cultures are sinners. It seems noteworthy that Locke's writings on government approximate Leibniz's position here. In his *First Treatise*, Locke condemns infanticide and the selling of children, concluding in section 58 that such atrocities become possible when one "quits his reason."[37] I conclude from this passage that Locke is not a cultural relativist: some acts are wrong, no matter how many people perform them. Although chapter 1.4 of the *Essay* cites the absence of certain principles in certain cultures in order to prove that they are not innate, Locke also admits that these principles are self-evident to those who cultivate reason. Why they would not be self-evident to the savage cultures Locke mentions, he does not here explain, but it would seem to follow that he, along with Leibniz, regards the members of such cultures as sinners.

Locke's view of instinct is much less optimistic than is Leibniz's: "Principles of Actions indeed there are lodged in Men's Appetites, but these are so far from being innate Moral Principles, that if they were left to their full swing, they would carry Men to the over-turning of all Morality" (1.3.13). In effect, Locke states that our desires are disordered, such that "Moral Laws are set as a curb and restraint to these exorbitant Desires" (ibid.). These statements sound like they comport with an orthodox Christian view of concupiscence, the postlapsarian disorder of our desires. But I agree with those scholars who insist that Locke's denial of original sin (at least in this doctrine's contemporary orthodox forms) was robust.[38] Still, Locke insists upon the importance of revealed law as a curb for our disordered wills. Locke's insistence that an innate morality would have to entail an innate Gospel raises a challenge for a fellow Christian philosopher such as Leibniz: if we have an innate Gospel, why do we need the written one? Locke seems to think we do need the written Gospel. Although natural law for Locke is something "that we being ignorant of may attain to the knowledge of, by the use and due application of our natural faculties" (1.3.13), having a Bible also helps: it is notable in this context that Locke's list of cultures behaving atrociously is composed primarily of pre- or non-Christian cultures. But having a Bible without applying one's natural faculties is also insufficient: "it is familiar amongst the *Mengrelians*, a People professing Christianity, to bury their Children alive without scruple" (1.3.9). One needs both biblical revelation and God-given reason. Locke and Leibniz agree on this fundamental point.

To the extent that Locke denies original sin, he must trace our disorders to some other source than the Fall of our first parents, Adam and Eve.[39] Against Paul and the natural lawyers who hold that God writes laws in our hearts, Locke in the *Essay* asserts that nurses, old women, and neighbors do so, along with parents and local communities. Drawing upon contemporary ordinary language, Locke maintains that moral principles do not originate from God's having stamped them upon us, but rather are taught: thus we say that we *principle* children. Our principles do not derive from the mind's natural endowment: they are located in the cultures into which children are socialized. Although Locke denies the *existence* of innate principles, he recognizes that *belief* in them is widespread and strong. His explanation of this belief involves a natural history, according to which people (1) are principled as children, (2) subsequently forget *how* they got their moral knowledge, (3) reflect on their own minds when grown up, (4) "cannot find anything more ancient there, than those Opinions, which were taught them" (1.3.23) and so (5) falsely conclude them to be innate.[40] Locke would have us fear this misapprehension: these opinions are "Idols," even "Monsters lodged in [the] Brain" (1.3.26) and yet people "entertain and submit to [them], as many do to their Parents, with Veneration" (1.3.23). Honoring one's parents is all well and good, but mistaken filial piety (for monsters in the brain posing as parents) is dangerous. Unfortunately, it is also quite common. Locke explains that most people are "exposed by their Ignorance, Laziness, Education, or Precipitancy, to *take them upon trust*. . . . This is evidently the case of all Children and young Folk" (1.3.24–25). Trust might be appropriate for children, who should at least for a time trust their elders, but it is not appropriate for mature human beings, who should *meditate* but are often unable or unwilling to do so.[41] For grown men, custom prevents this, along with business. Here, Locke sounds very much like Descartes in his praise of the few who "dare shake the foundations of all his past Thoughts and Actions" (1.3.25) and begin to extirpate errors gathered since childhood.

Locke's description of principling children is gendered; Locke scholarship has often overlooked this fact. Douglas Greenlee states that Locke's attack on innate ideas was directed at three groups: Cartesians, scholastics, and certain British theologians and moralists. On the final page of his article, Greenlee cites a passage in which Locke names nurses and old women as those who instituted certain flawed opinions in the child, and Greenlee provides this footnote: "Hence to the list of polemical adversaries a fourth can be added, that of unthinking custom and superstition."[42] Although he cites Locke's words ("nurse," "old woman"), Greenlee himself names them only through circumscription ("unthinking custom," "superstition") and in a footnote. He could have revised his previous summary, listing the four categories in the body of the article, yet he omitted doing so. Greenlee's conclusion — that Locke's attack on innate ideas is a rejection of "dogmatic appeals to authorities, whether those authorities consist in ecclesiastical or philosophical establishments or merely in blind human custom"[43] — is generally convincing, yet it also obfuscates. It replaces Locke's fourth target (nurses and old women) with a substitute term (blind human custom). By contrast, William Walker's interpretation of these passages highlights the originary presence of women in Locke's genealogy of opinion. According to Locke, many doctrines that grow to become moral or religious principles "have been derived from no better original, than the Superstition of a Nurse, or the Authority of an old Woman" (1.3.22). Feminine miseducation is the hallmark of childhood. But this fact is forgotten: thus children, having become "*Men*" (1.3.23), find these opinions in place but forget how they came to be there, and thus conclude "*That those Propositions, of whose knowledge they can find in themselves no original, were certainly the impress of God and Nature* upon their Minds" (1.3.23). Walker states that in Locke's account, "a real empirical origin is displaced and totally effaced by the posited origin: in the oblivion of the male mind, God usurps Woman as the origin of the oldest belief and makes it sacred. Empiricism liquidates this posited God by locating experience, the female, and time in what the mind senses as the atemporality in which divinity works."[44] I would argue that Locke's genealogy holds not for "the male mind," as in Walker's first sentence, but for "the mind," as in his second one. That is, I do not find that Locke here analyzes male vs. female belief. Locke's conclusion (that innate principles are not from God, but rather from nurses and old women) is not meant to uncover a truth that is either neutral or to be celebrated (that unexplored notions of divinity actually have a feminine origin), but rather one that is regrettable and should be overcome. In my view, Locke's polemic against the authority of old women and the superstition of nurses is intended to explain the origin of erroneous thinking in childhood. For Descartes, as we saw in chapter 1, the errors of cognition in childhood derive from the rational soul's being deeply immersed in the body. For Locke, childhood error derives from being immersed in women's superstitions and authority.[45]

An important distinction between Descartes and Locke requires comment. Descartes's view of the source of our childish cognitive ways involves an immutable human condition: our souls must suffer immersion in the fetal, infant, and then child's body. This immersion causes us to rely excessively on the senses and thus make erroneous judgments until adulthood. But Locke's attribution of error to children's being principled by superstitious women may be a cultural diagnosis. It is necessary that we be embodied as children before becoming adults; it is not necessary that we be raised by superstitious women. If children can instead be raised by those who would aim to stimulate their critical thinking skills, rather than principling them, then presumably these children will not have need of a demolition of their opinions in their 30s (as with Descartes). In Schouls's estimation, Locke is optimistic that education can avoid the problems of principling: "the only principle that ought to guide parents is not 'to principle' children but to encourage them to develop their power of questioning. . . . This manner of educating, according to Locke, is the only way for a new generation to have the best chance of maturing free from prejudice."[46] This optimism may well have informed Locke's *Some Thoughts*, but I find that the tenor of the *Essay* regards principling as a cultural constant. Recall that Locke said about taking opinions on trust: this is so for "*all* Children and young Folk" (1.3.25, my emphasis). Schouls himself admits later in his study that in Locke, "human beings are not prejudiced at birth but they are *all*, to a greater or lesser degree, prejudiced by their upbringing."[47] I would suggest that for Locke, moral progress is possible even without a reformed educational system; it is possible due to God's revelation of laws to guide us and due to our God-given understandings, which can actively formulate moral ideas (those of "mixed modes"). As Schouls emphasizes, the human condition for Locke may involve an initially deficient situation (being irrationally attached to childhood principles), but it also entails the possibility of progress beyond that deficiency: "we may say that to be prejudiced is human, that is, it is part of the human condition. But a being does not become truly human, does not actualize the potential of human nature, except by overcoming prejudice."[48] Anticipating my discussion in chapter 3, I should like to note that Schouls's remarks seem apposite to what Locke will call "moral Man," rather than to "Man," which is for Locke a biological term.

Whether the problem with principling is a cultural constant or a contingency, it takes place during childhood. While the Locke of *Some Thoughts* might imagine an alternative childhood that could avoid prejudice, the Locke of the *Essay* holds that childhood involves a feminine moral miseducation that can be overcome in maturity. As we shall now see, this view of childhood deficiency and subsequent progress into maturity characterizes Locke's view of intellectual life as well.

PROGRESSIVE DEVELOPMENT
FROM DEFICIENT BEGINNINGS

Locke's program, which the first developmental psychologists would begin to follow a century later, places great importance in identifying the first exercises, first beginnings, and first ideas: "Because several of these faculties being exercised at first principally about simple *Ideas*, we might, by following Nature in its ordinary method, trace and discover them in their rise, progress, and gradual improvements" (2.9.14). Locke's "short, and, I think, true *History of the first beginnings of Humane Knowledge*" seeks

to narrate the progress the mind makes from its first steps on (2.9.15).
One should not miss the contrast with Descartes, for whom "first philosophy" began with the meditations of a thirty-something year-old. But
the contrast is less stark with infant and adult cognition, about which
Descartes and Locke often write similarly, than with children's sensate
thoughts, to which they assign different value. Where Descartes saw
these thoughts as unfortunate accretions, sure to form impediments to
rationality, Locke saw them as building blocks for the edifice of knowledge.

Locke's map of development divides mental life into three phases:
first, the ignominious beginning, a time of presensate or minimally sensate fetal life; second, childhood, a time of sensation; third, adulthood, a
time of reflection and reason (along with sensation). As though anticipating his later discussion of what makes an identical plant, an identical
animal, and an identical human, Locke characterizes the beginning of
human cognition thus: noting that infants spend much of their time
sleeping, and that newborn children show "few Signs of a Soul accustomed to much thinking . . . and much fewer of Reasoning at all," Locke
finds "Reason to imagine, that a *Foetus in the Mother's Womb, differs not
much from the State of a Vegetable*" (2.1.21; see also 2.9.11). Lacking sensual stimulation, the fetus lacks ideas. (This view could not differ more
from Descartes's, for whom even the fetus is thinking always. It may
lack memory storage, but it does not lack ideas.) Locke does not explicitly state that the child is like an animal, but as I discuss below, an enumeration of the intellectual operations of which the *Essay*'s animals are
capable largely overlaps with a similar enumeration for the *Essay*'s
youngest children.[49] The postvegetable stage is defined as a time of sensation: "Follow a *Child* from its Birth" (2.1.22), Locke exhorts us, and
we will see that ideas are gained *by degrees* through the senses. Once impressions are made on the senses, "the Mind seems first to employ itself"
(1.2.23) about them. This self-employment, which seems to span childhood, involves "*Perception, Remembring, Consideration, Reasoning*, etc."
(2.1.23). But the endgoal is set at a later point: "In time, the Mind comes
to reflect on its own *Operations*" (2.1.24). This reflective capacity, which
marks the prerogative of human understanding, is proper to human
adulthood.

When he writes about cognitive acts, Locke switches between several
subjects: from "men" to "one" to "children." In the first two cases, Locke
invariably makes statements about the human mind in general; "men" in
Locke's use stands not only for men and women, but also for children

and adults. But when he speaks of "children" as cognitive subjects, Locke quite specifically refers to the beginnings of human cognition. Children get all their ideas via sensation; they are "born into the World being surrounded with Bodies" (2.1.6). The operations of children's minds "pass there continually; yet like floating Visions, they make not deep Impressions enough, to leave in the Mind clear distinct lasting Ideas, till the Understanding turns inwards upon it self. . . . Children . . . are surrounded with a world of new things, which, by a constant solicitation of their senses, draw the mind constantly to them. . . . Thus the first Years are usually imploy'd and diverted in looking abroad" (2.1.8). Reflection, for Locke as well as for Descartes, does not happen "till they come to be of riper Years" (2.1.8). Young children only perceive things, whereas older children and adults can also reflect upon things (and upon their own mental operations). Although Locke's tone does not match Descartes's aversion to childhood immersion in the body, children are nevertheless for Locke immersed in a world of bodies and things (along with early feminine miseducation). For both thinkers, being human means being rational. Both thus celebrate progress, that is, steps taken away from childhood. Of course, Cartesian progress entails a demolition of opinions, in contrast to which Lockean progress (via reflection, compounding of ideas, etc.) often appears less unsettling.[50] But common to both is the deficient beginning of childhood and the movement away from it.

Locke's agreement with Descartes on the uselessness of fetal cognition subtends his more famous disagreement with Descartes on the nature of the soul. Locke's challenge to the Cartesian view of the soul as a *res cogitans*, a thinking thing, proceeds on two fronts. First and most famously, Locke asserts that *"Thinking is the Action, and not the Essence of the Soul"* (2.19.4). Thus, there may be gaps in the soul's thinking. It seems often enough not to think (as in deep sleep, or in fevers), and if one says that the thinking took place but left no traces behind, this seems to Locke a bad argument: *"To think often, and never to retain it so much as one moment, is a very useless sort of thinking"* (2.1.15). Such a soul would be like a material mirror, keeping no traces of what goes across its surface, no "footsteps" of ideas, no "impressions" (2.1.15; see also 2.1.25). (Recall from chapter 1 Descartes's metaphor of footprints in the sand.) The second challenge is of more interest to my discussion: "Those who confidently tell us, That the Soul always actually thinks, I would they would also tell us, what those *Ideas* are that are in the Soul of a Child, before, or just at the union with the Body, before it hath received any by *Sensation*"

(2.1.17). Leibniz, willing to attempt an answer to Locke, thinks that "there is always a perfect correspondence between the body and the soul" (*NE* 116). Presumably, this correspondence holds for infancy as well. "The perceptions of the soul always correspond [*repondent*] naturally to the state of the body; and when there are many confused and indistinct motions in the brain as happens with those who have had little experience, it naturally follows that the thoughts of the soul cannot be distinct either" (*NE* 117, G 5:106). So Leibniz does not say that the fetus has *ideas*, as Descartes sometimes claimed. It can, though, have *perceptions*, the indistinctness of which results from the infant soul representing the young body's soft and humid brain. What interests me here is the agreement beneath the rationalist/empiricist polemic: for both Descartes and Locke (as well as Gassendi—see chapter 1), the cognition of very young children is "very useless" (2.1.25). On this topic, Leibniz emerges, perhaps surprisingly, as the defender of infant cognition. Against Locke's (but also Descartes's) dismissal of thinking-and-not-retaining as useless, Leibniz replies that "every impression has an effect, but the effects are not always noticeable" (*NE* 115). Indeed, it is an axiom for Leibniz that "anything which is noticeable must be made up of parts which are not" (*NE* 117). For Locke, there is nothing useful before the first conscious ideas. For Leibniz, infant and fetal cognition, even below the threshold of consciousness and before the first conscious idea, counts as the act of a mind that is human, not vegetable.

For someone who is famous for claiming that children may be regarded as rational creatures, Locke is quite expansive in cataloging ways in which children are intellectually lacking.[51] To list five such ways: first, *children are passive*. Sensation and perception produce actual ideas in the understanding, and so even a fetus in the womb can have ideas of warmth and hunger. (These are the first ideas, Locke repeats, not innate ones.) After birth, light is the next idea impressed upon children via sensation (see 2.9.5–7). These initial perceptions are passive, whereas later reflection is active. Second, *children lack judgment*. We learn that *"Ideas we receive by sensation, are often* in grown People *alter'd by the Judgement"* (2.9.8). Locke's emphasis in this phrase (marked by the absence of italics) indicates that in children, this alteration does not occur. For children, a bent stick in water is believed to be bent. Locke thereby states that adults have judgment to correct ideas of sensation; children lack this judgment. Third, *children lack consideration and reasoning*. Pleasure and pain make initially the deepest, most lasting impression. Pain, "supplying the Place of Consideration and Reasoning in Children, and acting quicker than Consideration in grown Men, makes both Young and Old avoid painful Objects . . . and in both settles in the Memory a caution for the Future" (2.10.3). Fourth, *children are heedless*. A passage on the lack of imprinting in memory yields another statement from Locke about children's deficiencies: Locke says that some objects have affected the senses too rarely, or "have yet been little taken notice of; the Mind, either heedless, as in Children, or otherwise employ'd, as in Men, intent only on one thing, not setting the stamp deep into it self" (2.10.4). In these cases, ideas fade and vanish, leaving no "footsteps." Men might not heed certain ideas, but they are not constitutionally heedless, as children are. Fifth, *children are confined to observation*. The mind is passive in its getting simple ideas, but active in getting complex ones, through combining, apprehending relations, and abstracting: these faculties go beyond what sensation and reflection can provide. Forming complex ideas seems to be a prerogative of the more mature mind: "when [the mind] has once got these simple *Ideas*, it is not confined barely to Observation." (2.12.2). By implication, children *are* so confined to the passive observation of things. It should be clear by now that for Locke, the distinction child/adult corresponds to the distinctions: passive/active, confined/free, lacking/having certain faculties.

Locke makes plain that children lack the liberty of intellectual beings. He begins a chapter on power, the contents of which Leibniz singled out as "the subtlest and most important in the whole work" (*NE* 164), by considering whether human powers in general (the will, the understanding) are free. Regarding the understanding, Locke states that "a waking Man being under the necessity of having some *Ideas* constantly in his Mind, is not at *liberty* to think, or not to think" (2.21.12). This condition entails children as well. Intellectual liberty consists in the choice to think of one thing vs. another, and men normally do have this choice. Regarding the will, liberty for Locke, as well as later for Kant, means being "determined by our own judgment" (2.21.48). It is the ability to suspend one's desires that "makes way for consideration" (2.21.47) and makes up "the liberty of intellectual Beings" (2.21.52). Children, who as we have seen lack judgment and consideration, are by implication not at liberty in this way. Although their wills may not be in bondage in quite the theological sense articulated by Augustine and Luther, children *are* for Locke in bondage to sensation.[52]

Discerning, or distinguishing between ideas, allows confused perceptions to become clear. Since it is absent in animals, discerning seems to Locke "to be the Prerogative of Humane Understanding" (2.9.5).[53] But this faculty and that of abstraction, which marks "a perfect distinction" (2.11.10) between humans and animals, can only be observed in later childhood. Thus, in earlier childhood, the distinction proves to be imperfect. (Abstraction begins with naming in childhood. As I discuss in chapter 3, it seems the child first exercises its human prerogative, thus showing that it is a Man, when it first forms the concept of "Man," Locke's example of an abstraction.) While a rationalist might quibble with Locke about how universal ideas are made (through induction or through anamnesis), that rationalist could certainly agree with Locke "that the having of general *Ideas*, is that which puts a perfect distinction betwixt Man and Brutes" (ibid.). In both Locke and Leibniz, the cognitions of children and animals are confused and particular, rather than clear and general. Animals, children and even many grown men rely entirely upon this inferior "analogy to reason" to guide their beliefs and actions: "This could be called 'inference' or 'reasoning' in a very broad sense. But I prefer to keep to accepted usage, reserving [*consecrant*] these words for men and restricting them to the knowledge of some *reason* for perceptions' being linked together" (*NE* 143, G 5:130). Grown men can and should cultivate the superior faculty of reason, which is inherently closed to animals and temporarily closed to children (so long as they are children).

Such is the normal map of cognitive development, according to Locke. But not all humans show that they possess the prerogative of human understanding, and this fact calls for explanation. Locke does not overlook the existence of defective cases, such as idiocy or insanity. (I discuss changelings and monstrosity in the following chapter.) Locke concludes "That mad Men put wrong *Ideas* together, and so make Propositions, but argue and reason right from them: But Idiots make very few or no Propositions, and reason scarce at all" (2.11.13). It seems that young children are more like idiots than like madmen. As they grow, normal children become less idiotic and more rational. As part of this process, they become persons.

CHILDHOOD AND PERSONHOOD

Given Locke's regular use of the terms *man, men,* and *he* when he means what we would refer to as *human* or *one*, it is striking how gender-neutral the chapter on personal identity is. This seems to be one reason that several early modern women philosophers (Damaris Masham, Catharine Cockburn, and Mary Astell) advocated Locke's *Essay* in general and this chapter in particular. As Kathryn J. Ready argues, these philosophers observed that Locke's alternative to dominant Christian theories of identity—which tied identity to the body and thus justified the subjugation of women—seemed to contain the seeds of liberation from traditional gender roles. That is, Locke's theory of personal identity, which decoupled identity from the body, could be very good for women.[54] My question is: what does Locke's theory of personal identity, which decoupled connected consciousness from infancy, do for infants and children? A full answer to this question would have to negotiate the massive amount of scholarship on personal identity since Locke; this lies beyond my present intent. A comparison with Leibniz, with which I conclude this chapter, will make a start.

Locke developed a theory of personal identity that comports with both the Christian doctrine of resurrection and Locke's profound skepticism about our ability to know substances. On the day of judgment, Locke believed, all persons will be resurrected and rewarded or punished for their deeds. But he was uncertain whether the bodies in which these persons will be resurrected would be the same bodies to which they were connected in life; he was similarly uncertain whether the spiritual substance would remain the same. Thus Locke wanted to ensure that we could understand the justice of God's rewarding or punishing each person, despite our inadequate knowledge of the material or spiritual substance that supports the person being rewarded or punished. This religious context, I believe, helps explain why Locke needed to develop a theory of identity that could tolerate (indeed repeatedly insisted upon) interruptions of consciousness. In *The Reasonableness of Christianity*, Locke upheld the doctrine that death entered the world through Adam's sin, but he took issue with orthodox interpretations that took the word "death" to signify a death of the human body and a continued life of the personal spirit in the torments of hell. "I must confess by *death* here, I can understand nothing but a ceasing to be, the losing of all actions of life and sense."[55] To use three important terms from Locke's chapter on personal identity, death for Locke signifies annihilation of the human, the spirit, and the person. And when people die, they would "remain under death forever, and so be utterly lost" (ibid. 5), were it not for their redemption by Jesus Christ. But this redemption undoes death only at the resurrection, when people "recover from death"[56] in order to be judged. Only at that point, if I read Locke correctly, do hell or heaven become possible fates. But the resurrection for judgment day can be reconciled with God's goodness only if the identity of the resurrected can be established, in spite of the intervening interruption of existence, which of course entailed an interruption of consciousness along with a likely change in the bodily or spiritual substance supporting that consciousness. If the question is what gets resurrected from nonbeing, Locke's answer is: certainly the same person; whether the same bodily or spiritual substance is also resurrected, we cannot know with certainty.

This religious concern may seem distant from what philosophers have lately debated concerning personal identity. In recent decades, there has been much discussion of personal identity in terms of survival: transplanted brains, transplanted consciousnesses, even fission, i.e., separating the right and left halves of a brain and placing them in two bodies to create (perhaps) two new persons.[57] But one could certainly view this modern secular discussion as continuous with Locke's early modern theological engagement with the doctrine of resurrection. Both aim to secure personal survival beyond bodily death.

This seems to bring us far afield of our topic, infancy and childhood, but Locke's treatment of identity as a forensic term (i.e. pertaining to reward and punishment) has several consequences for infants and young children. For as I presently show, infants and young children, according to Locke's text, are not persons. It follows that they cannot justly be judged at the resurrection. Famously enough, Locke denied the Augustinian theory of original sin, which ascribes personal guilt to every infant for Adam's disobedience, such that every infant deserves eternal punishment.[58] One might ask what Locke believed would happen to human beings who die before they can be said to have personhood. It would seem that neither reward nor punishment would be a just fate for the unaccountable. Being unaware of any statements by Locke on infant damnation, I can only draw conclusions regarding what infants and young children deserve (after death) based on Locke's statements about accountability. It seems to me that Locke's statements (in the *Essay* and *Reasonableness*) would incline him to believe in some version of the children's limbo, supposed to be a place of neither reward nor punishment, but something in between.[59] As far as I have seen, Locke says nothing explicit on this theological question. In any case, his developmental view of selfhood and personhood, as sketched in the *Essay*, would seem to have consequences for his thoughts on accountability in legal, ethical, and pedagogical settings. A thorough examination of Locke's writings on this topic would be instructive, but this exceeds my current project. In the remainder of this section, I restrict myself to accountability as articulated in the *Essay*.

Locke insists that human identity, like animal and plant identity, depends upon an uninterrupted organization of the body. This continued organization may involve different bits of matter, which enter into and exit from the organization, but the organization of that matter must be continuous and uninterrupted for that organization to qualify as identical. A plant or an animal is comparable to a ship under constant piecemeal repair. Even if every plank of wood is ultimately replaced, the ship still deserves the same name. (Locke refers here to the ship of Theseus.) Anyone attributing human identity to anything other than such bodily organization "will find it hard, to make an *Embryo*, one of Years, mad, and sober, the same Man" (2.27.6). That is, Locke's unnamed targets hold that human identity depends upon the identity of the soul, rather than the identity of the body; they are thus unable to exclude the possibility that the soul of Socrates has returned in the body of Cesar Borgia. A good definition of human identity has to exclude this possibility, yet still allow the embryo and adult to be identified as the same man. So Locke suggests that human identity should be located in the continuous succession of bodily states.

Against the scholastic definition of Man as a *rational animal*, Locke proposes a counter-definition of Man as "an Animal of a certain Form" (2.27.8), even if that man lacks reason. He may be "a dull irrational *Man*" (2.27.8), but this *irrational animal* is nonetheless a man. Locke thereby suggests that the rationality of a given man is accidental rather than essential. Whereas the Aristotelian definition places two terms into one concept, it seems to me that Locke regards *rational animal* as two distinct concepts proper to different times. With Man, that is, the animal comes first and (if all goes well) the rational comes later. This delay, I submit, is marked by Locke's differential use of the terms *self* (which comes first) and *person* (which comes later). The rational (the person, consciousness) can also survive the animal (the human, the body). Locke disassembled the Aristotelian scholastic definition to create one that would comport with his Christian eschatology. Understanding this helps us correctly read other statements where Locke highlights the connection, rather than the difference, between the rational and the animal. For example, Locke says that in most people's estimation, the same man is made up of "the same successive Body . . . as well as the same immaterial Spirit" (2.27.8). This "as well as," I suggest, must be understood as marking a temporary nonessential state.

Locke's short definition of personal identity is "the sameness of a rational Being" (2.27.9). And a person is "a thinking intelligent Being, that has reason and reflection, and can consider it self as it self, the same thinking thing in different times and places; which it does only by that consciousness, which is inseparable from thinking, and as it seems to me essential to it" (2.27.9). Let us recall Locke's previous statements that infants and young children lack reason, reflection, and the liberty of intellectual beings: it is then evident that this definition, which requires reason and reflection, excludes infants and young children from personhood. Whereas the identity of the *man* (i.e., the human body) can include the embryo and the adult (per 2.27.6), the identity of the *person* cannot. Embryos and infants are men but are not persons.

This conclusion is further supported by Locke's relating personal identity to consciousness: "And as far as this consciousness can be extended backwards to any past Action or Thought, so far reaches the Identity of the *Person*; it is the same *self* now it was then" (2.27.9). Although there is a textual basis for regarding Locke as a simple memory theorist—and this is precisely how most eighteenth-century critics interpreted Locke—it should be noted that "consciousness" is a more inclusive term than *memory*.[60] There is a difference of emphasis, at least, in what Locke considers a person vs. a self. I agree with Raymond Martin and John Barresi that Locke sometimes "uses the words interchangeably. However, often he seems to use *self* to refer to a momentary entity and *person* to refer to a temporally extended one."[61] Another emphatic difference pertains not only to the temporality but to the type of consciousness: some definitions (at 2.27.9 and 2.27.17) underscore that "persons are *thinkers*" of transtemporal self-reference, whereas "selves are *sensors*"[62] of punctual self-reference. It then seems to follow that infants and children, who exist in a world of sensation, are selves before they are persons. Martin and Barresi suggest that personhood is a temporal concatenation of selfhoods; they offer this reconstruction of Locke's stage theory:

> First, a human organism's experience of pleasure and pain gives rise to the idea of a self—its own self—that is the experiencer of pleasure and pain. Second, a human organism's experience of pleasure and pain also gives rise to concern with the quality of that self's experience (each of us wants more pleasure, less pain). In thus constituting itself as a self, the organism, in effect, creates what initially is "a momentary self." In creating this self, the organism does not create any new matter or spirit. Third, the momentary self thus constituted (or perhaps the organism) thinks of itself (or its self) as extended over brief periods of time (say, the

specious present). Then, through memory and the appropriation ingre-
dient in self-consciousness, it thinks of itself as extended over longer pe-
riods of time.[63]

In this fourth step, the self becomes "accountable" (2.27.26), that is, a
person. This reconstruction, while illuminating, provides more clarity
than Locke himself did. Locke is much more specific in defining *person*
than he is in defining *self*. For Locke, *human* is clearly a biological term
and *person* is clearly a forensic one; it seems to me that the term *self* hov-
ers between these two discourses. Martin and Barresi conclude their
discussion of "the origin of selves" by pointing out that according to
Locke's terms, it is unclear what the referent of the word *me* is: the or-
ganism, the self, or the person. I would suggest that this difficulty stems
from Locke's internal temporal division in the concept *rational animal*.

But where Locke was a splitter, Leibniz was a lumper: for Leibniz,
"me" (rendered in the following translations as: "I") refers to the monad,
which is at once self and person, and which is vitally attached to the or-
ganism. In a word, the monad is the principle of being for the rational
animal. Leibniz, a philosopher of the individual (against Locke, a
philosopher of the conceptually divisible human, self, or person), posits
in strong terms the identity of the human mind from conception into
eternity: "We have all these forms in our mind; we even have forms *from
all time*, for the mind always expresses all its future thoughts and already thinks confusedly about everything it will ever think about distinctly" (AG 58). Leibniz, the philosopher of continuity, marks precisely
one significant discontinuity in the existence of the human monad: conception. In Leibniz's settled view, all human monads were created as
souls along with Adam, in whose seed they lay dormant, encased one
within the other like Russian dolls, their perceptions very obscure.[64] At
the moment of conception, these souls are elevated to reason, and
henceforth count as spirits, as rational minds. And when the human
body dies, the monad merely folds up, remaining still attached to some
small body, but does not itself change in nature (see *NE* 233); it merely
slumbers as it awaits resurrection. (Since for Leibniz, death is not annihilation, the waiting period between death and judgment day does not
pose a serious continuity problem, as it did for Locke.) A consequence
of this view is that Leibniz tends to minimize all discontinuities other
than conception, such as the transition from infancy to childhood to
adulthood; or the transition from selfhood to personhood. Leibniz does
concede some of what Locke wrote about the self becoming a person,

but he is not overly concerned with identifying the person, since he has already located identity in the immaterial immortal monad. The difference between Leibniz and Locke on selfhood and personhood results not from a particular conceptual disagreement (there is none I discern) but rather from a difference of emphasis and approach: Leibniz is more concerned than is Locke with the prepersonal self, minimizing its being considered different from the personal self. To make a classic distinction, Locke is here the empiricist, writing about what we can observe (that personhood emerges under certain conditions), while Leibniz is the rationalist, writing about what we can assume and conclude about selves and persons (that they are two ways of regarding the same individual, the rational monad).

Responding to Locke's definition of the "same human" as a continuity of bodily organization, Leibniz asks a question Locke neglects to pose: who or what is behind the organization? For Leibniz, the principle of life that he calls a "monad" makes an individual such. The organic body continues to be the same only in appearance, like the ship constantly under repair or like water in a river. The monad directing this organization, Leibniz says, "makes the *I* in substances which think" (*NE* 232). Where Locke contests Aristotle's definition of man by insisting on shape alone (prioritizing observation over definition), Leibniz says that shape alone is insufficient: the inner working of reason is always to be assumed, even if its exercise is suspended and it cannot be observed (see *NE* 234). Always: that means in childhood, in infancy, even in utero, where the soul was elevated to reason. Leibniz agrees with Locke "that consciousness or the sense of *I* proves moral or personal identity" (*NE* 236) but balks at the memory criterion (whether this criterion is actually Locke's is an open question; Leibniz took it to be so): "I would not wish to deny, either, that 'personal identity' and even the 'self' [*le* soy] persist in us, and that I am that *I* [*ce* moy] who was in the cradle, merely on the grounds that I can no longer remember anything that I did at that time" (ibid., G 5:219). So for Leibniz, there was indeed an *I* in the cradle. But this is a separate question from whether there was also the *sense of I* or the *consciousness of I* in the cradle. These would be necessary for personhood to obtain in the cradle. Now there does have to be "a mediating bond of consciousness" (ibid.) for the *I* to extend back to infancy, so Leibniz keeps Locke's general criterion (consciousness), rejecting only what he takes to be Locke's specific criterion (memory). Leibniz notes that we forget things all the time, that others can fill in gaps in our recollection, and that we can be justly punished for what we have done, even if we cannot recall it. It is worth noting that Leibniz writes here about illnesses that erase memory, as opposed to an infancy that fails to store memory. Still, the lack of memory of infancy should not cause us to assume that we are not identical to the *I* who was in the cradle. I would emphasize here that Leibniz insists that there is an *I* in the cradle, even though we cannot observe the infant designate itself as such.

Over his career, Leibniz uses the term "I" to refer exclusively to intelligent souls. In the 1688 *Discourse on Metaphysics*, section 34, he says that only intelligent souls have "the ability to utter the word 'I' [*ce MOY*], a word so full of meaning" (AG 65, G 4:459). In the 1714 *Principles of Nature and Grace, Based on Reason*, section 5, we learn that these souls "are capable of performing reflexive acts, and capable of considering what is called 'I' [*Moy*], substance, soul, mind" (AG 209, G 6:601). Since infants cannot utter anything, and young children speak long before they refer to themselves in the first person, it might seem that infants by definition and young children by observation would not be included in the class of intelligent souls. This concern is dispelled by Leibniz's 1702 letter to Queen Sophie Charlotte, in which we learn that "since I conceive that other beings can also have the right to say 'I,' or that it can be said for them, it is through this that I conceive what is called *substance* in general" (AG 188). Even if infants and children lack the actual ability to say 'I,' they have the right to say it, and it can be said for them. One might say that Leibniz regards infants as wards, rather than as nonpersons. Thus, Leibniz can assert that there was an *I* in the cradle, even if that *I* was unable to refer to itself as an *I* at that time. And according to his criterion, this condition obtains not only in the cradle, but also in the uterus, as far back as the moment of conception, when the soul was elevated to reason with all the rights of that state, including the right to say "I." This leads me to conclude that Leibniz's *I* serves a similar function to Locke's *self*, a property Locke ascribed to infants and even to fetuses, in so far as they were able to have sensations and thus ideas and thus self-concern. If infants and fetuses are wards in Locke's system, protected from destruction in a way that animals are not, this is presumably by virtue of their selfhood rather than their personhood.[65]

In this chapter, I have explored Locke's views on what children deserve from adults and what persons deserve from God. The following two chapters continue this theme, considering Locke's views on what changelings deserve from human beings and from God, as well as Leibniz's views on what infants dying without baptism deserve from God. The theological dimension may be more obvious in Leibniz's case, but I submit that it is no less present in Locke; overlooking this dimension skews one's understanding of Locke's thought.

I stated earlier that Locke's skepticism about our ability to know substances motivated him to elaborate a theory of personal identity. It seems to me that Leibniz's concern with defending his notion of substance as knowable just as strongly motivated his reply to Locke on personal identity. In both cases, statements about infants and children seem to have emerged from this epistemological concern, rather than from a focused reflection upon infants and children. Perhaps this is why neither Locke nor Leibniz considered in this context language acquisition in general or pronoun acquisition ("I," "Me") in particular. Regarding personal identity, both Locke and Leibniz were considering substance, not language. It is all the more notable, then, that Locke's dim view regarding human knowledge of substance found expression in terms of a debate about language; the following chapter begins with this topic.

3

Locke: Children's Language
and the Fate of Changelings

This chapter continues my examination of Locke's *Essay*, focusing on books 3 and 4. I begin with book 2's discussion of figurative language, which has received much attention by philosophers and literary scholars. Because Paul de Man's reading of Locke turns on his understanding of childhood, I engage it at some length. I argue that the figure of *the child* that de Man constructs obfuscates what Locke wrote about children. Given Locke's stature in the history of childhood, it seems self-evident that one would want to know what Locke wrote about children. And yet the material I examine in most of this chapter is glaringly absent from histories of childhood. Books 3 and 4 of the *Essay* contain discussions of children's language, Adamic language theory, and the childish ways in which we speak of substances. As readers of the *Essay* will recall, the two most recurring examples of substances in that text are *gold* and *man*. I submit that a full understanding of childhood in Locke's *Essay* must involve consideration of both substances. The results may yield a surprising picture of Locke on species boundaries, with weighty implications for his moral philosophy. I conclude this chapter by considering what the defective children called changelings deserve, according to Locke's classifications. Most studies of Locke I have consulted assure us that by *changeling* Locke meant a mentally handicapped person. My analysis may provide a corrective to Locke scholarship; close reading has suggested to me that for Locke, changelings are neither persons nor human.

Ways of speaking: metaphorically, in plain English, like an Indian philosopher, like children

Locke makes not one, but several distinctions between plain English and its others. The most famous such distinction is that between plain

speech and eloquence. Locke says he would gladly banish metaphorical
and figurative speech from philosophy, and yet he often describes the
mind metaphorically: as a sheet of paper, as a wax tablet, as a chamber
room. The manner in which one explains this discrepancy can say as
much about the scholar doing the explaining as it does about Locke.
After considering two explanations of this discrepancy, I go on to consider less well-explored distinctions that reveal a developmental dimension to Locke's view of ways of speaking.[1]

"Locke is eloquent in defense of plain speech."[2] As Susan Haack recognizes, Locke's eloquence seems out of place in a passage that pro-
motes linguistic exactitude in philosophy, and more generally in "all discourses that pretend to inform and instruct" (3.10.34), as opposed to
"Harangues and popular Addresses" (3.10.34), in which eloquence is allowed. In order to explain the appropriateness of this apparent impropriety, she recalls Locke's distinction (from 3.9.3) "between the *civil* and
the *philosophical* use of words."[3] The former refers to communicating
thoughts and ideas, the latter to conveying precise notions and expressing truths in general propositions. The figurative language Locke uses in
the *Essay* would not conflict with Locke's ideal of figure-free discourse
if, as Haack suggests, the *Essay* is a civil communication, rather than a
philosophical one: "Perhaps Locke's ubiquitous use in the *Essay* of the
figurative language he officially deplores in serious discourse may be explained, not as simple inadvertence, but as an indication that he doesn't
regard the *Essay* as philosophical discourse in the strictest sense."[4] There
are some things to be said for this solution: certainly, the *Essay* has a
more informal feel than do most enquiries of other early modern
philosophers; and the application of Locke's distinction between two
ways of speaking (instruction on the one hand, popular address on the
other) allows one to banish the paradox of an eloquent defense of plain
speech by regarding the *Essay* as belonging to the one side (popular address), where rhetoric is allowed, rather than to the other (instruction in
general, philosophy in particular), where it is not. But Haack does not
name any other metaphor-free text by Locke that *would* count as philosophy strictly speaking, and so it then seems that Locke, who is on all
lists of great philosophers, himself wrote no philosophy.[5] Surely this conclusion cannot satisfy. And as I discuss presently, Locke drew not one,
but several distinctions regarding ways of speaking, and I argue that an
adequate reading of Locke on language must negotiate them.

"Nothing could be more eloquent than this denunciation of eloquence."[6] Although this statement addresses the same discrepancy as

does Haack's, its formulation highlights the paradox. In Paul de Man's reading, Locke opens Pandora's box when he considers language and its tropology. Locke the philosopher "would have wanted nothing better than" to limit the role of rhetoric; this desire is evident in any number of statements he makes.[7] Locke's text, though, is carried along by the tropological movements he wished (but failed) to master. For de Man, the text was able to escape Locke's wishes because Locke was a "scrupulous and superb writer."[8] This is another attractive solution, for it also, like Haack's, turns the paradox of an eloquent denunciation of eloquence into a contradiction that can be examined from one side or the other: Locke the philosopher denounces eloquence, but Locke the writer is eloquent. To the extent that Locke writes, he opens himself to the endless play of figures, even though his philosophizing would try to seriously minimize that play. Two souls, alas, reside in John Locke's breast. But some of de Man's premises are not self-evidently true. For example: "Once the reflection on the figurality of language is started, there is no telling where it may lead."[9] All well and good, but this "no telling" quickly turns into a telling: "Locke has deployed . . . the anamorphosis of tropes which has to run its full course whenever one engages, however reluctantly or tentatively, the question of language as figure."[10] The hidden premise ("has to") seems to be that any engagement with figural language effects a total destabilization of meaning, that any attempt at understanding the limits of figures leads inexorably—at least for the scrupulous writer—toward nonunderstanding or incomprehensibility (in German: *Unverständlichkeit*, which negates *Verstand*, understanding).[11] Here it seems fitting to consider Haack's claim that "both the friends and the enemies of metaphor . . . exaggerate."[12] But because de Man's reading of Locke turns on his understanding (actually, his misunderstanding) of childhood in the *Essay*, it warrants further discussion here.

Locke begins with a distinction between simple and complex ideas. In the case of simple ideas, word and thing (nominal and real essence) fall together; simple ideas cannot be defined, since definition means using nonsynonymous words to indicate meaning. Rather, simple ideas emerge due to sensations, and each simple idea has a single word attached to it. If one has never had the sensation, one could never understand the word. In the case of complex ideas, nominal and real essence do not coincide; these ideas are appropriately bound to discourse. It seems to me that de Man's reading aims to show that Locke's simple idea is actually complex, and that Locke's complex idea leads to the simple. The details of de Man's argument need not concern us here. (For the curious, I sketch them at this note.)[13] When de Man states that simple ideas are "simpleminded," he is using an adjective that applies to the idiotic child, that is, a human being who lacks reason.[14] The acts of definition in which scholastics, among others, engage, are those of adults who fail to realize that their ratiocination does not capture the simplicity of the simple ideas. But against the grain of Locke's official concepts, de Man attempts to show that these supposedly simple-minded, childish ideas, are in fact discursive, i.e. adult, entities. And on the other side, category problems of complex ideas turn "us," that is, adults engaged in rational discourse, into "a philosophical changeling," that is, into a child, and a defective one at that.[15] De Man's deconstruction (however successful) of Locke's distinction simple/complex depends upon de Man's distinction child-idiot-changeling/us. In one passage of his article, de Man associates "the child" with a "wild figuration which will make a mockery of the most authoritarian academy."[16] I believe that de Man is correct to note the importance of childhood in Locke's discussion of language. However, as I stated above, de Man's account of "the child" in Locke's book 3 is incomplete: the epistemologically happy idiot, who can perhaps teach adults how much they really don't know, is only *one* of Locke's children. For as soon as Locke moves from simple to complex ideas, the role played by children reverses: now, children are deficient speakers, whereas the careful adult is as adequate a speaker as one can hope for. By conflating various child figures in the *Essay*, de Man constructs a figure, *the child*, that obscures the *children* of Locke's text. And when de Man identifies "the child" who confuses the literal and the proper as one of the "barely disguised figures of our universal predicament," he overlooks Locke's developmental view of knowledge, according to which "our" predicament is not universal, but rather unfolds in stages.[17] De Man would have it that we all speak an uneven English, and that the belief (Locke's, for example) that some English might be plainer than others is merely an avoidance of the recognition that all language is figural, i.e., not plain. Even if this is true, such an insight overlooks an age-based distinction that contributes significantly to the organization of Locke's text. The universal predicament that interests de Man ignores Locke's view of childhood as one sort of predicament and adulthood as another. I sketch this view in the following sections with specific examples of speaking about the substances *gold* and *man*.

Locke has little hope for useful discussion about substance. Here, there is indeed a universal predicament: to understand what substances are, we would have to be able to see beyond ideas we have from sensation and reflection, and penetrate into their causes.[18] But we cannot do so: all the mind discovers is "its own short-sightedness" (2.23.28). These two fountains of knowledge mark "the Boundaries of our Thoughts" (2.23.29), beyond which "we fall presently into Darkness and Obscurity," discovering "our own Blindness and Ignorance" (2.23.32). As soon as we inquire *how* bodies communicate motion by impulse, or *how* thought excites motion, "we *are equally in the dark*" (2.23.28). This darkness has not stopped some from talking, but Locke clearly thinks that such talking should not take place. But Locke parses this universal predicament: he says that those who talk of substances know not of which they speak, and are no better than "an *Indian* Philosopher" (2.13.19), later referred to as "the *Indian* before mentioned" (2.23.2) who said that the world is supported by an elephant, which stood on a tortoise, which stood on something, he knew not what: "And thus here, as in all other cases, where we use Words without having clear and distinct *Ideas*, we talk like Children; who, being questioned, what such a thing is, which they know not, readily give this satisfactory answer, That it is *something*; which in truth signifies no more, when so used, either by Children or Men, but that they know not what; and that the thing they pretend to know, and talk of, is what they have no distinct *Idea* of at all, and so are perfectly ignorant of it, and in the dark" (2.23.2). This unknown support we call *substantia*, "which, according to the true import of that Word, is in plain *English*, *standing under*, or *upholding*" (2.23.2). This translation was certainly possible before Locke, but his rendering substance as *standing under* in a passage on our not understanding substance, in a book on human *understanding*, seems to want explanation. Locke's scathing tone indicates his feeling that the terms mystify rather than clarify. They amount to an unconscious word game that masks the lack of determinate ideas. De Man said that Locke's child mocked authority; in this scene, Locke mocks children (along with the Indian philosopher and those who talk of substances).[19] What the latter say with conviction (that they understand substance) turns out to be an absurdity, when translated into plain English (that they understand standing under). Locke draws attention to this paradox not to show the absurdity of *all* speaking (as it appears de Man would have Locke's stuttering child do), but rather in order to show the absurdity of *certain* ways of speaking.

As I mentioned previously, Locke's specific targets seem to be the ways of speaking of scholastics, Cartesians, and certain British theologians and moralists. The doctrine of the Trinity may not have been an intended target, but Locke hit it. The trinitarian statement of the Nicene creed, namely that Jesus Christ is "of one being with" (or "consubstantial with") the Father, presumes that we can speak meaningfully about substance. It was inevitable that a theologian like Edward Stillingfleet would raise the objection to the *Essay* that its results are antitrinitarian.[20] These targets (intended and unintended) and Locke's aim (to promote the way of speaking of the corpuscularians and of the Royal Society) have been discussed in various scholarly treatments.[21] Since Locke's *manner* of mocking his targets is to say that they speak like children, it seems clear that "children" here represent deficient speaking. Such a depiction of children dominates book 3 as well.

ADAM'S CHILDREN:

BEGINNERS AT THE WRONG END

Children are epistemologically happy to the extent that they inhabit a world of things. Their linguistic shortcomings correspond to their proximity to a fullness of meaning, to a tight connection between the few words they know and things, as opposed to adult wrangling over empty words. This cognitive advantage of childhood, the proximity to particulars, Locke articulates in book 2. But in book 3, Locke presents children as immersed in not only a world of things, but also a world of words. The same capacities and lacks of book 2 recur here: in the case of simple ideas, children understand things without definitions, and quickly learn the words designating simple ideas: "For if we will observe how Children learn Languages, we shall find, that to make them understand what the names of simple *Ideas*, or Substances, stand for, People ordinarily shew them the thing, whereof they would have them have the *Idea*; and then repeat to them the name that stands for it, as *White, Sweet, Milk, Sugar, Cat, Dog*" (3.9.9). This level of language and idea acquisition is deficient from a discursive perspective (uttering nothing but particular adjectives and nouns like "sweet!" and "dog!" amounts to stammering), but their learning names while being shown the thing is good from a cognitive perspective (children really do understand simple ideas; words, things, and ideas happily coincide). Childhood is both poor in reason and rich in understanding. In the case of complex ideas, though, the situation is much more troublesome, for children typically learn the words before they actually have the ideas. When using words for complex ideas, children seem to be reasoning, but without understanding. This premature reasoning is bad from both a cognitive and a discursive perspective: when it occurs, children understand nothing and talk nonsense.

This is bad not only for children, but also for the adults they become: "Though the proper and immediate Signification of Words, are *Ideas* in the Mind of the Speaker; yet because by familiar use from our Cradles, we come to learn certain articulate Sounds very perfectly, and have them readily on our Tongues, and always at hand in our Memories; but yet are not always careful to examine, or settle their Significations perfectly, it *often* happens that *Men . . . do set their Thoughts more on Words than Things. . . .* Some, not only Children, but Men, speak several Words, no otherwise than Parrots do (3.2.7). Descartes could have written the preceding passage. Childhood—to the extent that this age now represents for Locke an attachment to words without ideas, to words without things—contaminates adult cognition. In the *Essay*, then, children are epistemologically ambivalent and discursively deficient.

A refrain of book 3 is that children, as beginners, are bad observers. For example, the same word, gold, in the mouths of different speakers, refers to different ideas: a child has only the idea of color, thus applying the same term to a metal and to a peacock's tail. "Another that hath *better* observed" (3.2.3, my emphasis) adds the idea of weight, a third better observer adds the idea of fusibility, and a fourth adds the idea of malleability. Of these four, children are clearly the worst observers; their word is the least tied to a good idea of gold. A later passage presents three sorts of observers: "The yellow shining Colour, makes *Gold* to Children; others add Weight, Malleableness, and Fusibility; and others yet other Qualities, which they find joined with that yellow Colour, as constantly as its Weight and Fusibility" (3.6.31). Locke's explicit point here is that each sort of observer has equal justification in forming the complex idea of the substance or essence of gold based on the simple ideas (or in the case of children: the simple idea) each observes in it. This being the case, one must conclude that nature does not distinguish between essences and accidents; rather, we do so, arbitrarily. Nature certainly makes properties, such that we can have various simple ideas when confronted with gold or experimenting upon it. Nature even makes similarities, such that talk of species differentiation (as I discuss in the next section) is not entirely idle. But it is up to us where to draw the line and decide what belongs to the essence of gold (or of Man), and what might be considered an accident instead. In a word, Locke is a nominalist.[22] The first point I would emphasize here is that children have as much a right to have an idea of the essence of gold as do adult chemists. No progress in science will ever give any group of adults purchase on nature's essences, such that inquiry can cease. Rather, talk of essences shuts down useful discussion, gets us nowhere, and should be abandoned. In this respect, Locke's point is not that children should grow up, become chemists, and thus be able to speak authoritatively about gold; children and adults are in the same class (nonauthoritative knowers of gold). But while denying that anyone can speak *authoritatively* about gold's essence, Locke states that the complex idea is made "by some more, and others less *accurately*" (3.6.31, my emphasis). And his presentation of three groups of increasingly better observers ("children," who observe one property; "others," who observe four; and "others yet," who observe more than four) suggests progress in being able to speak accurately about gold's properties. What Locke denies is a foreseeable end to that progress. Locke's future-oriented view of words slowly coming to approximate things must be understood in contrast to a rival view: Adamic language theory, which looked to the past, at the origin of language, for a vital connection between words and things.

One could imagine similarities, but Locke usually highlights differences between "the first Beginners of Languages" (3.1.5) and children as beginners in language learning. The fact that he speaks of beginners, in the plural, already indicates Locke's resistance to the Adamic theory of language, with its singular beginner. In chapter 3.6, sections 44–51, Locke contrasts Adam's language with the language of Adam's children.[25] Adam is supposed to be "in the State of a grown Man, with a good Understanding" (3.6.44). He invents complex ideas of mixed modes as well as the words signifying them. Mixed modes occasion no uncertainty with Adam, because he always forms the ideas before coining the words. By contrast, all subsequent language learners are not at *this* beginning. Adam's children are still free, in principle, to name mixed modes as Adam did (3.6.45). But in order to communicate, they must conform to existing terms for certain combinations of ideas. Mixed modes cause trouble for all children after Adam, in that the names thereof are generally gotten before the ideas for which they should stand. At least, this is true ever since languages existed. "I confess, that in the beginning of Languages, it was necessary to have the *Idea*, before one gave it the Name" (3.5.15). This felicitous situation is to be contrasted with "the ordinary Method, that Children learn the Names of mixed Modes, before they have their *Ideas*" (ibid.). But in the following thought experiment, Adam's children are luckier than all subsequent children, since the former are able to witness the original invention of words for complex ideas. When one of them finds in the mountains "a glittering Substance, which pleases his Eye" (3.6.46), he silently carries

it home to his father. (Locke here says nothing of Eve.) Unlike his child
in particular and children in general, who, as Locke previously stated,
refer only to the color, Adam himself "upon consideration . . . takes notice of" (3.6.46) its color, hardness, and weight, and gives it the name
Zahab. Now Adam has certainly noticed more properties of gold than
the first sort of observers, children; but he barely belongs in Locke's second sort of observers (of 3.6.31), who noticed malleability and fusibility.
Luckily, it was possible to make progress beyond the superficial considerations Adam had in mind when he coined names: "But the inquisitive
Mind of Man, not content with the Knowledge of these, as I may say, superficial Qualities, puts *Adam* upon farther Examination of this Matter.
He therefore knocks, and beats it with Flints, to see what was discover-
able in the inside" (3.6.47). This discontent on the part of unnamed children of Adam, who spurred him on to further discover the properties of
ductility, fusibility, and fixedness, helped Adam progress from his initial
inadequate enumeration of properties to a less inadequate one. At least,
according to the narrative, it would have to be Adam's children doing
the prodding; but it rather sounds like corpuscularians of the Royal Society in a dialogue with the dead. This "inquisitive Mind of Man" is presumably not content with the enumeration of properties from either the
first sort of observers (children, who notice one property because it
pleases the eye), nor with the second sort (Adam, who at first notices
three surface properties, then is able to notice three more depth properties after being prompted by his discontented children). I submit that
Locke's ideal of science aligns this inquisitive mind with the third sort of
observers, who progressively find "yet other Qualities" (3.6.31) in gold.
In the transition from the initial "consideration" of 3.6.46 to the "farther
Examination" and "farther Trials" of 3.6.47, Adam ceases to be an
Adamic namer and starts to be an assayer.

   The enumeration of gold's properties could go on forever. Adam's
names, which are slightly less inadequate than are the child's, do not really get at the essence of things, but rather just at three properties (and
then six). By stating this, Locke controverts Adamic language theory,
which said that Adam's language was powerful precisely because his
words did correspond to the essences of things.[24] Locke aligns Adam
rather with the "ignorant and illiterate people" (3.6.25) who were the
beginners of languages. Locke suggests that authoritative talk of
essences, as in Adamic language theory, is meant to shut down this bad
infinity of progress, but because it lacks actual knowledge of essence, it
amounts to authoritarian discourse. It is thus not the child (as de Man

concluded), but rather the scientist finding ever more properties of gold, who mocks the authoritarian discourse of substances. Everyone's idea of the substance called gold is legitimate: that of the child, who sees one property, that of Adam, who initially sees three, that of the inquisitive mind of man, who helps Adam to see six, and that of the inquisitive mind of future generations of man, who will see more than six properties. The problem for Locke lies in the arbitrariness of deciding which properties belong to the essence and which ones belong to the accidents of gold. Locke thinks that no such decision can be considered expressive of the real essence of gold. However, Locke does distinguish within this class of legitimate observers: it is notable that children are content with one property, as Adam is initially content with three. Children and Adam thus help show that not every mind of man is inquisitive: "Though the Mind of Man, *in making* its *complex Ideas of Substances*, never puts any together that do not really, or are not supposed to co-exist. . . . Men generally content themselves with some few sensible obvious Qualities" (3.6.29). By contrast, the observers aligned with the *inquisitive* mind of man—and I think with Locke and the Royal Society—settle on no specific number of properties with which they are content. For them, the number should be listed as 6+, and one should underscore the "+." That is, Locke esteems the assayer's activity of finding ever more properties, as opposed to children's "being pleased by" one superficial property or Adam's premature designation after "considering" three superficial properties. Based on my reading of 3.6.44–51, I submit that Locke's resistance to being content (that one has discovered the essence of a substance) and his commitment to the process of inquiring (into the properties of things) are reflected in the very title of his book: *Essay*. In Locke's time, the verbs essay and assay were equivalent.[25] It is as though human understanding were a metal to be assayed. This title, I believe, must be read with chemical experiments on gold in mind.

If the discourse of substances and essences represents a bad way of speaking, then what are the good ways of speaking? Locke has much less to say about this. Despite the fact that names were established long ago by ignorant, illiterate nonscientists, Locke maintains that we should nevertheless retain received names for things, at least for common commerce. Although we enter the world with empty minds awaiting furnishing—recall that "the Senses at first let in particular *Ideas*, and furnish the yet empty Cabinet" (1.2.15)—we are "furnished already with Names for [our] Ideas" (3.6.51). We are just as free as Adam was to name things anew, but being born into languages, we abuse communication when we exercise this freedom. Still, one wonders how our tainted words can be put to better use. In the end, Locke vaguely suggests that serious intent is sufficient to ward off imperfections and abuses. It seems to follow from his discourse on assaying that our discontent can lead us to improve the enumeration of properties of things. Perhaps this can help us improve our words.

It may be difficult to identify good speaking; Locke has no trouble identifying sources of bad speaking. Locke's specific polemic with other adults—academics engaged in fruitless debates that turn on eloquence—seems to suggest that choice is all that is necessary to speak in plain English. Famously, Locke defines modern philosophers as those "who have endeavored to throw off the *Jargon* of the Schools, and speak intelligibly" (3.4.9). But speaking intelligibly is not just something that one can will to do. As we have seen, men speak like parrots because children learn words before significations. Locke's natural history of unintelligible speech leads him to an anthropological view of childhood as the source of error. To speak intelligibly, then, one would have to undo this damage from childhood.

Locke is clearer on the damage childhood does than on how to remedy it. Mixed modes, especially moral concepts, are typically learned imperfectly in childhood. Children learn the words for religion, murder, church, and incest long before they have collected the ideas that these names should signify. They learn the sounds first, and to get the ideas, "they [children] are either beholden to the explication of others, or (which happens for the most part) are left to their own Observation and industry; which being little laid out in the search of the true and precise meaning of Names, these moral Words are, in most Men's mouths, little more than bare Sounds" (3.9.9). Note that in the preceding quote, the subject switches from children to men. The result of this imperfection from childhood is the endless, infinite, bad commentary upon commentary, for example in biblical exegesis. It is interesting to note that endless discussion is precisely what Locke calls for in natural history, though he rails against endless discussion in moral discourse. In the latter case, it seems that scripture trumps commentary and discussion. This abuse of words derives from men's being content with the imperfect ideas they formed in childhood, or with the imperfect method, begun in childhood, of associating names and significations. *"Men*, having been *accustomed* from their Cradles" (3.10.4) to learn words before complex ideas usually continue to learn words in this manner all their lives, thus fail to form determined (that is, distinct) ideas, instead maintaining confused notions and "contenting" (ibid.) themselves with the same words other people use.[26] This "insignificancy in their Words" (ibid.), when they come to Reason, fills their discourse with empty unintelligible noise and jargon, especially in moral matters.[27]

The remedies of this imperfection and abuse derive from discontent. With substances, we should neither rest with the ordinary received ideas, nor retain the results of our childish method of concept formation, "but must go a little *farther*" (3.11.24, my emphasis)—recall the "farther Examination" (3.6.47) of the assayer—and inquire into the properties of things, thus improving (if not settling, though Locke sometimes does use this term as well) our ideas of substances and their distinct species, and perhaps thus eventually improving our words. But since Locke regards the process of improvement as interminable, we have to make due with existing words. One might have expected Locke to suggest that we could start over "at the right end," having once identified it. But Locke seems to distrust the project of constructing a formal language free from historical accretions and linguistic ambiguities. Still, Locke's goal is to progress toward a good way of speaking. The point of assaying substances is, as we have seen, to enumerate the various simple ideas each one can evoke. With simple ideas, we are on more certain ground than with complex ideas. This is why Locke thought that natural history, which investigates things to enumerate these simple ideas, could help "rectify and settle" (3.11.24) our complex ideas. Regardless of how successful this remedy might be, Locke is clear on why it is needed: in forming complex ideas, children "begin at the wrong end" (3.11.24), that is, with words. Natural history, which begins at the right end (with things), amounts to a reversal of childhood's method. Locke's similarity to Descartes, for whom method involved overcoming childhood cognitive habits in general, is notable, but one should recall that the names for Locke's simple ideas, which begin at the right end (ideas and things), are never in doubt: not for children, not for adults. In Locke, one must be an adult to be a natural historian, but since the natural historian enumerates simple ideas, he could in theory speak a language that even a child could understand.

Adamic language theory was oriented toward a past fullness of meaning, a tight fit between word and thing, since lost but perhaps recoverable. Locke on language is oriented toward the future: he seems to always describe linguistic development as progress from an ignoble origin. This holds both for the species (see the story of Adam naming the gold found by his son) and for the individual: from an ignoble origin in childhood's misunderstanding of mixed modes and complex ideas, men grow up with imperfect ideas that contaminate their understanding and reasoning. Yet with the help of natural history, complex ideas can be rectified and perhaps settled. This optimistic picture of progress, which emerges from Locke's passages on the substance gold, is disturbed by the other substance treated in book 3, namely Man. The upshot is that men cannot know for certain what beings count as men.

MAN AND CHANGELING:
SHAPE AND NOMINAL ESSENCES

Throughout book 3, Locke presents various hybrids and puzzle cases as challenges to taxonomies that assume a fixed number of species with a clearly knowable essence; he returns most often to the figure of the changeling. Formerly considered the spawn of a demon, left as a substitute for one's real child, the term had come in Locke's day to refer to the congenital fool, the idiot.[28] Still, Locke uses the two terms in different contexts.[29] He writes of the idiot when he is concerned with intellectual deficit, thus mental life; he writes of the changeling when he is concerned with species boundaries, thus physical life. Mermaids, mules, and bipedal birds are also mentioned in the latter context, but their function in Locke's argument is fulfilled rapidly. The substitute child, by contrast, raises not only epistemological, but also ethical problems. What is the appropriate relationship between Man and changeling? To answer this, we must first consider what the term Man signifies. Although Locke's initial intent was, I think, to challenge scholastics, who believed that we can determine species boundaries on the basis of real essences, his puzzle cases came to look fairly puzzling to Locke as well. Thus at the end of book 3, Locke tried to demonstrate moral certainty regarding what makes a (moral) Man, as though that would dispel the physical uncertainty he had evoked in preceding chapters. As we shall see, this palliative was unsuccessful, such that he returned to these problems in book 4.

The first third of chapter 3.3 describes the usual way in which human beings form general concepts, such as that of Man. This way is more natural, less arbitrary, than the way of the academies. This earliest stage in Locke's natural history of general concepts deserves quotation in full:

> But to deduce this a little more distinctly, it will not perhaps be amiss, to trace our Notions, and Names, from their beginning, and observe by what

degrees we proceed, and by what steps we enlarge our *Ideas* from our first Infancy. There is nothing more evident, than that the *Ideas* of the Persons Children converse with, (to instance in them alone,) are like the Persons themselves, only particular. The *Ideas* of the Nurse, and the Mother, are well framed in their Minds; and, like Pictures of them there, represent only those Individuals. The Names they first give to them, are confined to these Individuals; and the Names of *Nurse* and *Mamma*, the Child uses, determine themselves to those Persons. Afterwards, when time and a larger Acquaintance have made them observe, that there are a great many other Things in the World, that in some common agreements of Shape, and several other Qualities, resemble their Father and Mother, and those Persons they have been used to, they frame an *Idea*, which they find those many Particulars do partake in; and to that they give, with others, the name *Man*, for Example. And *thus they come to have a general Name*, and a general *Idea*. Wherein they make nothing new, but only leave out of the complex *Idea* they had of *Peter* and *James*, *Mary* and *Jane*, that which is peculiar to each, and retain only what is common to them all. (3.3.7)

Since Locke's history begins with the particular names of Nurse and Mamma, one might expect the child's first general name to be Woman, rather than Man. One might have also expected Locke to draw such a conclusion: in his *First Discourse*, a refutation of Robert Filmer's *Patriarchia*, which often misquoted the biblical commandment as "Honor thy father," Locke recalls multiple times that the injunction continues "and thy mother." Although father and mother are both listed in this passage of the *Essay*, Locke seems not to have extended his critique of patriarchy far enough that he would find the term Man problematic as the name of a species. Locke's child annexes the idea of nurse to the name Nurse, and the idea of mother to the name Mamma. But Locke mentions no name (nor idea) that would be annexed to the father, who emerges late in the paragraph (as though he had just returned home from work). A mere two lines after the appearance of the unnamed father, Locke's child designates the human species with the name Man. (One might suggest that the idea of father, unattached in this passage to the name of Father, becomes attached to the name of Man instead.) Several gendered implications of this passage have been discussed by Walker.[30] What has not been discussed, to my knowledge, is the curious position that infants and young children occupy in this passage: they have ideas of particular persons, yet as we have seen previously, they are themselves not persons. In any case: when considering that infants have the particular ideas of

nurse and mother (along with Peter, James, Mary and Jane) before
they have the general idea of Man, one should recall that Locke believes
that only particulars are real.[31] Indeed, this chapter begins — "All things,
that exist, being Particulars . . ." (3.3.1) — and ends — "were their words
and Thoughts confined only to Particulars" (3.3.20) — with particulars.
When children enter the world of general concepts, perhaps beginning
with "Man," their particular hold on reality loosens, though their ability
to sort and communicate simultaneously increases.

This usual process by which general concepts are formed, abstraction, is not correctly understood by the schools. If scholastic definitions
are composed of two terms (genera and differentia), this has nothing to
do with the nature of things, but rather follows a pragmatic consideration: such definitions are quickly communicated. This speed is advanta-
geous, but we are deluded if we think that such definitions give us actual
purchase on particulars. Having just described the usual way in which
the general name *Man* is formed, Locke now refers to an influential, yet
still conventional and arbitrary, definition of Man: that of Aristotle. The
upshot of Locke's discussion is to assert that the essence of any species
(including Man) *is* the abstract idea one has of that species. If Aristotle's
"rational Animal" (3.3.10) is a good definition, this is not because it correctly names the real essence of humanity (rationality and animality),
but rather because it quickly signifies a collection of ideas that most people have in mind when they hear the term Man.[32] Locke insists that we
deal with nominal essences, not with real ones.

Reality does provide similarities. Our nominal sorting of real existing
things does relate to — Locke says that abstract ideas *"take occasion from"*
and even *"have their foundation in"* (3.3.13) — real similitude, but a gap between nominal and real still obtains. Though real essences exist, our
words relate not to them but to our ideas of them. This being so, we
should not pretend to know real essences. But if we orient our speaking
toward abstract ideas (vs. toward realities we cannot directly access),
then we can have as much confidence in sorting things as human beings
can have. In making this distinction between those who know that our
sorting is nominal and ideational, and those who falsely believe that our
sorting is real, taken from and authorized by the things themselves,
Locke begins to marshal cases that the latter evidently cannot explain:

> Nay, even in Substances, where their abstract *Ideas* seem to be taken
> from the Things themselves, they are not constantly the same; no not in
> that Species, which is most familiar to us, and with which we have the

most intimate acquaintance: It having been more than once doubted, whether the *Foetus* born of a Woman were a *Man*, even so far, as that it hath been debated, whether it were, or were not to be nourished and baptized: which could not be, if the abstract *Idea* or Essence, to which the Name Man belonged, were of Nature's making; and were not the uncertain and various Collection of simple Ideas, which the Understanding puts together, and then abstracting it, affixed a name to it. (3.3.14)

Nature makes particulars (including normal and defective children), but we make generals (and thus species, such as Man). Against the view that nature itself has created a fixed number of species, which differ in essence from one another, Locke evidences "the frequent Productions of Monsters, in all the Species of Animals, and of Changelings, and other strange Issues of humane Birth" (3.3.17). Since changelings and defective births have properties different from normal human children, they cannot "partake exactly of the same real *Essence*" (3.3.17). These puzzle cases absolutely puzzle *real essentialists*; Locke seems to want to say that *nominal essentialists* can make better sense of them. (I use these terms, rather than *realists* and *nominalists*, out of a desire to follow Locke's terms closely.) Determining if something is a horse or lead is "easy to resolve" (3.3.13), as long as our determination is oriented toward our abstract ideas; determining whether a changeling or a strange issue of human birth is human may or may not be easy to resolve, but since we cannot know the real essence of the creature in question, we have no choice but to "content our selves" (3.3.17) with the way of abstract, complex ideas. Expecting us to be content with an "uncertain and various Collection of simple ideas" (3.3.14) may be asking a lot, but Locke maintains that this way of sorting things is the only viable one.

Given all the uncertainty, it is notable that Locke presents what he calls *his* definition of Man, though he does so almost in passing: "For though, perhaps, voluntary Motion, with Sense and Reason, join'd to a Body of a certain shape, be the complex *Idea*, to which I, and others, annex the name *Man*; and so be the *nominal Essence* of the *Species* so called: yet no body will say, that that complex *Idea* is the *real Essence* and Source of all those Operations, which are to be found in any Individual of that Sort" (3.6.3). The only essence worth discussing, so Locke, is nominal rather than real. In order to dramatize his tenet that essence, in human conversation, is a sortal term, rather than something real, he imagines himself as a bare individual and denies that anything is essential to him. An accident such as a fall, or a disease such as a fever, could take away his reason, his memory, his sense, his understanding, and his life. As an individual, he is alterable; all properties he may have are subject to change. However, Locke still asserts that reason is essential to Man. That is, reason is a sorting term (one of four, according to the preceding quote) that allows Locke to distinguish Man from not-Man. This assertion begs the question of how certain we can be that our sorting somehow answers to (or "takes occasion from" or "has its foundation in") the real essence of Man. A closer examination of Locke's polemic against real-essence classification may help us situate the positive claims he makes for his nominal-essence way of sorting and for his definition of Man.

In a famous image, Locke depicts the difference between nominal and real essence in terms of two perspectives. Human beings see the things of the world as the "gazing Country-man" (3.6.3) sees the clock of Strasburg. Just as he "barely sees the motion of the Hand, and hears the Clock strike, and observes only some of the outward appearances" (ibid.), so we only observe simple ideas that things occasion in us, and must do our best to determine what makes the mechanism run. Angels, perhaps, and God, certainly, can see inside the mechanism, that is, can converse in terms of real essences. Such a possibility is foreclosed to us. Given that our lot is that of the Country-man, it is worth noting that Locke highlights his ignorance (as in the clock example) and his illiteracy when comparing him to superior celestial beings, but within the mundane human species, Locke often emphasizes the greater wisdom and superior knowledge of "those ignorant Men, who pretend not any insight into the real Essences, nor trouble themselves about substantial Forms, but are content with knowing Things one from another, by their sensible Qualities, [who] are often better acquainted with their Differences . . . than those learned quick-sighted Men, who look so deep into them, and talk so confidently of something more hidden and essential" (3.6.24). Locke's primary aim in this chapter is to show the failures of real-essence classification systems, which are hubristic in their attempt to access a perspective only possible for superior beings.

To show that the individuals we often group into one species, according to our nominal essences, do not in fact share real essences, Locke refers to "Chymists" who often "by sad Experience . . . sometimes in vain" (3.6.8) seek common properties in differing samples of the supposedly same mineral. The sadness, of course, derives from discovering the gap between nominal and real essences. Locke believes that the chemist's lesson needs to be learned by zoologists as well: "He that thinks he can distinguish Sheep and Goats by their real Essences, that are unknown to him, may be pleased to try his Skill in those *Species*, called *Cassiowary*, and *Querechinchio*; and by their internal real Essences, determine the boundaries of those *Species*, without knowing the complex *Idea* of sensible Qualities, that each of those Names stands for, in the Countries where those Animals are to be found" (3.6.9). The cassowary, in its current spelling, is a bird native to New Guinea; Locke observed several of them in St. James Park.[33] It is bipedal, and its feathers have a hair-like appearance. These qualities are notable because the bird very nearly fits Plato's definition of the human being: "*Animal implume bipes latis unguibus*" (3.6.26, see also 3.11.20), "*a two-leg'd Animal with broad Nails, and without Feathers*" (3.10.17). Only the lack of wide toenails excludes the cassowary from being human by that definition. The quirquincho, in its current spelling, is an armadillo native to the Andean mountain region.[34] I know neither whether Locke ever encountered one, nor which of its properties Locke had in mind when he presented it as a puzzle case, but it is clear he felt it to be one of those peculiar links in the chain of being that real-essence taxonomies could not explain.

Locke's commitment to the notion of the chain of being has been generally noted, but some scholars, such as Lovejoy and David Wiggins, have taken Locke to say that the continuity consists in nature creating *species* that differ from one another by steps. Against this view, I agree with those Locke scholars, such as W. L. Uzgalis, who hold that Locke's notion of the chain of being is more radically gradational: the continuity consists in nature creating *individuals* that differ from one another by steps. Locke's mention of amphibians, mermaids, man-apes, and creatures spanning the animal and vegetable kingdoms seems designed to demonstrate the irreality of fixed species by showing the reality of individuals that do not fit into our existing ideas of species. The works of creation do magnify God's power and wisdom, but certain of these works tend to betray our lack of insight. In addition to hybrids, "irregular and monstrous Births" (3.6.16) also challenge taxonomies that presume a fixed number of real essences and a corresponding fixed number of species. Against the taxonomies of real essentialists, Locke marshals another set of problem cases: "Creatures in the World, that have shapes like ours, but are hairy, and want Language, and Reason . . . Naturals amongst us, that have perfectly our shape, but want Reason, and some of them Language too . . . Creatures . . . that with Language, and Reason, and a shape in other Things agreeing with ours, have hairy Tails;

others where the Males have no Beards, and others where the Females have" (3.6.22). Here, Locke does not explicate why these puzzle cases would not form a problem for nominal essentialists like himself. In a final challenge to the belief in a fixed number of species, Locke refers to cross-breeding in vegetables, in animals such as mules and gimars, in a creature he once saw "that was the Issue of a Cat and a Rat, and had the plain Marks of both about it" (3.6.23) and even in humans: "for if History lie not, Women have conceived by Drills" (ibid.), or in the current spelling, mandrills (West African baboons). These all result in species not distinguished by generation; from this Locke concludes that existing species are not "distinct and entire" (ibid.). The real boundaries are mobile, as well as unclear, and anything other than a strictly nominalist taxonomy will fail when confronted with such cases.

But how successful is a taxonomy based on nominal essences? When Locke is not engaged in a polemic against real-essence classification, his tone is hardly triumphant: "all we can do is to collect such a number of simple *Ideas*, as by Examination, we find to be united together in Things existing, and thereof to make one complex *Idea*" (3.6.21). And in substances, we have to deal with a combination of distinct simple ideas (which we can name and understand) and the confused idea of substance (which we cannot understand). Such a situation hardly seems to lead to an "easy resolve" and "contenting ourselves." Furthermore, we have different ideas of Man, and this lack of consensus causes problems. Against the earlier confident claims made for nominalism, Locke later stresses that the definition of Man is not "setled" (3.6.26) nor can any definition thereof "satisfie" (3.6.27) the considerations of an inquisitive person. Locke briefly turns confident again, stating that although nominal essences of substances are made by the mind, they are "*not* yet *made so arbitrarily, as those of mixed Modes*" (3.6.28). At least the mind "only follows Nature" (ibid.) in forming these essences. Immediately, though, he recalls that the number of properties considered to be constitutive of the essence depend upon us and us alone, "*upon the various Care, Industry, or Fancy of him that makes it*" (3.6.29). But despite the arbitrariness of the number of properties one should observe in order to accurately identify a Man, Locke seems to favor rationality over shape as the leading characteristic of the human species.

Human shape is the more usual criterion; it determines whether an infant will be kept or destroyed. Although Locke cautions us that rationality "can be no more discerned in a well-formed, than ill-shaped Infant, as soon as born" (3.11.20), he recognizes that we tend to look to the infant's shape in order to identify it as either human or nonhuman. Against usual custom, Locke seems to hold that rationality is a better criterion than shape. He refers to a hypothetical interlocutor who "annexes the name *Man*, to a complex *Idea*, made up of Sense and spontaneous Motion, join'd to a Body of such a shape" and thereby has "one" (3.6.26) essence of the species. The beginning of the next sentence is of interest: "And he that, *upon farther examination*, adds rationality . . ." (3.6.26, my emphasis). We have seen that for Locke, "farther" examination is always the sign of the better knower. According to 3.6.3, where Locke gives his definition of Man, which includes rationality, Locke himself is this better knower of 3.6.26. Further evidence that Locke favors rationality over shape as a leading criterion is given in his explicit advice on how to handle cases of misshapen infants. "The learned Divine and Lawyer, must, on such occasions, renounce his sacred Definition of *Animal Rationale*, and substitute some other Essence of the humane *Species* (3.6.26). Why "must"? Presumably, this renunciation of the sacred definition follows an ethical imperative to be cautious. The anecdote Locke then relates supports such an interpretation: the Abbot of St. Martin was born misshapen, and was nearly considered a monster, but he grew to become a significant Church dignitary. This example shows that rationality, which does not manifest itself in children until late, is a better indicator of humanity than is shape. Indeed, Locke states, a number of beings spared on the basis of their shape (changelings, that is) never showed reason all their lives (3.6.26). Locke does not state a conclusion that seems to follow from his definition of Man and his preference for rationality as a leading characteristic of the essence of Man: that changelings, which lack all rationality, could be destroyed without it being considered murder. Locke seems to say that we should be cautious—when in doubt, change the definition of Man. Even the misshapen child should be given a chance to demonstrate its rationality and, thereby, its humanity. A "substitute" definition (which makes Man a changeling in another contemporary sense of the term) gives the child a chance to show that it is indeed human.[35]

In a polemic against maxims, in book 4, Locke gives this list of increasingly less deficient concepts of Man: first, a British "Child can demonstrate to you, that *a Negro is not a Man*, because White-colour was one of the constant simple *Ideas* of the complex *Idea* he calls *Man*" (4.7.16). "*Secondly*, Another that hath gone farther . . . and to the outward shape adds *Laughter*, and *Rational Discourse*, may demonstrate, that Infants, and Changelings are no Men. . . . And I have discoursed with very Rational Men, who have actually denied that they are *Men*" (4.7.18). While it is unclear who Locke has in mind in this second class, he refers elsewhere to the Roman who gave us a trifling proposition: that the word *Homo* signified "*Corporeitas, Sensibilitas, Potentia se movendi, Rationalitas, Risibilitas*" or "*Sense, Motion, Reason*, and *Laughter*" (4.8.6). Locke's list continues: "*Thirdly*, Perhaps, another makes up the complex *Idea* which he calls *Man*, only out of the *Ideas* of Body in general, and the Powers of Language and Reason, and leaves out the Shape wholly" (4.7.18). Locke seems to have the least reservations with this third definition, as it allows human beings without hands to still count as human. But unfortunately, it also includes talking parrots (one was described in a travelogue Locke cites at 2.27.8) and talking asses (a hypothesis from 3.6.29 and 4.4.13) in the category human, so it seems to be deficient as well. I want here to underscore Locke's rejection of (1) the child's concept of Man, which excludes people of a different color, and (2) the concept of Man that excludes infants and changelings. But I suspect that Locke rejects (2) because of its exclusion of infants, *not* because of its exclusion of changelings.

The uncertainty about knowing the physical nature (or real essence) of Man, which leads to ethical dilemmas regarding defective babies, may have motivated Locke to present a more certain knowledge in the final chapter of book 3:

> For as to Substances, when concerned in moral Discourses, their divers Natures are not so much enquir'd into, as supposed; *v.g.* when we say that *Man is subject to Law*: We mean nothing by *Man*, but a corporeal rational Creature: What the real Essence or other Qualities of that Creature are in this Case, is no way considered. And therefore, whether a Child or Changeling be a *Man* in a physical Sense, may amongst the Naturalists be as disputable as it will, it concerns not at all the *moral Man*, as I may call him, which is this immoveable unchangeable *Idea, a corporeal rational Being*. For were there a Monkey, or any other Creature to be found, that had the use of Reason, to such a degree, as to be able to understand general Signs, and to deduce Consequences about general *Ideas*, he would no doubt be subject to Law, and, in that Sense, be a *Man*, how much soever he differ'd in Shape from others of that Name. (3.11.16)

The term "moral Man" is a forensic term. Like "personal identity," it functions irrespective of knowledge of corporeal (and spiritual) substance. The upshot of this discussion in book 3 is that something may not have human identity, yet it can have moral (personal) identity. Even in cases of obvious nonhuman identity that could be imagined (such as the talking ass) or that could present themselves (such as the intelligent parrot), Locke means to say that a rational animal, though not human, could reasonably be expected to obey human laws. But the cases of nonobvious nonhuman identity (misshapen children and changelings) are troubling. Despite Locke's concluding claim that "the Names of Substances, if they be used in them, as they should, can no more disturb Moral, than they do Mathematical Discourses" (3.11.16), it rather does matter, when a "moral Man" is on trial for killing a changeling, whether the changeling be considered a "Man," or no. Consider Locke's example of an absolutely certain moral precept: "*Murther deserves Death*" (4.4.8). This will be true "in Reality of any Action that exists conformable to that *Idea* of *Murther*" (ibid.). Shortly after the triumphant announcement at 3.11.16 of certain knowledge of morality, Locke returns to the Platonic and Aristotelian definitions of Man, and seems to oscillate between which one he prefers. It is an open question how good an indicator of humanity shape is. But without certain knowledge, one can neither readily charge someone who destroys a monster or changeling with murder nor readily defend them from this charge.

One difference between Locke's discussion of "moral Man" and his chapter on personal identity is rather striking. The point in the latter chapter was that we could have certain knowledge of persons even in the absence of certain knowledge of what material or spiritual substance houses persons. This lack of human knowledge was not troubling, because God does have that certain knowledge. God's justice is beyond question: there is no reason to think that on judgment day, God could make a mistake in classifying those deserving heaven vs. those deserving hell. But in considering moral Man, Locke is concerned with fallible human justice: a man could indeed make a mistake in classifying a newborn as either a human child, who deserves to be "preserved and cherished" (per 1.3.12), or a nonhuman changeling, who may possibly not deserve such care.

Near the end of chapter 3.6, Locke returns to the clock analogy, stating that one's relative insight into the mechanism of things determines the number of species one can observe. "No body will doubt, that the wheels, or springs (if I may so say) within, are different in a *rational Man*, and a *Changeling*, no more than that there is a difference in the frame between a *Drill* and a *Changeling*" (3.6.39). But as human observers, we cannot state with certainty or authority what those differences are. Locke says that it depends upon one's abstract idea of Man (and not upon the unobservable underlying reality of Man) whether one includes the drill or the changeling into that classification. Locke does not here state whether *he* regards either drill or changeling as human. But earlier, he did state that his definition of Man includes the property of rationality. It seems to follow that drills and changelings, both lacking reason, would be excluded by Locke's definition from the category of Man. A later passage supports this conclusion: Locke rejects as inappropriate the interlocutor who regards the changeling as being "something between a Man and a Beast" (4.4.13). In place of this vaguely defined intermediate species, Locke suggests that it would be more accurate to posit four sortal terms: (1) Man, (2) Beast, (3) Changeling, described as a "Man without Reason" (ibid.), and (4) an "*Ass* with Reason" (ibid.). Locke regards the last of these as a fiction, although it seems he also believed that real animals with reason (such as the intelligent parrot) might exist. But children who never manifest reason, i.e. changelings, are depicted by Locke as real cases.

A long passage in book 4 (4.4.14–16) pertains to justice for changelings in this world and the next. Locke explicitly wards off the question: what do they deserve in the next life?, answering that "it concerns me not to know or enquire" (4.4.14). And only obliquely does he negotiate the question: what do they deserve in this life? In this passage, which turns into an imagined dialogue between Locke and the reader, the changeling is used in order to create uncertainty in the reader, who at the outset of the passage was certain that the changeling is human, whereas misshapen monsters are not. Locke says that such monsters are everywhere destroyed, and yet he suggests that there may be less reason to destroy monsters than there is to destroy changelings. The conclusion toward which Locke guides the reader is that shape is not a reliable leading characteristic of the idea of Man, whereas reason is such a characteristic. By the end of the passage, the reader should have become uncertain whether misshapen monsters are inhuman. But neither the implied reader nor Locke openly pose or answer the question whether changelings are human. Locke never says explicitly that it is *not* murder to destroy a changeling, but I submit that this conclusion follows from everything Locke says and omits saying. It seems to me that Locke considers the changeling to be neither (physically) human nor (morally) a person. This does not dispel the question of infanticide; it does show Locke's allegiance to rationality as central to the definition of Man (as person).[36]

Knowledge of what is human is limited, inadequate, and uncertain. This seems to qualify in advance any triumphant reading of the title of book 4, "On Human Knowledge." How certain could human knowledge be if we lack certain knowledge of what is human? As a species, we fail the delphic oracle's injunction ("Know thyself").

INTUITIVE KNOWLEDGE OF PARTICULARS:
MAN VS. SCHOLAR, CHILD, AND CHANGELING

Compared to what precedes it, book 4 has strikingly little to say about children. It does contain extended passages on changelings, but if my preceding argument is correct, Locke did not regard changelings as human children. Whereas (normal) children and adults alike can form ideas (book 2) and acquire names for them (book 3), it seems that reasoning—the activity of combining and separating ideas, comparing and contrasting them, testing them for their connections to one another—is strictly for adults (book 4). It is not that Locke places the greatest trust in this faculty: after all, he states explicitly that we find general certainty in our ideas (therefore in *understanding*) rather than in our propositions (therefore in *reasoning*) (4.6.16). But Locke's epistemological ideal seems to be expressed in several forms of adult knowledge. Against this ideal, children and scholars prove to be lacking.

Locke's statements about the advantages and shortcomings of three forms of knowledge (intuitive, demonstrative, sensitive) consistently emphasize the importance of knowing particulars, the only real existents. When he contrasts intuitive knowledge (which perceives connections immediately) and demonstrative knowledge (which discovers connections through syllogistic reasoning), Locke depicts the former as being perceived "at the first sight of the *Ideas* together . . . the clearest . . . like the bright Sun-shine" (4.2.1), against which the latter pales by comparison.[37] Demonstrative knowledge, though "it has a great mixture of Dimness" (4.2.6), is nevertheless still knowledge, provided every step of the demonstration itself involves intuitive knowledge. But this last statement already makes evident that Locke regards intuition as most deserving of the name *knowledge*. The knowledge of discoverers in the world exceeds that of teachers in the schools. "When we find out an *Idea* . . . this is a Revelation from God to us, by the Voice of Reason" (4.7.11). No intermediary authority is necessary to produce knowledge. Locke's antischolastic stance is clear in his reference to a time "when Schools were erected, and Sciences had their Professors to teach what others had found out" (ibid.), as well as his preference for "the rational part of Mankind not corrupted by Education" (ibid.). The corruption seems to consist in a preference for winning disputations over discovering truths, an attachment to words as opposed to things. But Locke's demotion of professors is not accompanied by a promotion of children. Locke states that sensation—the only initial source of ideas in childhood—is a legitimate source of knowledge, but a much more imperfect one than either intuitive or demonstrative knowledge (4.2.14). The problem with scholars' demonstrative knowledge is that it is overly attached to general concepts, and children's sensitive knowledge is exclusively attached to particular concepts. Now since only particulars exist, strictly speaking, sensitive knowledge is quite certain, but we still need general concepts to communicate. It seems that intuitive knowledge has the optimal balance between particular and general ideas. The intuition of a healthy Man speaking plain English is superior to both the scholar's demonstration and the child's sensation.

Locke's polemic with scholastic syllogism should not be misunderstood as part of an antirational stance. I will venture this claim: Locke is a rationalist (of a sort), but he emphasizes often that reason is the property of Man in general (perhaps also Woman), not just scholars in particular. Indeed, he underscores his anthropological concern when he names reason "that faculty, whereby Man is supposed to be distinguished from Beasts, and wherein it is evident he much surpasses them" (4.17.1). Given that reason makes the Man/Beast distinction, it would appear that changelings, lacking reason all their lives, fall more to the side of beasts than of men. In any case, Locke holds that syllogisms merely describe what a good healthy mind does naturally, even (and especially) lacking explicit knowledge of syllogistic logic. The source of this healthy mind is divine goodness: "But God has not been so sparing to Men to make them barely two-legged Creatures, and left it to *Aristotle* to make them Rational" (4.17.4). Locke is silent on the source of the defective mind, that of the irrational, barely two-legged changeling. It seems Locke considered it possible that changelings are not God's children.

In addition to three forms of knowledge, book 4 also treats three forms of nonknowledge (probability, opinion, faith). As most of the *Essay* has made abundantly clear, there is rather little of which we can be certain. In most cases, we must content ourselves with probability. Lacking knowledge, we must exercise our best judgment. Although we may lack certainty, Locke held that reason helps us sift through claims, and thus order our opinions as well as our assent or dissent. In short, reason helps regulate faith. Referring to an old Christian distinction (dating at least to the medieval period) between (1) propositions according to reason, (2) propositions above reason, and (3) propositions contrary to reason (4.17.23), Locke insists that faith is compatible with (1) and (2), but not with (3). Those who oppose reason to faith are guilty of "a very improper way of speaking" (4.17.24), and are likely to fall into grave errors, such as enthusiasm. Indeed, reason and faith are compatible to such an extent that Locke can identify reason and revelation: "*Reason* is natural *Revelation* . . . *Revelation* is natural *Reason* enlarged" (4.19.4). Whoever goes against reason to make way for revelation actually "puts out the Light of both, and does much the same, as if he would perswade a Man to put out his Eyes the better to receive the remote Light of an invisible Star by a Telescope" (ibid.). True light, for Locke, is that of the self-evidence of true propositions. To admit any other light, such as the false light of enthusiasm (revelation without reason), is "to put our selves in the dark, or in the power of the Prince of Darkness" (4.19.13), whose existence Locke here affirms. The chapter ends with a distinction between true revelation, "an Offspring of Heaven, and of divine Original" (4.19.16), and false revelation, "a Fondling of our own" (ibid.). Irrational faith substitutes a real child, divine revelation, for one of our own construction, or possibly of diabolic origin. Once again, the substitute child fares badly in Locke's philosophy.

Not long before Locke's time, changelings were considered to be the offspring of demons or of the devil. Book 4, which contains extended passages on categorizing changelings, regularly asserts that particular knowledge best deserves the name *knowledge*, and true reasoning is reasoning about particulars. General concepts are only useful if they help us with particulars. I have argued that Locke's *general* definition of Man seems to exonerate those who destroy changelings from the charge of murder. But since Locke is always more certain of the particular than of the general concept, he might not draw this conclusion. Recall his express statement that the general definition of Man is malleable; it can be made to fit the particulars in questionable cases such as that of the misshapen infant, a monster who grew up to become a churchman. But despite Locke's urging toward caution, as in the latter case, changelings as a class do not fare well in Locke's classifications. Lacking reason, they certainly lack any personal identity, and are thus not subject to law in the same way that persons are. And the changeling likely lacks human identity, as Locke defines it. Book 4 fails to answer the question left open from book 3: do those who destroy changelings commit murder?

When Locke discusses Man late in chapter 4.6, his examples avoid the question of infanticide and species boundaries. His assertion that we mostly deal with probabilities, rather than with certainties, and that we must "appeal to trial in particular Subjects" (4.6.15) would suggest proceeding cautiously with changelings, but Locke says nothing more explicit than this.

God, Locke is certain, will treat changelings justly in the next life, whatever this will mean. Moribund human infants will also receive their just deserts, though it remains unclear whether Locke's premises would place them in limbo or elsewhere. Leibniz's reply to Locke on what changelings and idiots deserve, in this life and the next, seems a fitting way to conclude this chapter: "If this human-shaped animal is not a man, no great harm will come from caring for it while we are uncertain about its fate. And whether it has a rational soul or one which is not rational, God will not have created that soul for no purpose. As for the souls of men who remain always in a state like that of earliest infancy: one would think that they might have the same fate as the souls of infants who die in the cradle" (*NE* 395). This tentative statement may seem a relief to the relatives of such infants (and by extension to the relatives of those men who remain in an infant-like state). But it is not obvious what Leibniz believed that fate to be; the following chapter aims to answer this question.

4
Leibniz:
Against Infant Damnation

For doubtless there is nothing more shocking to reason than
the statement that the sin of the first man has rendered guilty
those who are so far from the source as to seem incapable of
participation therein. This transmission seems to us not only
impossible but very immoral [*injuste*]; for what is there more
contrary to the laws of our poor justice than to damn eternally
an infant, incapable of will, for a sin in which he seems to have
so little say that it was committed six thousand years before he
was born?

— Blaise Pascal

REASONS BEYOND SHOCK:
REFUTING THE JANSENISTS

EVEN THOSE WHO BELIEVE IN THE DAMNATION OF INFANTS WHO DIE
unbaptized admit that the doctrine explaining this fate shocks reason.
But what must follow from this admission? Pascal asserts that we cannot understand the human condition without accepting the doctrine of
original sin. As hard as it may be to grasp the related tenet, that the souls
of dead unbaptized infants are damned, this must be believed. For "it is
not through the proud notions [*les superbes agitations*] of our reason, but
by simple subordination of reason, that we can truly get to know ourselves."[1] Several late seventeenth-century theologians (including, but
not limited to, Jansenists such as Antoine Arnauld and Pierre Nicole)
agreed with Pascal that the demands of faith always trump those of reason.[2] Arguing against such fideism in his 1710 *Theodicy*, Leibniz held that
faith and reason are compatible, and that if reason is shocked by a religious doctrine, then that doctrine must be false, rather than mysterious.[3]

107

His showcase example of such a false doctrine is that of the damnation of innocents, specifically non-Christian virtuous adults and infants.[4]

This rejection has an exceptional status in Leibniz's argument. Typically, Leibniz exonerates God for allowing all sorts of evil to exist. Leibniz offers reasons or at least speculates why God permits evil, or else he states that God must have His reasons, even if we don't understand them. In the latter case, Leibniz offers *consolation*, a mode of explanation made famous by Boethius's *Consolation of Philosophy* (written in 524). Consolation calls for trust in Providence: one must assume that one's own perspective is too limited to comprehend the reasons for the existence of evil, that God's perspective is perfect, and that there are reasons for evil that are compatible with belief in God's absolute power and absolute goodness. The existence of apparent and real evils need not shake our optimism: although it contains evils that may be hard to fathom, our world is nonetheless the best of all possible worlds. But the damnation of the innocent, specifically infants, forms an exception. Here, Leibniz abandons the consolation mode, and instead rejects a doctrine outright as false. There is another sign of the exceptional status of Leibniz's treatment of this particular evil: when considering it, Leibniz seems to lose his composure. Beyond giving reasonable objections, Leibniz also expresses "disapproval" with this cruel doctrine, which he says is "shockingly" harsh. As though he were slightly traumatized, he repeats the word "harsh" several times on the same page. It seems that Leibniz rejects this doctrine not only due to considered reasons, but also due to a gut reaction. Since the damnation of the innocent is one of the very few evils that Leibniz cannot stomach, it is worth our while to explore the status of infants and children in his *Theodicy*. (I leave the finer details concerning the status of virtuous adults, such as pagans and Jewish prophets, for others to explore.)

This doctrinal rejection forms an exception to his rule of optimism; Leibniz clearly considered it significant, since he included it in his *Abrégé de la controverse, réduite à des arguments en forme*. This mercifully short presentation of his argument in syllogistic form condenses all of *Theodicy* into eight objections and replies; the sixth set of these considers the souls of moribund pagans and infants. The objection reads: "Whoever punishes those who have done as well as it was in their power to do is unjust. God does so. Therefore, etc." (*Theodicy*, 385). The major premise can stand, but Leibniz denies the minor premise: "I believe that God always gives sufficient aid and grace to those who have good will, that is to say, who do not reject this grace by a fresh sin. Thus I do not admit the damnation of children dying unbaptized or outside the Church, or the damnation of adult persons who have acted according to the light that God has given them" (ibid.). Although he denies that these souls are damned, Leibniz does not clarify in this text what he means by damnation, nor what the alternatives might be: do these souls languish in limbo, enjoy natural bliss in an earthly paradise, or enter into the kingdom of heaven? Thus one must complicate the claim that Leibniz "rejects" "infant damnation," as this doctrine admits of variety. According to some, unbaptized infants go to hell, where they suffer physical torments (*poena sensus*) for all time. According to others, these infants suffer only mental anguish (*poena damni*), cognizant of being shut out of the kingdom of heaven, left on the threshold, as it were.[5]

The history of baptism seems to me to be structured by this question: are there two possible fates after death (heaven or hell), or three (heaven, hell, limbo)? Focusing on a fifth-century turning point in the history of Christianity, I will overlook baptism in the centuries preceding.[6] At the risk of oversimplifying, I submit the following historical sketch: in 418, Augustine prompted a council of bishops in Carthage to pass nine canons against "Pelagianism," a set of doctrines (attributed to Pelagius, Caelestius, and others) that (1) emphasized the freedom of human will to do and be good, (2) stated that Christ came to set a good example, and (3) asserted that infants dying unbaptized were not condemned, since sin is not contracted through birth. Caelestius had also argued that newborn children were in the state of Adam before the Fall; Pelagius had rejected this view, since infants could not reason as Adam could, but both Pelagius and Caelestius agreed that it was possible to live a sinless life if one truly willed it. That is, the "Pelagians" held that humans are not born with corrupt wills; this happens through bad examples.[7] Against the Pelagians, Augustine (1) emphasized the bondage of human will to sin and the necessity of God's grace to do and be good, (2) stated that Christ came to redeem us from our sinful nature, and (3) cited biblical passages showing that one went either to heaven or to hell, concluding that the unbaptized are thus indeed among the damned. Now, this fate can be just only if they deserve damnation; thus, the doctrine of original sin served to justify God's damnation of the unbaptized. It also helped strengthen the institution of the Roman Church and its sacraments.[8] The result of the Council of Carthage was that Augustine's voice held sway in Latin Christianity, Pelagianism was branded a heresy, and the necessity of infant baptism was made Catholic doctrine. The council's ninth canon explicitly denied that children dying without baptism go to a middle place. Interestingly enough, some reports list only eight canons, omitting precisely this one.[9] Eight centuries later, Aquinas argued for a milder view, relegating those who die guilty only of original sin to limbo, where they would not suffer physical pains and might enjoy a kind of natural bliss, due to ignorance of the divine grace of which they are deprived. Although there were always some adherents after Aquinas for the harsher Augustinian view, they tended to be labeled *tortores infantium*, or *baby torturers*. But with the Protestant Reformation, a renewed consideration of Augustine occupied all Western Christian denominations. The controversy between Augustine and Pelagius set the terms for the later debate between Luther and Erasmus on the question of free vs. enslaved will, and Luther's Augustinian view of a will enslaved by original sin held the greatest sway within Protestantism for two centuries. For Luther, grace is a response to faith alone [*sola fide*] and not to innocence. It is fitting that he regarded baptism as a sacrament that allowed actual faith to be instilled in newborns.[10] Although Luther defended the practice of infant baptism, he also stated that parents' prayers for stillborn or miscarried infants would suffice for God to save their souls.[11] Johann Gerhard's *Loci Communes Theologici* (9 vols., 1610-22), still consulted by some Protestant pastors today, describes this loophole for some lucky infants: "If a question be moved concerning infants departing without Baptisme: we must proceed distinctly. Those which are without the Church, are left to the judgement of God. But those which being born of Christian parents, by reason of some case of urgent necessitie, could not be baptized; or those which die in their mothers wombe: those, I say, by the prayers of their parents and the Church may be commended unto God; but are not excluded from the fellowship of the kingdome of heaven."[12] The Catholic Church's response to the Protestant revival of Augustine was not unified: some like the Jansenists (whom Leibniz refers to as the "disciples of Augustine") generally favored a return to Augustine's binary view on infant damnation, whereas others maintained Aquinas's ternary view.[13] Such was the state of discussion by circa 1700.

To clarify Leibniz's position on the fate of infant souls, one must read the unmercifully long text of *Theodicy*. And one must read carefully, for Leibniz tries to be an orthodox Christian with reservations. The question is whether the reservations make him unorthodox, the answer is "yes," but Leibniz downplays this fact, whether out of fear of being labeled a heretic (as Bertrand Russell would argue) or out of a sincere desire to unify the warring Christian factions.[14] Toward the end of his preface, Leibniz claims that he generally approves of Protestant theology, which considers the unregenerate to be corrupt, to be considered as dead. But this general approval comes with an important caveat: "Yet this corruption of unregenerate man is, it must be added, no hindrance to his possession of true moral virtues and his performance of good actions in his civic life, actions which spring from a good principle, without any evil intention and without mixture of actual sin. Wherein I hope I shall be forgiven, if I have dared to diverge from the opinion [*sentiment*] of St. Augustine: he was doubtless a great man, of admirable intelligence, but inclined sometimes, as it seems, to exaggerate things, above all in the heat of controversies" (*Theodicy*, 70; G 6:46). This passage may be read as doublespeak: Leibniz claims to accept original sin and the corruption of human nature, but goes right on to posit that one may act virtuously without grace and without the sacraments: the "good principle" seems to be sufficient. What Ernst Cassirer wrote about humanism seems to hold for Leibniz's *Theodicy*: "Humanism never dared openly assail the dogma of the fall of man but its basic intellectual tendency was toward undermining the force of this dogma [*dieses Dogma gewissermaßen aufzulockern und seine Gewalt abzuschwächen*]."[15] Cassirer reports that eighteenth-century German Protestantism would undergo a sea change: many enlightened Protestant theologians increasingly returned to the Pelagian-Erasman position concerning human nature and free will, and formally rejected the doctrine of original sin. Cassirer credits Shaftesbury and especially Rousseau for indirectly helping bring about this new development, whereas he regards Leibniz as having exhausted all the old options of theodicy.[16] I submit that a careful reading shows that Leibniz also deserves credit for redirecting the debate between Luther and Erasmus, such that in eighteenth-century Protestantism, it was decided in favor of the latter. But it should be stressed that Leibniz himself did not wish to decide, that he did not see these positions as mutually exclusive: "Man has behaved badly, he has fallen; but there remains still a certain freedom after the fall. . . . Thus it is that free will and will in bondage are one and the same thing" (*T* 277). Leibniz could not be clearer here: he regards the Augustinian/Pelagian, Lutheran/Erasman debate as fundamentally misguided. Let us recall that Pelagius and Erasmus argued for free will, while Augustine and Luther argued for will in bondage. Leibniz says yes to both sides: he claims to affirm original sin and the fall, but there is always a supplemental clause in which Leibniz affirms that the natural light (as opposed to the supernatural one) can suffice for salvation. In his attempt to mediate between warring theological factions, Leibniz made it his task to present a doctrine of original sin that would be acceptable to reason. (In Leibniz's day, formulating Christian doctrines that would be "acceptable to reason" meant that they would be acceptable to Catholics, Lutherans, and Calvinists. This diplomatic mission may help explain why Leibniz, a Lutheran, often sounds like a Catholic and finds Aquinas's positions sympathetic. Nevertheless, it should be noted that Leibniz never converted to Catholicism.)[17]

But reason requires that one reject certain beliefs of Augustine. His denial that pagans can be virtuous, for example, "shocks reason [*choque la raison*]" (*T* 259, G 6:270). In general, though, Leibniz says he can accept the system of Augustine's disciples, the Jansenists, "provided one exclude certain obnoxious things [*choses odieuses*], whether in the expressions or in the dogmas themselves" (*T* 280, G 6:283). Leibniz could not be clearer about what provoked his distaste: "In the dogmas themselves held by the Disciples of St. Augustine I cannot approve [*je ne saurois gouster*] the damnation of unregenerate children, nor in general damnation resulting from original sin alone. . . . Save for these points, and some few others, where St. Augustine appears obscure or even repellant [*rebutant*], it seems as though one can conform to his system" (*T* 283–84, G 6:285). Clearly, Leibniz takes distance from several harsh views of Augustine and the Jansenists. But as I argue in the conclusion of this chapter, Elmar J. Kremer is mistaken in characterizing Leibniz's rejection of these views as dogmatic, put forward without evidence, and grounded solely in shock: "In the *Theodicy*, Leibniz does not explain why he denies that an infant, who is innocent of actual sin, could be in a state that would merit damnation to hell. . . . He ignores the Augustinian position that human beings are not innocent at birth, but rather are born in a state of sin that was initiated by Adam's sinful action. He does not try to show that the position is logically incoherent. He simply declares that it is shocking."[18] Far from ignoring the doctrine of original sin, Leibniz rewrites it. As I outline below, Leibniz recasts original sin as not a moral evil, but rather a metaphysical one, resulting from Adam's having been physically poisoned. That is, Leibniz denies that a depraved will, which merits damnation, necessarily follows from original sin. I argue that Leibniz's laborious attempt to decouple the human condition from any depravity of the will is clearly a response to and a refutation of Augustine and his followers, the Jansenists, on this one point concerning the unbaptized. Leibniz is certainly shocked by their harshness, but he also reasons against it.

A rejection of Augustine's view of infant damnation can go several ways: (1) one accepts that infants are excluded from heaven, do suffer from this knowledge (*poena damni*), but at least do not suffer *poena sensus* with the adult damned, (2) one follows Aquinas in accepting that infants are excluded from heaven, but denying that they are fully aware of their state; accordingly, they suffer neither *poena sensus* nor *poena damni*, but rather live in a state of natural happiness in an earthly paradise, or (3) one denies limbo and thus concludes that if these infants do not go to hell, they must therefore go to heaven. In Kremer's estimation, Leibniz concludes (2): he follows Aquinas and rejects the physical torment of infants as too cruel to be just but accepts their exclusion from heaven as something for which God must have had his reasons. In the final section of this chapter, I present evidence to support my argument that Leibniz concludes (3): he rejects *both* infant damnation *and* the infant's limbo. Although Leibniz does not explicitly state this conclusion, I submit that his arguments locate the souls of unbaptized innocents in heaven.

LEIBNIZ VS. BAYLE ON FAITH
AND REASON, TRIAL PROCEDURE

It has always been a central concern of monotheism to explain the existence of evil, which seems incompatible with God's goodness, power, and/or wisdom. The 1702 publication of William King's *De origine mali* had resparked debates on this topic, but Pierre Bayle's reviews of King seem to have had even more effect than King's text per se.[19] Since Bayle argued reasonably enough for the mortification of reason when it comes to questions of faith, Leibniz found him to be a perfect sparring partner. As Austin Farrer wrote, "if we had not evidence of [Bayle's] historical reality, we might have suspected Leibniz of inventing him" (*Theodicy*, 35).

Although Bayle has been overlooked in many surveys of the Enlightenment, his *Historical and Critical Dictionary* galvanized eighteenth-century and subsequent thought.[20] In short articles devoted to various biblical and historical figures, Bayle provided long footnotes, and even notes to the notes, all of which provide occasion for philosophical and theological discussions. For example, the notes to the article Rorarius discuss various theories on the souls of animals; remarks H and (in the second edition) L review Leibniz's new system of preestablished harmony.[21] As he began replying to Bayle, Leibniz quickly sensed the importance of addressing other articles in the *Dictionary*, especially those touching on the question of evil. After a later friendly letter to Bayle, Leibniz conceived the idea of writing a systematic discussion of interesting passages in Bayle's work, which ultimately led him to produce *Theodicy*.[22]

It is notoriously difficult to say what Bayle believed; he presented himself as a fideist. Accordingly, he aimed to show that reason cannot clarify our lives, that only faith can do so, and that reasoned arguments can never square with the requirements of Christian belief. Why he did so is an open question: certainly, he had personal motivations to argue that if knowledge cannot be certain, then religious toleration would be imperative.[23] But many contemporary and later thinkers suspected or concluded that Bayle actually aimed to show that Christianity is incoherent. Although his stated intent was to sway his readers away from reason and toward faith, the *Dictionary* came to provide various Enlightenment thinkers with ammunition for their criticisms of religious institutions. Whether this would have horrified or pleased Bayle is open to debate; regardless of the answer to this question, Bayle's finessed use of reason to demonstrate the weakness of reason has received a great deal of attention. Bayle argued that our experience shows us and our reason tells us that if God exists, he must be either impotent (God cannot save us from the evil choices we make), ignorant (God does not know what choices we will make, and thus cannot be held accountable for them), or malevolent (God wishes us to make evil choices and be damned).[24] Evidence for the last point is so compelling, Bayle argues, that it seems most reasonable to conclude with the Manicheans that there are in fact two separate cosmic powers, one good and the other evil. This solution would at least defend God's goodness, if not his power. But Bayle, I submit, was hardly arguing for Manicheism. Rather, by showing that Manicheism is the most reasonable stance one can hold, Bayle wished his readers to conclude that one should not hold a reasonable stance; one should instead submit one's reason to the demands of faith. (Here I provisionally solve the Bayle enigma for the present study by regarding him as a fideist. I am fully aware that one may with equal justification regard Bayle as a closet atheist.[25] But since Leibniz took Bayle to be a fideist, so I shall treat him in the following.) According to Bayle, one should simply decide to believe in the Christian God in the face of so many reasons not to.

One of the major reasons not to believe is that God permits human beings to sin. If God is capable of not letting us sin, then Bayle claims that it reasonably appears monstrous that He allows us to do so, only to redeem (some of) us later through Christ. To illustrate this point, Bayle calls to mind what a good parent would do:

If God did not foresee the fall of man, he must at least have judged that it was possible; therefore, since he saw he would be obliged to abandon his paternal goodness if the fall ever did occur, only to make his children miserable by exercising upon them the role of a severe judge, he would have determined man to moral good. . . . This is where we are led by the clear and distinct ideas of order when we follow, step by step, what an infinitely good principle ought to do. For, if a goodness as limited as that of a human father necessarily requires that he prevent as much as possible the bad use which his children might make of the goods he gives them, much more will an infinite and all-powerful goodness prevent the bad effects of its gifts.[26]

A number of unorthodox views regard God's power as limited. The Manichaeans saw it limited by a rival deity; the Socinians saw it limited by God's ignorance of the choices we will make; as I discuss further below, Leibniz sees it limited by God's own wisdom. In contrast to all of these positions, Bayle views God's power as unlimited. But granting God's omnipotence seems to entail questioning His goodness. A human father, with good intentions but limited in power, seems to do better than God does. According to Bayle, reasoning here entails invoking the experiences one has with good fathers in order to judge God's conduct. That the outcome is negative supports Bayle's ultimate claim that one should abandon reasoning for faith, at least regarding theological articles. For Leibniz, reasoning does not depend upon appeals to experience, so Bayle's analogies should not lead one to fideism. Continuing his analogy, Bayle seems to suggest that reason is least offended by Manichaeism: Susan Neiman states nicely that "if this view makes God into a large and long-living parent, well-meaning but bounded, it does less violence to our intuitions than do other options. It may be hard to acknowledge God's limits, but it's less frightening than denying His goodwill."[27] But fright is precisely what Bayle wished to evoke in his readers, and his parent analogy is perfectly suited to this aim. Any reason one might give to justify God's permission for sin leads one to extremely unpalatable conclusions:

For example, if you say that God has permitted sin in order to manifest his wisdom . . . you will be answered that this is to compare God . . . to a father who allows his children to break their legs so that he can show everyone his great skill in mending their broken bones. . . . The conduct of this father . . . is so contrary to the clear and distinct ideas by which we judge goodness and wisdom and in general all the duties of a father . . . that our reason cannot conceive how God could act in this way. . . . Those who say that God permitted sin because he could not have prevented it without destroying the free will that he had given to man, and which was the best present he made to him, expose themselves greatly. . . . There is no good mother who, having given her daughters permission to go to a dance, would not revoke that permission if she were assured that they would succumb to temptations and lose their virginity there. And any mother who, knowing for sure that this would come to pass, allowed them to go to the dance and was satisfied with exhorting them to be virtuous and with threatening to disown them if they were no longer virgins when they returned home, would, at the very least, bring upon herself the just charge that she loved neither her daughters nor chastity. It would be in vain for her to try to justify herself by saying that she had not wished to restrain the freedom of her daughters or to indicate that she distrusted them. She would be told this type of behaviour was preposterous and was more indicative of a provoked, cruel stepmother than of a mother, and that it would have been better to keep her daughters in her sight than to give them the privilege of freedom and the signs of her confidence for such a bad end.[28]

God's permission to sin cannot be reasonably defended. With one argument, one must conclude that God suffers from Munchhausen Syndrome By Proxy; with another argument, one must conclude that God is a pimp. As Bayle depicts it, reasoned argument leads us to conclude that God is a cruel father, a wicked stepmother, a horrible parent. Bayle does seem to take pleasure in shocking his readers with such descriptions, which may be one reason why he has been suspected of atheism (and why atheists have gladly read Bayle). But I think it just as likely that Bayle intended to shock the reader into abandoning reason, if the result of reasoning is to shake all confidence in the goodness of God the father (or mother). All the more motivation to turn to faith, which tells us that God is a loving parent (never mind original sin, damnation, etc.).[29] A rationalist could not read such things and sit by idly. Leibniz wanted, in the only philosophical book he published, to reclaim reason from Bayle, and effect a conciliation between philosophy and theology, between reason and faith. Thus the conformity of faith with reason is the subject of an eighty-seven paragraph "Preliminary Dissertation" preceding the three essays of *Theodicy*.

Before turning to Leibniz's explicit answers to Bayle, where he asserts the compatibility of faith and reason in a discursive manner, I would like to submit that Leibniz does so in an implicit, even cryptic manner as well. That is, Leibniz provides a double answer to the ques-

tion: who is the child of God? In the Latin summary, Leibniz refers to
Jesus Christ as the son of God. But the summary given at the conclusion
of the French text discusses instead Pallas Athena, goddess of wisdom,
daughter of Jupiter. What should one make of this equivalent status of
Greco-Roman and Christian deities? In a fictive dialogue, Jupiter in-
structs Theodorus, the questioning human, to go to his daughter, Pallas
Athena, because she can explain what Jupiter "was bound to do" (*T*
413) when he created the world. She gives Theodorus a Leibnizian account concerning Jupiter's choice of the optimal world. Had he not chosen this world, he would have thereby renounced his own child: "Else
would Jupiter have banished me, me his daughter" (*T* 416). It seems
noteworthy that Leibniz does not write here about Jesus Christ, the
child of God who was paradoxically sacrificed (but resurrected), thus
seemingly (though not in truth) abandoned, just as Isaac was seemingly
(though not in truth) threatened with death by God's will at the hand of
his father, Abraham. That is, *Theodicy* is not oriented toward the mysterious Christ, whose death and resurrection Bayle could cite as one of the
mysteries that exceed reason. Instead, the child of God in Leibniz's text
is Wisdom herself. The universe admits of rational organization and explanation. By contrast, the *Causa Dei*, a Latin summary of *Theodicy*,
names Christ the head of the created world and signifier of a freedom to
come, in which we all become the children of God; there is no mention
of pagan gods here (G 6:446, sec. 49). I would like to suggest that this
omission is not simply an expression of cautious prudence, although it
should be noted that the censors were much more likely to read the independent Latin summary than the embedded French one. One might
be tempted to assert (following Russell) that Leibniz's self-presentation
as a man of faith is belied by his actually being a man of reason. But
since Leibniz published *both* texts, the charge of prudence or cowardice
here fails to convince. I submit that Leibniz's belief in the compatibility
of faith and reason explains his having placed Christ and Pallas Athena
in complementary positions in the two summaries.

Where Bayle would have reason attack faith (and seemingly win)
and conclude from this terrible victory that God's authority must triumph over human reason, Leibniz points out that reason and faith, like
Athena and Christ, both come from God: "Since reason is a gift of God,
even as faith is, contention between them would cause God to contend
against God; and if the objections of reason against any article of faith
are insoluble, then it must be said that this alleged article will be false
and not revealed: this will be a chimera of the human mind. . . . Such is

the doctrine of the damnation of unbaptized children, which M. Nicole would have us assume to be a consequence of original sin; such would be the eternal damnation of adults lacking the light that is necessary for the attainment of salvation" (*Theodicy*, 96–97).[30] Leibniz's denial of the damnation of innocents displays (or betrays, one might prefer to say) his belief that human beings, including heretics, schismatics, pagans, and above all infants and children, are naturally good. Leibniz's defense of God is no less a defense of human nature.

"Theodicy," a term Leibniz coined, means "justness of God." Leibniz's early training was in law, and the three essays of *Theodicy* read much like a brief for the defense. Bayle had also, in his own way, aimed to defend God, as though human reason were holding God on trial. Leibniz in turn aims to defend God not against reason, presumed to be the plaintiff, but against His inept defense lawyers, such as Bayle, who mistakenly hold that reason must be in conflict with theology. Leibniz's rebuttal of Bayle commences by noting that Bayle puts God on trial using juridical terms and procedures that are appropriate for human beings:

> Bayle will not have it that one can justify the goodness of God in the permission of sin, because probability [*vraisemblance*] would be against a man that should happen to be in circumstances comparable in our eyes to this permission. God foresees that Eve will be deceived by the serpent if he places her in the circumstances wherein she later found herself; and nevertheless he placed her there. Now if a father or a guardian did the same in regard to his child or his ward, if a friend did so in regard to a young person whose behaviour was his concern, the judge would not be satisfied by the excuses of an advocate who said that the man only permitted the evil, without doing it or willing it: he would rather take this permission as a sign of ill intention, and would regard it as a sin of omission, which would render the one convicted thereof accessary in another's sin of commission. (*Theodicy*, 92–93; G 6:69)

Leibniz concedes that a human being who allows bad things to happen to good people is guilty of a sin of omission. In taking up his role as advocate, Leibniz states that with God, the *rules* must be the same (God must be just, and we must understand what we mean when we state this; otherwise it is a meaningless statement), but it is a wholly different *case*. That is, with God, we do not deal with probabilities and initial presumptions of innocence. Rather, whatever God does *is* right, even if it does not appear to us to be so. But this is where Leibniz differs from the

Jansenists: if one can prove beyond reasonable doubt that something is not right, then one must conclude that God did not do it. Accordingly, Leibniz maintains that certain points of faith do not require rational proofs to be believed. Rather, Christians who accept revelation are supposed to believe them *unless* someone provides a compelling reason not to believe them. This point is significant, for it refutes the Jansenist argument for total submission of reason to faith, even when a doctrine contradicts reason. Against this argument, Leibniz distinguishes along with the scholastics between doctrines *above* reason, which should be accepted, and doctrines *against* reason, which must not be accepted.[31] We must always believe God, but we must also always trust the use of our God-given reason. Leibniz's general rule in arguing for the justness of God is to make the first point: whatever God does is right, although it may appear to be evil. But there are exceptional passages, as in his denial of infant damnation, where Leibniz makes the second point: God did not do this thing.

Bayle depicted God as being on trial before the court of human reason. Accepting this depiction as an heuristic fiction, Leibniz points out that the preponderance of evidence must come from the prosecution, not from the defense; the defendant is under no compulsion to prove His innocence. Rather, we must presume His innocence unless He is proven guilty. (And if God's "guilt" is proven, then one must conclude that the charges are baseless, i.e., the doctrine in question is false.) It is fascinating (even sobering) to observe Leibniz, who is remembered as an early Enlightenment philosopher, clarify that enlightenment is purely a matter for the prosecution, given that Leibniz represents the defendant (see *Theodicy*, 116). The defense attorney must of course argue according to the rules of reason, but what he defends (God and his ways) does not yet admit of enlightenment. In this life, we can see only with the light of nature, and perhaps that of grace, which still amounts only to seeing through a glass, darkly, in comparison to the coming light of glory in the next world. Leibniz concludes his preliminary discussion by citing Augustine, who believed that mysteries of faith might be clarified on earth, by a limited number of holy men, and Luther, who held that only the celestial academy would understand what we terrestrials may find incomprehensible. Leibniz specifically cites Luther, who maintained God's justice despite the reservations raised by reason, given that God apparently damns those undeserving of such a fate.[32] For Luther, our inability to comprehend God's justice should translate into an imperative to believe in it, despite our incomprehension. Clearly, Leibniz's book was meant to refute Luther's argument that God's justice must be wholly mysterious to us. But this early in his text, Leibniz does not yet correct Luther's premise that one can be justly damned without deserving it. Indeed, he never explicitly says that he is correcting Luther, and yet this is the effect of his book. Leibniz concludes his "Preliminary Dissertation" by expressing the charitable hope that the deceased Bayle is now illuminated by the light of glory. Presumably, the now-illuminated Bayle can see the question of damnation in its true light.

But Bayle the writer is another matter: he did not see so clearly, and Leibniz's text aims to clarify the perspective we should take when considering the evidence against God. This is the divine perspective, and since we can't actually assume it, we must instead trust it. This trust has a venerable history, and is classically expressed in Boethius's *Consolation of Philosophy*. Most of the time, Leibniz argues in this mode: we may not always understand the reasons for our suffering, but we cannot doubt that there must be such reasons. If one accepts this argument, one can maintain belief in God's infinite goodness, power, and wisdom. In our own microcosms, we may perceive disorder. But these innumerable small worlds add up to the best universe, where order reigns. If we could take a universal perspective, we would see this clearly. We are like children, Leibniz writes, whom adults secretly direct in ways they cannot see, and when we go astray, it is appropriate that God punishes us, as parents and teachers do their children (*T* 147). Bayle's arguments that God appears unjust are framed within the child's perspective; against Bayle's limited vision, Leibniz reminds us to use our mature reason and thus posit the larger perspective, even if we can't (yet) see it.

But Leibniz's consolation has its limit: when it comes to the damnation of virtuous pagans and children, guilty only of not having been baptized, Leibniz does not wish any longer to console: he holds this doctrine to be against reason, and concludes that it is false. Leibniz addresses the question whether being ready and able to sin is sufficient to damn the soul lacking regeneration through baptism: "St. Gregory of Nazianzos is supposed to have denied this; but St. Augustine is for the affirmative, and maintains that original sin of itself is enough to earn the flames of hell, although this opinion is, *to say the least*, very harsh. [My emphasis.] . . . Gregory of Rimini, General of the Augustinians, with a few others followed St. Augustine in opposition to the accepted opinion of the Schools of his time, and for that reason he was called the torturer of children, *tortor infantum*" (*T* 92). So far, Leibniz has indeed said the least, but as his historical sketch moves toward the present, he becomes bolder in rejecting the eternal physical torment of unbaptized infants. He refers to a large group of contemporary French prelates and theologians who side with Augustine, "who condemns to eternal flames children that die in the age of innocence before having received baptism" (*T* 93). The conclusion Leibniz draws certainly seems clear enough:

> But it must be confessed that this opinion has not sufficient foundation either in reason or in Scripture, and that it is outrageously harsh [*une dureté des plus choquantes*]. M. Nicole makes rather a poor apology for it in his book on the *Unity of the Church*, written to oppose M. Jurieu, although M. Bayle takes his side in chapter 178 of the *Reply to the Questions of a Provincial*, vol. III. M. Nicole makes use of this pretext, that there are also other dogmas in the Christian religion which appear harsh. . . . We must take into account that the other dogmas mentioned by M. Nicole, namely original sin and eternity of punishment, are only harsh and unjust to outward appearance, while the damnation of children dying without actual sin and without regeneration would in truth be harsh, since it would be in effect the damning of innocents. (*T* 93, G 6:154)

Voltaire must have overlooked or ignored this passage when he composed his 1759 *Candide: ou l'optimisme*.[33] His parody of Leibniz involves a figure (Pangloss) who can justify *any* apparent injustice as conforming to divine justice. As I discuss below, Leibniz is willing to accept original sin and even eternal punishment as part of an optimal world. But Leibniz's optimism has its limit here: he will not entertain the idea that the damnation of babies merely appears to be harsh; he insists that it would be in truth harsh. It is therefore a false doctrine.

Although it is certainly true that Bayle appreciated Nicole's demolition of Jurieu's arguments, Leibniz is not quite correct when he claims that Bayle agrees with Nicole. For his own part, although he criticizes Nicole's reasons, Leibniz is careful not to explicitly align himself with Jurieu's position. Nevertheless, Leibniz's terms to describe Nicole's views (as "harsh" and "shocking") derive directly from Jurieu. Clearly, then, Bayle's review of the Jurieu-Nicole debate was very important for Leibniz's elaboration of his own position. Because this text has seen much less reception in anglophone scholarship than has Bayle's *Dictionary*, I will quote from it at some length in the following section.[34] My translation of the entire review is given as an appendix to the present study.

REASON DIGESTING CRUELTY:
REVIEWING THE JURIEU-NICOLE DEBATE

In *Reply to the Questions of a Provincial*, Bayle continues the critical de-
bunking work he began in the *Dictionary*. His primary target is the bad
argumentation of liberal Christians who would combine faith and reason.[35] In chapters 177–78, Bayle reviews a debate between Pierre Jurieu
and Pierre Nicole (Bayle typically spells his name "Nicolle") on the
unity of the Church.[36] Initially, Bayle does not take sides; he indicates
that he is merely presenting opposing arguments. But it quickly becomes evident that Bayle pits Nicole against Jurieu in order to expose
the logical flaws of Jurieu's reasoning.[37] The opening paragraphs are
typical of Bayle's style; his own voice involves the words of Nicole (here
in double quotes) as well as those of Jurieu (here in single quotes):

> It is a Papist dogma that all children who die before having received
> Baptism are damned, and that all adults who die in heresy or in schism,
> that is, separated internally or externally from the Communion of Rome,
> go to hell. "This doctrine is so odious" to Mr. Jurieu (I am using Mr.
> Nicolle's words) "that when he thinks about it, he loses his composure
> and he cannot speak of it except with great emotion and convulsions. In
> one passage, he says: 'When one begins to speak to us of similar things,
> we shudder [*nous frémissons*] and we deplore the blindness of those who,
> instead of drawing a veil over the passages of ancient writers, spread
> them and glorify them. These are amazing cruelties which we can never
> believe that a single person of good sense could digest [*digérer*] today.' In
> another passage, he says: 'It is this question that I have said is the most
> cruel, and most absurd one ever asked, and so absurd that one can never
> persuade me that those who defend it actually believe it.' This is what
> makes him say in the same passage that 'supporting this doctrine without
> believing it must be political and a demonic ruse.' Elsewhere, he says: 'I
> will say once more that imagination is the most foolish thing installed in
> the human spirit.' Finally, he is so outraged by this point that he declares
> 'that it is one of those things that even if one swears a thousand times that
> one believes them, one could never persuade people of good sense.'"[38]
>
> It was not possible to more skillfully take advantage of [*profiter de*] Mr.
> Jurieu's thought than Mr. Nicolle has, but I must warn you that this
> moderation, this honesty that has been praised so much, and of which
> one finds many indications in his book, hardly appears in this passage:
> here, he employs harsh and injurious terms that he certainly could have
> omitted. His response could be just as strong and brilliant without them.
> (*RQP* 1197–99)

Infant damnation was not a "Papist" dogma; it was Augustine's and that of the Jansenists. It is unclear to me whether Bayle was simply mistaken (I find this unlikely), was ventriloquizing Nicole's position, or for some other reason wished here to conflate Nicole's position with that of the Catholic Church. In any case: Bayle goes on to list, in eight points, Nicole's refutations of Jurieu's criticisms of Catholic doctrines. For Bayle, the most serious charge was the first: Nicole claimed that Jurieu copied the Socinians in denying the eternity of suffering, an article firmly accepted in all of Christianity. Bayle points out that although Jurieu replied to the other points, albeit in an angry manner, he "kept profoundly silent regarding Mr. Nicolle's first observation. It may well have been odious: it was a shot at point-blank range [*un coup à brûle-pourpoint*]" (*RQP* 1212). Around 1700, being labeled a "Socinian" meant that one put too much trust in human reason unaided by God's mysterious grace.[39] Since Jurieu would jettison a doctrine because it seems cruel to reason, Nicole and Bayle could discredit him from the outset as an overly rational heretic. Jurieu fails to see that reason is a threat to the very existence of the Church:

> If it is permitted to reject dogmas accepted by the entire Church based on the fact that the human spirit unilluminated by faith finds there something shocking and harsh, what doors will not be opened to the Socinians to shake up and reverse the foundations of Christianity? What could appear more harsh than the condemnation of all infants for the crime of a single man, when they had no part in it with their own wills? And if one gives human reason liberty to rise up against the authority of the Church and against Scripture as interpreted by the Church, how much will reason strongly counter this article, as well as countering the judgement held by the Roman Church concerning the state of heretic and schismatic sects, and concerning the damnation of the unbaptized children of the faithful? (*RQP* 1200)[40]

Nicole began by stating that it appears to be cruel to damn infants, but went on to assert that there is actually no cruelty at all "in that which the ancient Church decided regarding the state of unbaptized infants, even those born of the faithful, supposing, as faith obliges us to believe, that God justly treats all infants whom he has not graced with baptism in a similar manner" (*RQP* 1203–4).[41] (The qualifier "even" signals that by "ancient," Nicole means the fifth-century church after the Augustinian solution to the Pelagian problem.) Nicole's conclusion is worth citing, because Leibniz will accept the first sentence but contest the second one: "Everything that God does can not be cruel, since he is sovereign justice itself. We must therefore limit all our research to that, and not pretend to judge whether he has done or has not done something, according to the feeble ideas we have of justice and of cruelty" (*RQP* 1204).[42] Leibniz objects that our ideas are not feeble, at least not in the sense Nicole means. They may be less extensive, but cannot be wholly different. Otherwise, we use terms like justice without knowing what we mean. (See *T* 176.) Reason comes from God; thus we can judge of what is just and what is not.

It seems that reason is particularly outraged by infant damnation. Be this as it may, Nicole recalls that St. Paul's long list (in Galations 5:19-21) of those who will be excluded from heaven also appears quite harsh to human reason, and yet Jurieu accepts St. Paul's authority. Thus, Nicole can both remind us that the Christian Church (insofar as it rests upon Paul) is not and was never meant to be rational, and also accuse Jurieu of being inconsistent. Nicole thus disqualifies in advance a rationalist critique of orthodox theology, but he also shows that Jurieu's argument is not even well reasoned:

> At the same time that Mr. Jurieu accepts and embraces the two dogmas of original sin and the eternity of suffering, maintained by the Church against the Socinians, which are like the triumph of God's authority over human reason; at the same time that he renounces his feeble understanding to adore the incomprehensible judgements of God's justice: he is not aware [*il ne prend pas garde*] that his animosity against the Roman Church leads him to form reckless accusations against two parts of these dogmas which he professes to believe as a whole. For what is the doctrine of the Church, which teaches that the children of the faithful who die without baptism are excluded from the kingdom of God and punished by eternal damnation; what, I say, is this doctrine other than a small part of the general doctrine of original sin which condemns to eternal damnation all unbaptized children? And what is it that the same Church teaches regarding heretics and schismatics, that those who die in schism and in heresy will never enter the kingdom of heaven, but will share the fate of hypocrites and reprobates, other than a small part of that which is contained in the letter of St. Paul, which excludes from the kingdom of God all crimes, explicitly including schisms and heresies? What harshness, what cruelty is there in these two particular dogmas that is not contained in the general dogmas? The children of the faithful, when they have never received baptism, are they not guilty of original sin? (*RQP* 1201–2)[43]

Nicole depicts infant damnation and original sin as having a part-whole relationship. Since Jurieu accepts the whole and rejects the part, his theology is illogical. As Bayle put it, Jurieu is a blind guide, guilty of "straining out the gnat after having swallowed the camel" (*RQP* 1233).[44] Jurieu's reply to Nicole aims to recast the doctrines as representing not a whole and a part, but rather a rule and an exception. Let us be perfectly clear: Jurieu is not shocked by the damnation of all unbaptized infants. He is only shocked at the notion that even the unbaptized children of believers must be damned. "Are the general rules violated by the exceptions that God has himself set? What follows from this? All children are deserving of death; thus children who are born in the alliance of grace must be damned. Is this what follows?" (*RQP* 1211–12). The Calvinist theory of election would seem to save certain unbaptized children, but Nicole will not have it: either the unbaptized are damned, or they are not. If one believes the former, one is steadfast in faith; if one believes the latter, one is a heretic. Interestingly, and *pace* Leibniz, Bayle does not take sides on this particular point: "[Jurieu] leaves us all the burden of examining whether it is correct or incorrect to place in the same class all children who die before baptism. He wants that those who are born within Christianity should be saved, even if their fathers and mothers are not married, have committed incest, and are destined to eternal damnation. He has his reasons, but they have been disputed; this is a very complicated controversy" (*RQP* 1229). I find Bayle's reticence here noteworthy, for it is the only place in the review where he seems to distance himself from Nicole's Jansenist Catholicism. (The title of *Reply to the Questions of a Provincial* clearly alludes to the Jansenist Blaise Pascal's *Lettres d'un Provincial*.) Recall that when Bayle discussed God's permission for us to sin, he reveled in imagining God as a child abuser or a procurer. Why this reserve now? It seems that Bayle distinguishes, after all, between God's treatment of adult sinners (who could be described *metaphorically* as abused children, according to the reason Bayle says should fall silent when we consider their damnation) and God's treatment of *actual* children (on which Bayle is here uncharacteristically silent).

Bayle generally shows that Jurieu's hypotheses prove more than they want to and have irrational consequences. He admits that "our reason prefers [*goûteroit mieux*] the ideas the Roman Catholics give to the Church less than those Mr. Jurieu forms of it" (*RQP* 1215). Nevertheless, Bayle concludes that "it is necessary that our reason sacrifice here its understanding to divine authority" (*RQP* 1219). Specifically, Jurieu's weak attempt to show the rationality of original sin (he argues that children's conditions follow those of their parents) is easily dismantled:

Bayle recalls that beautiful parents can have ugly children, that according to Jurieu's logic, human beings after Adam should have inherited
Adam's post-Edenic reconciliation with God, rather than his sin, and
that human laws always despise rulers who condemn all relatives of a
criminal to death. In short, Bayle argues that original sin cannot be rationally explained, and that one should rather avow with Zanchius that
"one cannot give another reason for original sin than the will of God"
(*RQP* 1219). Leibniz found this explanation deficient, and aimed to
show that the will of God cannot be the final ground of explanation. (In
this respect, Leibniz is consistent with his metaphysical explanation of
mind-body relations, which Descartes and his followers located in divine will. Leibniz argued that the ultimate ground of this explanation
must instead be in the divine intellect.) In the following section, I suggest that Leibniz's depiction of original sin as a physical evil is meant to
refute Bayle's claim that one cannot provide a reason other than that
God willed it.

Bayle and Nicole misidentified Jurieu as a rationalist theologian.
They wanted to show that reason cannot clarify our lives, that it leads
us in circles, that in questions of faith, it must necessarily fall silent before God's authority. They aimed to present Jurieu's logical missteps
as examples of this inherent weakness of reason. I submit that Leibniz
wrote *Theodicy* because Jurieu's arguments were not rationalist
enough. The more one reads from Bayle's summary of this debate, the
clearer it becomes that Leibniz's central arguments were designed to
escape Nicole's criticisms and redeem reason better than Jurieu was
capable of doing. Where Nicole claims that a dogma may shock human
spirit and yet must be believed, Leibniz insists on a distinction between dogmas that *appear* harsh but are not (the eternity of damnation)
and dogmas that appear harsh because they *are* harsh (the damnation
of innocents). Reason helps us distinguish between the two; and where
reason remains shocked, the doctrine in question is false. And where
Nicole contrasts the Socinians, who find the doctrine of original sin irrational, with his own Jansenist belief in the triumph of authority over
human reason, Leibniz rationalizes original sin, thus showing that the
premise of this contrast is false. That is, in proposing his own theory of
original sin as a physical evil, Leibniz takes away the irrational aspect
that the Socinians saw therein, thereby also removing the *triumph* over
reason that the Jansenists saw therein. Where reason is not shocked,
no authority (God's or the church's) can be said to triumph over reason.

Leibniz set about to depict original sin as no camel to be swallowed, but rather as a doctrine compatible with the salvation of infants, which is no insignificant gnat to be strained out. Where Jurieu was willing to save only some children from damnation, Bayle asked: "Wouldn't it be necessary, then, following the example of the Socinians, to save all children?" (*RQP* 1233). As repugnant as this eventuality might be to Nicole, Jurieu and (perhaps) Bayle alike, Leibniz's arguments do tend to save all children.

Bayle concludes that Jurieu's charge of Catholicism's cruelty is baseless. If the charge of cruelty should truly lead one to judge dogmas, then one should rather "abandon the doctrine of original sin and the eternity of infernal suffering, against which the objection of cruelty would be much more plausible than against the doctrine that Mr. Jurieu attacks" (*RQP* 1233). Leibniz intends to show that one can reasonably retain both doctrines and still uphold God's justice. To do so, of course, Leibniz had to make the doctrine of original sin digestible, if not palatable, to reason.

JUSTIFYING EVILS
(IMPERFECTION, SIN, DAMNATION OF SINNERS),
RATIONALIZING ORIGINAL SIN

If one attributes everything existing to one benevolent creator, as a Christian thinker must, then evil becomes a pressing problem requiring explanation. Leibniz follows medieval scholastics in viewing evil as consisting in distance from God, in privation; in scholastic terms, evil does not have an efficient cause as much as a deficient one (*T* 20). Thus, one cannot place the Devil right at the origin of evil. Rather, as Leibniz's *Causa Dei* states, "the root of the Fall is in the original imperfection or feebleness of creatures" (G 6:451, sec. 79, my translation). The three essays that make up *Theodicy* generally correspond to the three types of evil Leibniz distinguished: metaphysical, moral, and physical. In brief, it is a metaphysical evil that we are imperfect creatures, a moral evil that we are made such that we can sin, and a physical evil that we suffer punishment by our creator. I shall discuss each in turn. As we shall see, Leibniz's greatest difficulties in depicting reasonable notions of justice as compatible with Christianity arise as he considers original sin, which he presents as a hybrid of metaphysical and moral evil, and damnation, the worst form of physical evil. His solutions may have given rise to doubts about theodicy in general, and even doubts about Leibniz's sincerity, but

that is another story.[45] My concern here is to show that Leibniz's solutions are always concerned with the salvation of the innocent, that is,
virtuous pagans and infants.

If sin is based first and foremost in metaphysical evil, as Leibniz argues, then one must conclude that human nature is not originally depraved, but rather originally imperfect. This imperfection precedes the
fallen state of original sin, which in turn can lead us to commit actual
sins, but the fact that two steps precede any actual sin demonstrates that
Leibniz does not regard the human being as a sinner at root. Against
those who ascribe sin to the depravity of human will, Leibniz ascribes
sin to the limitations of human intellect. Accordingly, the clearer and
more distinctly one can recognize the good, the more one will gravitate
towards it. Sin for Leibniz consists in turning towards what seems to be
a good but is not correctly recognized as inferior to a greater good (*T*
289). Leibniz explicitly criticizes the notion that human will could be
truly neutral, in a state of equipoise, and could incline indifferently toward either good or evil. Leibniz will not have a neutral middle ground,
and he disputes the depravity of will, so only one option is left: that
human will inclines toward the good. The evident fact that we do not always arrive there is explained through a specific metaphysical limitation: temporality. God is above and beyond time; being in time is an imperfection of creatures. We may perceive that something is good, but
since it takes time to think about what we are doing, new perceptions or
inclinations can emerge and redirect our attention or desire away from
the previously perceived good (*T* 311). Our will, indeed our nature, is
good; sin is possible primarily because our vision is bad.[46]

But—secondarily—"original sin" takes hold of every human being at
conception. This doctrine seems to contradict our idea of God's goodness, according to which "his justice prevents him from condemning innocent men [*des innocens*]" (*T* 85, G 6:149). The difficulty of this contradiction resulted in various theories on the origin of the soul, three of
which Leibniz reviews. He repudiates the theory of the preexistence of
souls in other lives, which has it that guilt in a former life can lead to
punishment in this one. He also (initially) rejects the theory of traduction, according to which the souls of children are engendered from those
of their parents in the moment of conception, thus during sexual intercourse, a sinful activity that contaminates these new souls. Leibniz
points out that Augustine and most Protestants believe in traduction,
but notes that several Protestant universities are opposed to this explanation. The third theory, which Leibniz affirms, is that all souls were

created by God in the beginning. He notes that this theory is hardest to accommodate to the doctrine of original sin, but he goes on to attempt just this.

According to Leibniz, all human souls and bodies once existed in Adam's seed, one encapsulated in the other. When the time is right, namely at conception, each spermatic body begins to develop and becomes a fetus. Within the continuity of existence, conception marks an important discontinuity: before conception, the soul (or *monad*) perceives things most obscurely. But at conception, the soul is "elevated" and receives the faculty of reason. (Leibniz never states definitively whether this elevation occurs through natural or supernatural means.) At this point only does the soul become a being capable of free choice and therefore capable of sinning. That all human beings become potentially culpable even before birth might appear to be a harsh fate, but for Leibniz, the glass is half full: "it is much more appropriate to divine justice to give the soul, already corrupted *physically* or on the animal side by the sin of Adam, a new perfection which is reason, than to put a reasoning soul, by creation or otherwise, in a body wherein it is to be corrupted *morally*" (*T* 91). The physical corruption of which he speaks involves the following speculation, crucial for Leibniz's defense of God, about the effects of Adam's first sin.

Leibniz would have us believe that the forbidden fruit was poisonous. God's command not to eat of it was no different from the commands of parents who forbid children to play with knives. Such decrees are not arbitrary, but rather follow logically from the nature of wise and good beings, who desire that children avoid the natural consequences that follow from handling something harmful. This comparison is meant to discredit Bayle's depiction of the seeming arbitrariness of God's command. Leibniz criticizes Bayle for comparing God to the Athenians, who compel their condemned to drink hemlock. Leibniz specifically counters this specter of a willful God with this image: "if drunkards begot children inclined to the same vice, by a natural consequence of what takes place in bodies, that would be a punishment [from] their progenitors, but it would not be a penalty of law. There is something comparable to this in the consequences of the first man's sin" (*T* 112).[47] Where Bayle depicts God as a monarch, Leibniz refers to God's intellect and wisdom (rather than God's will) as the ultimate explanatory principle. We may not understand why God allowed the human race to be infected, but we may console ourselves in knowing that this infection is not actually a *punishment* God placed upon us. Only when we acquire reason (at conception) does our original metaphysical imperfection become a capacity to sin, and only if or when this capacity is acted upon does one sin and thereby become deserving of punishment. It is crucial to note that, for Leibniz, original sin alone does not cause one to be deserving of punishment. At least this is the impetus of the French text, which compares original sin to hereditary alcoholism. The Latin summary states that since we suffer from original sin, our intellect is subject to our senses, and our will is oriented toward our flesh, so that according to nature (read: without grace, which in most orthodox Western Christian denominations first comes with baptism) we are "sons of wrath [*filii irae*]" (G 6:452, sec. 86, my translation). This latter description is more orthodox than what Leibniz writes in the *Theodicy*, which regards us as *physically ill children*, but not as *morally wicked* ones. And to be clear: Adam, not God, is to blame for this sickness. Thus God is not only excused for original sin, but praised for deigning to bestow upon us the salutary gift of reason at conception. This defense does not address whether God can be reasonably blamed for Adam (or Eve) having contracted this illness; still, Leibniz's aim here is to maintain God's goodness by depicting original sin as a physical evil rather than a moral one. If we have inherited original sin, at least we can be assured that we don't deserve it.

Bayle depicted God as a negligent parent who failed to childproof his garden; Leibniz shifts the blame to our first father instead. This response to the charge of negligence is not very robust, and so Leibniz quickly returns to the explanation of optimalism. Could God have created a world in which we did not sin? Perhaps, Leibniz answers, but that world would not have been as good a world as the actual one is. He does not specify *how* it would be worse; rather, he concludes a priori *that* it would be worse. Several times in this discussion, Leibniz mentions a book on predestination by one Cardinal Sfondrati. He notes that "the cardinal appears to prefer even to the Kingdom of Heaven the state of children dying without baptism, because sin is the greatest of evils, and they have died innocent of all actual sin" (*T* 11; see also *T* 92). Leibniz claims to distance himself from this view, arguing that a world with sin and redemption must be better than a world entirely without sin. Would the latter world have been better, God would have made it. Because he did not, we must conclude that it would not have been better, and thus we should not envy deceased babies.[48]

Maintaining optimalism requires Leibniz to make the strong claim that physical suffering—whether brought on by a cold or an earthquake[49]—is always a result of sin; it always amounts to a punishment by

God (*T* 241). Since this may sound harsh, one should recall Leibniz's nonharsh claim that original sin, which is more a metaphysical than a moral evil, does not itself necessarily lead to punishment. But Leibniz is prepared to defend the worst form of physical evil: damnation (*T* 266). He discusses three difficulties concerning damnation that have regularly troubled belief in God's justice: the eternity of punishment, the great number of the damned—both of which Leibniz accepts—and the damnation of the unbaptized (infants and virtuous pagans), which he rejects. The first difficulty is quickly managed: Leibniz suggests that no one damned will ever experience remorse. Rather, the damned renew their hatred of God in every moment, such that they continue to sin forever; this explanation neatly justifies the eternity of their punishment. (See G 6:447-48, sec. 59.) The second difficulty requires greater finesse.

There are false ways to be optimistic. Leibniz alludes to various thinkers who have believed that the number of the damned would be very small, that there exists a middle space between heaven and hell—Leibniz does not specify whether this refers to purgatory or limbo, but the context suggests to me that he means the former—that all Christians would ultimately be taken into grace, and even, following Origen, that all rational creatures, including the fallen angels, would one day find their way to God (*T* 17). Compared to such beliefs, Leibniz's early modern optimism is much less rosy: he states that he holds to "the established doctrine that the number of men damned eternally will be incomparably greater than that of the saved" (*T* 19). Leibniz attempts to justify this seemingly harsh outcome by stating that the wickedness of these damned will be much smaller in comparison to the goodness of the blessed. In a further speculation, Leibniz says it is possible that even if the majority of human beings are damned, this may not be true of all rational creatures in the universe. There might be innumerable worlds where creatures swim in seas of happiness. (Reading such passages, Voltaire's parodic depiction of the Leibnizian Pangloss in *Candide* does come to mind.) Leibniz also helpfully offers the image of cities being laid to waste in order to inspire terror and capitulation in an opponent's remaining cities, as a way of suggesting that the damnation of the wicked of our globe might intimidate the wicked on other globes, thus leading them to mend their ways. Ultimately, though, Leibniz's rebuttal of Bayle does not consist in attempting to actually enumerate God's reasons, but rather "to show that he cannot lack such" (*T* 133).

But I submit that Leibniz was not completely at ease with this sort of explanation. He expresses awareness that the great number of the

damned appears to be unjust. After all, there can be no personal guilt involved if "countless men, in childhood or maturity [*enfans ou adultes*] . . .
have never heard or have not heard enough of Jesus Christ, Saviour of
the human race . . . [and thus] are condemned" (*T* 5, G 6:105). Bayle
was also aware of this appearance of injustice, and, as usual, he gave a
rather pointed description of it: "when a whole great people has become
guilty of rebellion, it is not showing clemency to pardon the hundred
thousandth part, and to kill all the rest, not excepting even babes and
sucklings [*sans excepter les enfants à la mamelle*]" (*RQP* 824–25, cited in *T*
133, G 6:184). Despite Leibniz's clear affirmation of the truth of this
seemingly harsh doctrine at several points in *Theodicy* (see *T* 19, 119 and
237), he seems at other points to back away from so harsh a conclusion:
"It seems to be assumed here that there are a hundred thousand times
more damned than saved, and that children dying unbaptized are included among the former. Both these points *are disputed*, and especially
the damnation of these children" (*T* 133, my emphasis). Despite his use
of the passive voice, I would like to suggest that Leibniz himself began
to dispute at least one of these points as he composed *Theodicy*. Raising
some doubt about the sincerity of his confession of faith elsewhere in the
text, Leibniz ultimately does refer to the exceeding number of the
damned as "a supposition which is nevertheless not altogether certain"
(*T* 263). Voltaire's ungenerous conclusion comes to mind: "Is this really
the best of available lots? . . . Leibniz sensed that he had no reply to this:
so he made fat books in which he disagreed with himself."[50] If consistency is desirable in a philosopher—Leibniz thought so—then one
should attempt to observe where Leibniz agreed with himself and where
he did not.[51] Whereas Leibniz merely fluctuated on the question of the
number of the damned, it seems that Bayle's reference to the murder of
babies struck a nerve, ultimately leading Leibniz to reject the doctrine of
infant damnation.

SAVING THE INNOCENT:
GRACE AND REASON VS. BAPTISM

Leibniz's expressions of shock seem to derive directly from Jurieu's own
shudders. But Leibniz does more than let Jurieu's shock speak through
him; in two ways, he attempts to provide counter-arguments. First,
Leibniz refers—if vaguely—to "moderate theologians" who are content
to "surrender these souls [of moribund infants] to the judgement and the
clemency of their Creator" (*T* 93). Second, he goes on to speculate that

these infants, those who lived before Christ, and contemporaries who have not heard of him, may perhaps receive this knowledge in the moment they are dying, which then opens the path to their salvation:

> Supposing that to-day a knowledge of Jesus Christ according to the flesh is absolutely necessary to salvation, as indeed it is safest to teach, it will be possible to say that God will give that knowledge to all those who do, humanly speaking, that which in them lies, even though God must needs give it by a miracle. Moreover, we cannot know what passes in souls at the point of death; and if sundry learned and serious theologians claim that children receive in baptism a kind of faith, although they do not remember it afterwards when they are questioned about it, why should one maintain that nothing of a like nature, or even more definite, could come about in the dying, whom we cannot interrogate after their death? (*T* 98)

Such a gracious dispensation cannot, of course, be observed, but it does not conflict with our ideas of God's power and goodness. Leibniz presents himself as being in good company: Aquinas and Francis Xavier had professed that those who followed their natural light, even outside of Christianity, would be given grace by God and thus be saved. And Friedrich Spee held that divine love could blot out sin even without the Catholic Church's sacraments.[52] Thus Leibniz posits the possibility of one mystery (faith received *in hora mortis*) to parallel another one (faith received in infant baptism) that has wide theological acceptance, at least in Protestantism. Of course, it then follows that all human beings, not only unbaptized infants but also pagans and heretics, may receive faith through divine intervention in their hour of death. Following Augustine, the 1547 Council of Trent had maintained that baptism was the normal means to salvation, but that there were notable exceptions (Elijah, Moses, et al.).[53] Leibniz effectively suggests that for the innocent (infants and virtuous adults), salvation might be the rule rather than the exception. Since this eleventh-hour gift of grace can obviate baptism, Leibniz holds open the possibility that no infant whatsoever need be damned.

In addition to possibly receiving grace at the end of life, we have all been supplied with reason since conception. This gift exonerates God for permitting us to sin, since reason for Leibniz is an adequate shield against vice: "by granting us the light of reason he has bestowed upon us the means whereby we may meet all difficulties" (*T* 265). Though Leibniz does not use these terms, the context suggests that reason may be regarded as an antidote for the poison Adam ingested with the apple. I submit that Leibniz replaces the gift of grace bestowed in baptism, which only some people receive, with reason, which all people receive. In this respect, Leibniz might seem to be a latitudinarian: one who would save as many as possible. But if reason is supposed to be an adequate defense against the effects of original sin, why are not all people saved? Why do so many sin and become damned? "God, in giving [man] intelligence, has presented him with an image of the Divinity. . . . [Man is] like a little god in his own world or Microcosm, which he governs after his own fashion: he sometimes performs wonders therein, and his art often imitates nature. . . . But he also commits great errors, because he abandons himself to the passions, and because God abandons him to his own way" (T 147). Those who err are then deservedly punished. The small evil of this punishment, Leibniz explains, serves to adorn the optimal universe. Leibniz's explanation of how actual sin is possible, given that we have all been supplied with reason, is rather underdeveloped. But by depicting reason as an adequate counterbalance to original sin, at least until one has the opportunity to actually sin, Leibniz does provide a coherent argument that the innocent are shielded from punishment. Reason may not serve to keep us all from abandoning ourselves to the passions, but at least we have all been given a fair chance at the beginning of our individual lives.

Leibniz clearly rejects the physical torment of babies in hell. Does he also deny, with Aquinas, the pangs of loss that might accompany exclusion from the kingdom of heaven? Evidence for an affirmative answer is located in implicit clues. One way in which Leibniz expresses his disapproval of the harsh Augustinian doctrine is by referring to three milder views held by various theologians: that these souls suffer a purely privative punishment in limbo, that they may experience a natural bliss, even that their state of happy innocence might be preferable to the fallen state of those who have lived past infancy. Regarding this third view, Leibniz states: "that, however, seems to go too far" (T 91). Should one take Leibniz to be assenting to either of the first two views? Both of them place infants in limbo, rather than in hell. Elmar J. Kremer, to my knowledge the only other scholar who has written about the fate of unbaptized infants in Leibniz, draws this conclusion. From Leibniz's reference to a distinction between physical suffering and a sense of deprivation, Kremer concludes that "Leibniz holds that it would be unjust for God to impose suffering upon infants who die unbaptized, but not that it would be unjust for him to exclude such infants from heaven."[54] But I submit that at this point of Leibniz's text, one can only conclude that Leibniz denies the sensory punishment of infants who die unbaptized. There is insufficient evidence in this passage alone to conclude whether Leibniz accepts or denies either the first mild view (a nonsensory, privative damnation) or the second one (natural bliss, without awareness of exclusion from heaven). Kremer goes on to note that Leibniz "mentions"[55] scholastics who would send these infants to limbo rather than hell. But then Kremer interprets Leibniz's *mention* as an *endorsement* of this position. The final four pages of Kremer's analysis then attempt to make sense of this endorsement; but if that interpretation is mistaken, then several of Kremer's conclusions must be reexamined.

As Kremer reads Leibniz, the permanent exclusion of infants from heaven is a metaphysical evil, but one that is necessary for the world to be the best of all possible ones. He presents as evidence for his conclusion the dialogue at the end of Leibniz's text in which Pallas Athena recounts that Jupiter had given Sextus a choice to give up the crown and find salvation, or be crowned ruler in Rome and die a sinner. Sextus chooses the latter course, things end badly for him (he is damned), but this is for the best, since the world thereby gains a great empire. According to this example, the damnation of one may serve the greater good. Kremer views this as a model for understanding Leibniz on the fate of infants dying unbaptized: "whether someone who dies as an infant gains or loses heaven is determined, in Leibniz's view, by what is required in order that this world be the best of all possible worlds."[56] But this dialogue presents an *adult*, someone whose will is actively engaged in a sin freely chosen. Such a person *deserves* damnation, in Leibniz and in any orthodox Christianity. Certainly, this dialogue provides evidence that Leibniz believed in exclusion from heaven and generally argued in terms of optimalism (too bad for the damned; all the better for the universe), but this dialogue provides no evidence to support the conclusion that Leibniz could regard infants as excluded from heaven. Rather, the principle of justice Leibniz articulates in *T* 241 and which the early Augustine had articulated in *De libero arbitrio*, which holds that *undeserved* suffering prepares the way for greater happiness, is true not only for the world as a whole, but for individuals as well. Thus I would suggest that nothing in Leibniz's text compels us to conclude that he believes in the existence of limbo; rather, his text is consistent with the belief of the early Augustine that infants' sufferings would be recompensed in the next life, i.e., in heaven.

I submit that Leibniz's explicit rejection of infants' physical suffering in hell and his implicit nod toward a more lenient theology can be accurately interpreted only when read together with this passage: "Many in the past have doubted, as I have already observed, whether the number of the damned is so great as is generally supposed; and it appears that they believed in the existence of some intermediate state between eternal damnation and perfect bliss. But we have no need of these opinions, and it is enough to keep to the ideas accepted in the Church" (*T* 113). It is unclear whether Leibniz here has purgatory or limbo in mind; he explicitly claims to have no need of an intermediate state. Taking this claim seriously may facilitate identifying Leibniz's position on the fate of infants dying unbaptized. Let us calculate: Leibniz accepts the existence of heaven and hell, denies the existence of an intermediate state between them, and rejects the damnation of infants dying unbaptized. If no infant souls are in hell, then logically they must all be in heaven.

At this point, one might recall Kremer's salient observation regarding Leibniz's attempt at factional conciliation within Christianity:

> The fact that Leibniz's argument commits him to an unorthodox position regarding the nature of original sin does not show that his argument is unsound. But it does spoil his attempt to present his position as theologically acceptable to almost all of the Christian denominations and theological factions—extremists, he would add, like the Jansenists, aside. Leibniz was a master at hiding the theologically controversial aspects of his philosophy in the service of his efforts to reunite the Christian churches. But his claim that it would be unjust to condemn infants who die unbaptized to hell because such infants are innocent commits him to a position on original sin that would be unacceptable to many of the churches he wanted to reunite.[57]

Leibniz's attempt to champion a rationalist Christian theology may have been quixotic. His explanation of evil certainly seemed inadequate to Voltaire and many others after the earthquake, fires, and tsunami of Lisbon in 1755.[58] My goal here is not to defend Leibniz's overall project. I wish to salvage but one consequence from Leibniz's *Theodicy*: it tried to save virtuous adults and all infants from the hell—and if my argument is sound, from the limbo—of early modern Western Christianity.

5

Wolff:
The Inferiority of Childhood

THE WORKS OF CHRISTIAN WOLFF, EASILY THE MOST SCORNED OF German philosophers, have been summarized as "Leibniz and water."[1] One of his translators described him as "indefatigably prolix. . . . He illustrates what needs no illustration . . . and proves what needs no proof."[2] In philosophy today, he is generally nothing more than a footnote to Kant, whose critical philosophy reportedly awoke Germany from its Leibnizian-Wolffian dogmatic slumber. But the historian of thought must recognize that Wolff taught the Germans philosophy, and that he taught philosophy to speak German.[3] The same blandness of style that occasions boredom in modern readers was once praised (even by Kant) for its clarity and precision. Wolff's exposition of many fields of knowledge in his sprawling German, and then Latin, texts commanded the attention of philosophers in the German lands, and beyond, from the 1720s until at least the 1750s. The bounds of my study preclude examining how the reception of Wolff helped shape European discourse on childhood before Rousseau, but any such examination must proceed on the basis of an accurate presentation of Wolff's understanding of childhood. The few studies that have addressed this topic focus on Wolff's views on education and center on his *Politics*.[4] By considering a range of statements on infants and children in several of his texts, this chapter provides the most complete presentation yet of Wolff's views on childhood. (All translations in this chapter are mine.) I find that Wolff's statements on infants and children consistently return to the same concern: the lack of rationality in infancy and childhood. Wolff supposes human beings to be rational in kind, but we must all pass through this irrational phase of life. As Descartes, Locke, and Leibniz before him, Wolff was bound to provide some explanation for this discrepancy. I argue in the following that his metaphysical writings grapple with this problem, but that his theory of education does little more than express the hope that rationality will express itself as quickly as possible. In ushering children to be more like adults as soon as they are able, Wolff's theory of childhood quickly becomes little more than an exhortation to precocity. Thus, I aim to show that Wolff's words and silences concerning infants and children point to several inconsistencies in his rationalism.

When Wolff sketched his autobiography in 1739–40, he missed a chance to consider himself as an infant, a child, an adolescent, and an adult. Instead, he wrote the life of a thinking thing. This hundred-page, five-part text is concerned primarily with tracing Wolff's academic career, outlining his studies at school (part 2) and university (part 3), his subsequent encounter with the works of Leibniz and development of his own philosophy (part 4), and finally his expulsion from Halle, due to Pietist intrigue, and his welcome reception in Marburg (part 5).[5] In part 1, by far the shortest of the five parts, Wolff condenses his infancy and childhood into six paragraphs. The first paragraph discusses the astrological constellation of his birth; this constellation enabled the prophecy that Wolff would fall into disfavor with a king who would later retract his disfavor. Since this prophecy more or less came to pass (in 1740, Frederick II revoked his father's order of 1723 to banish Wolff and invited him back to Prussia), the narration of his birth functions primarily as an announcement of his academic career. After a second paragraph about the location of his father's house, Wolff writes the following, third paragraph: "I was baptized on the Feast of Mary Magdalene, January 25, the day of Paul's conversion. Already in early childhood [*gleich in der ersten Kindheit*] I had a desire to study. So when I received an ABC book as a Christmas gift, I asked everyone I could what the letters were called and so forth, until I was able to read, before I started school."[6] The same sentence that first mentions his childhood also links it to the activity of study that would structure his adult career. The fourth paragraph details how he learned Latin from his father, who had desired to go to university but was not allowed to do so. In the penultimate paragraph, we learn that Wolff was also passionate about religion, such that he "read the Bible at home on a daily basis and quickly learned by heart the songs that were then typical in church."[7] His passion for religion manifests itself not in pious feelings, but in the cognitive activity of reading and memorizing. The sixth and final paragraph of part 1 cements Wolff's determination for an academic career: "Before I was even born, my father swore an oath that I would become a scholar, and thus he did all in his power in order to support his plan."[8] Given the size of his collected works—sixty-two volumes of his German and Latin writings, ninety-eight volumes thus far of supplemental materials and documents—one may conclude that Wolff did not disappoint his father. It appears that Wolff was a precocious child. But other than that it prepared him for his adult career, Wolff had nothing to say about his childhood as a distinct period of life.[9]

While his autobiography entirely avoids discussion of mental development, Wolff's "theoretical philosophy" (especially his *Metaphysics*) explicitly considers childhood a deficient condition, one in which the use of reason is absent. The consequences of this basic tenet are partially unfolded in his "practical philosophy" (in his *Ethics* and especially his *Politics*). There, childhood marks what one might call a semi-blind spot of Wolff's philosophy. That is to say, Wolff attends to understanding and reason, but seems to often avert his gaze from inferior faculties (sensation, memory, imagination) and inferior persons (children). There is a reason that Wolff is not famous for his philosophy of childhood, and yet his statements on children often form, willy-nilly, the most interesting passages in his texts. Many of Wolff's comments on childhood are made in passing; accordingly, my discussion involves some degree of "reading and raiding." That is, in order to reconstruct Wolff's philosophy of childhood, I juxtapose statements made in a number of different contexts. To do so coherently, I have endeavored to explain how these fragments are embedded in the explicit discourses in which they occur. For this reason, I have taken some pains to present a more than cursory overview of Wolff's metaphysics, moral philosophy, and political philosophy. While it would be instructive to compare Wolff's German texts of the 1720s with his Latin ones of the 1730s and 1740s, this exceeds my capacities. Still, my treatment of his German-language texts can help clarify what the *praeceptor Germaniae* had to teach Germany about childhood.

REASONABLE THOUGHTS ON THE HUMAN SOUL: THE CHILD'S BODY AND LACK OF REASON

Wolff generally denies that the body and the soul act upon each other, though he recognizes that they seem to act in harmony. But sometimes, Wolff seems to suggest that the body can actually limit the operations of the soul. In a superb study, Eric Watkins has discussed a gradual shift between two theories of mind-body interaction from 1700 to 1750 in the

German lands. Watkins argues that Wolff's own career demonstrates an increasing distance from Leibniz's theory and a corresponding openness to Physical Influx: "although Pre-established Harmony is central to Leibniz's system, during the course of his career Wolff increasingly demotes it to the periphery of his philosophy."[10] Curiously enough, I observe a fluctuation between these two theories in a single text by Wolff: his 1719 *Reasonable Thoughts on God, the World and the Human Soul, and on all Things in General* (referred to in this study as *Metaphysics*).[11] The fluctuation occurs when he considers two groups of humans who lack reason: infants on the one hand, the old and sick on the other. For the former group, infants, he relies on the theory of Pre-established Harmony; for the latter, his argument seems to allow for bodily action upon the mind, thus relying on the opposed theory of Physical Influx.[12] It seems that Wolff has difficulty producing consistent reasonable thoughts on human beings who lack reason.

Wolff is often seen as a compartmentalizer of the soul, an architect of a vertical split between cognitive and volitional powers and a horizontal split between the "inferior" and "superior" parts of these powers. In *Metaphysics*, we learn that various powers or "faculties" are housed in these quarters: reason and understanding make up the superior parts of the cognitive faculties, and will is the superior part of the volitional faculties. There are a number of inferior parts of the faculties: attention, memory, imagination, sensation, et al. on the cognitive side, and appetites, affects, pleasure and displeasure on the volitional side. The inferior parts are sensual, whereas the superior parts are soulful. We humans share the inferior parts of the faculties with animals, but our possession of the superior parts of the faculties distinguishes us as a species. Wolff's empirical psychology (chapter 3 of *Metaphysics*, later expanded into his 1732 *Psychologia empirica*) does indeed suggest that the soul is doubly divided and filled with many discrete faculties. However, Wolff states from the outset of his rational psychology (chapter 5 of *Metaphysics*, later expanded into his 1734 *Psychologia rationalis*) that this multiplicity is *only* an appearance. Fundamentally, we have a unified power, a source from which various faculties are manifested. That is, our basic power of mind, representation, appears now as sensation, now as memory, now as reason. Although Wolff is often called the father of faculty psychology, his theory attributes no metaphysical reality to the faculties, which he also repeatedly calls "changes [*Veränderungen*]." (See E 1.2.2:464–69; secs. 744–55.) He always adds that a basic power subtends these changes, "the foundation . . . of all changes occurring in the soul [*was veränderliches in der Seele vorgehet*]" (E 1.2.2:469; sec. 755). The source of the basic power beneath faculties and changes is the unified soul: "Because each self-subsisting thing has a power from which all of its changes flow, as from a wellspring, thus the soul must have a similar power, from which its changes flow" (E 1.2.2:464; sec. 744). The object of rational psychology is to trace these changes back to a common source, namely the power of the soul to represent the universe. One qualification, which will become important to my argument later, should be noted: this power is that of the soul to represent the universe from the particular standpoint of the body it inhabits. Here, Wolff follows Leibniz: "Thus, although each created monad represents the whole universe, it more distinctly represents the body which is particularly affected by it, and whose entelechy it constitutes" (AG 221). For Wolff, most of the time, the soul never changes because of any bodily events; rather, the soul's changes well forth from itself. Following Leibniz's monadology, Wolff's rational psychology regards change as self-modification.[13] Thus, the soul *suffers* no changes; rather, it *enacts* them. Such a view of the unitary nature of the soul and of its basic power entails a denial of intersubstance causality. This denial is consistent with Wolff's rejection of Physical Influx and his tentative acceptance of Pre-established Harmony. However, as I discuss below, Wolff sometimes seems close to supporting Physical Influx, especially when he writes about sick and old people.

In a 1726 report on his German writings, Wolff briefly addresses the question of how the faculties develop.[14] He states that the superior faculties cannot "express themselves" until the inferior faculties are exercised, for there are no leaps in nature: "The superior [*das Obere*] does not express itself without previous use of the inferior [*des Unteren*], and from the use of the one, one does not arrive at the use of the other through a leap [*durch einen Sprung*]" (E 1.9:257; sec. 93). But in discussing the unity of faculties shortly thereafter, Wolff states that "both the inferior faculty of knowing and willing, as well as the superior one, derives [*entspringet*] from the representational power of the soul" (E 1.9:287; sec. 103). In the earlier passage, a chronological story is told: the superior parts of the faculties achieve expression due to the prior exercise of the inferior parts. That is, Wolff briefly sketches a rudimentary developmental psychology. But in the latter passage, a logical (not a chronological) relation is privileged: from the basic power to represent the universe, one does not make a transition to the empirically observable faculties through development, but rather through derivation (*entspringen*). Whereas the concept of continuous development refers to a nature that tolerates no leaps, derivation has a leap-like quality to it ("ent-*springen*"). There is no contradiction here. In Leibniz and Wolff, nature indeed makes no leaps, but the basic power of mind is our portal to the supranatural. For this reason, derivation interests Wolff much more than does development. That is, Wolff focuses on the metaphysical source (*Quelle*) of mental powers rather than on the experiential (and therefore temporal) development of those powers. This atemporal, logical relation to the source is the privileged object of Wolffian rational psychology.

Wolff's privileging of derivation over development determines his understanding of the relation between body and soul. Wolff touches upon the body-soul relation at the end of the chapter on empirical psychology (E 1.2.1:323–29; secs. 527–39), but only to defer discussion of that relation to the chapter on rational psychology: "We perceive nothing more than that two things are simultaneous [*zugleich sind*], namely a change that occurs in the sense organs, and a thought, through which the soul is conscious of the external things that cause [*verursachen*] the change" (E 1.2.2:323–24; sec. 529). Wolff repeatedly insists that we may only observe in experience *that* the body and the soul harmonize. We do not see *how* they do so, not in experience. Influxionists, whom Wolff here criticizes, argue that this connection is given in experience, that either the soul directly influences the body (*influxus spiritus*) or the body the soul (*influxus corporis*). Wolff explicitly admits neither possibility. (See E 1.2.2:472–75; sec. 762.) For Wolff, body and soul must be respected as discrete substances, each with their own laws.[15] This recognition of the autonomy of physical vs. mental realms explains Wolff's provisional choice of Pre-established Harmony over either Physical Influx or Occasionalism (which locates the harmony of body and soul in the continuous exercise of God's will). Pre-established Harmony may concede that existence itself follows from the continuous exercise of God's will, but this theory regards the body-soul connection as an appearance deriving from a singular exercise: God's decision at the beginning of time to "tune" body and soul, such that they would subsequently act synchronously. This philosophical orientation on a decision made at the beginning of time entails abstracting from the data of experience, which occur in time. For example, Wolff seems to spare the soul *any* significant relation to time, as it does not significantly change over time. Closely following Leibniz, Wolff states that because souls are simple things, they neither evolve nor devolve naturally; they are not born and they do not die. Rather, they must be created or destroyed, and thus are only created or destroyed by God. (See E 1.2.2:569; sec. 921.)[16] Given this supranatural provenance of the soul, Wolff is able to comment on the soul's development over time without concern that this development might contribute to or take away from the soul's identity. In short, Wolff regards development as a form of unfolding rather than as a process in which new faculties actually emerge; he holds to Preformation, not Epigenesis.[17]

Wolff speculates that before conception, the souls of humans and animals must have been in a state in which they represented the world only obscurely. (See E 1.2.2:560; sec. 900.) Referring to a proof (in his 1723 *Physics*)[18] that the body emerges from "the transformation of an animalcule [*Thierleins*]" (E 1.2.2:572; sec. 925), Wolff states that the soul, before the moment of conception, had to arrange its thoughts according to the small spermatozoic body to which it was attached: "In this state, the soul's sensations have little clarity, and after this state they come to a higher degree of clarity. With the higher degree, the lower degree is also present: for we still do have indistinct thoughts, when we are elevated to having distinct ones. And accordingly, the soul retains in great changes what it has, and receives even more than it had before" (ibid.). At conception, a sort of progress begins: as the fetus grows and is born, the soul steadily accedes to clear and then distinct cognition. After conception, things only get brighter for the soul. This linear, progressive model of development informs one of the few remarks Wolff makes about children in this text:

> One finds further that the soul increases along with the body. For as long as children are small and still weak in body, their understanding is also very bad and there is no use of reason present. This is why people say: understanding and reason doesn't [*sic*] come prematurely. [*Man befindet ferner, daß die Seele mit dem Leibe zunimmet. Denn so lange die Kinder klein und noch schwach vom Leibe sind, so lange ist auch ihr Verstand sehr schlecht und kein Gebrauch der Vernunft vorhanden. Deswegen saget man: Verstand und Vernunft komme nicht vor den Jahren.*] (E 1.2.1:325; sec. 532)

This is how Wolff makes sense of children's being less reasonable than adults: they are smaller and weaker. Presumably, their souls have not enacted enough changes to accede to a reasonable state. The bodies of children and adults differ along what appears to be a continuum (small–large, weak–strong); it seems Wolff views the soul as unfolding along a similar continuum from infancy to adulthood. The difference between animal and human is much more significant for Wolff than any differences within the human species. Anticipating the objection that species classification on the basis of representational power would seem to entail that the soul of each human being must essentially differ from that of every other human being, and even that "one's soul must be different from itself after some time" (E 1.2.2:556; sec. 895), Wolff calmly states that not every degree makes an "essential difference" (ibid.). The difference between childhood and adulthood appears to be one of the inessential differences, a merely quantitative difference in strength and size that a seven-year wait will level.[19] Wolff's most interesting claim here is that the soul "increases" along with the body. Note that Wolff's explanation adheres, thus far, to Pre-established Harmony. He does not say that the child's weak body limits the soul or prevents it from having distinct thoughts. Rather, he highlights coincidence ("as long as"), not causality. Still, the brightness of the monad's representation is variable according to the body type that belongs to it. Let us recall that the basic power of the soul consists in representing the universe from the standpoint of the body it inhabits. Thus, any differences in the cognitive abilities of souls should be parallel to differences in bodily state. In Wolff, the "small and still weak" state of children's bodies corresponds to a limitation on the amount of light available to the soul. The presumably large and strong state of adults' bodies coincides with more optimal cognition. And angels, lacking bodies (or at least our sort of body) and the limitation on thought associated with (human) bodies, have a more perfect perspective. Accordingly, the human being's death is for Wolff timed with a freeing of the soul, which is then able to represent even more clearly and distinctly than during life: "Since many higher degrees [of cognitive clarity] still remain than [the soul] has already attained while embodied, but in the decline of the body there is absolutely no reason to assume that the soul should lose what it already has; thus one has not the slightest cause to doubt that the soul not only retains what it has, but also reaches as well a greater perfection. And accordingly, the soul not only remains in the state of distinct thoughts, but receives therein in addition greater clarity and distinctness" (E 1.2.2:572–73; sec. 925). When the body lacks strength, in childhood due to size and in adulthood due to illness, the soul will be limited (or more precisely: will limit itself) in a corresponding way. After recalling that children are less reasonable than adults, Wolff continues:

> It is similar when man becomes very old and weak; he then often becomes childish again. Yes, the maladies that affect the head in particular not only take away the sharpness of his understanding, such that he can

no longer reflect as he recently used to, but can also sometimes take away reason, such that he becomes stark raving mad. [*Ja, die Kranck-heiten, welche sonderlich das Haupt einnehmen, bringen den Menschen nicht allein um die Schärfe des Verstandes, daß er nicht mehr wie vorhin nachdencken kann, sondern unterweilen auch gar um die Vernunft, daß er toll und rasend wird.*] (E 1.2.1:325–26; sec. 532)

Here, Wolff's explanation seems more influxionist than Leibnizian. Wolff does not state that the decline of the body, in the form of advanced age and illness, corresponds to a decline in mental capacities. (Accord-ing to Pre-established Harmony, he should have given just such an ex-planation.) Rather, Wolff states that age and illness can "take away" the sharpness of understanding and can even "take away" reason itself. Such language at least suggests a causal relationship, rather than a preestablished one. This discrepancy in Wolff's explanation of the lack of reason (in all children vs. in aged or sick adults) lends support to Richard J. Blackwell's claim that Wolff's solution to the mind-body problem, as Descartes had left it, was ultimately ambiguous.[20] But since these opposed explanations occur in the very same section (532), it is hard to believe that this opposition reflects an inconsistency in Wolff's thinking. The consistent explanation might be as follows: Wolff specifies that there is no *use* of reason present in young children, which might imply that he regards reason as present, just not in use. Hence Wolff's adherence to Pre-established Harmony in the case of children: the soul, operating in noncausal synchronicity with the body, unfolds along with it. Whereas in sick and old people, reason is taken away, which might imply that reason is absent: hence Wolff's adherence to Physical Influx in this case. If I read this correctly, then Wolff's section 532 indicates that his philosophy of mind differs according to an age-based distinc-tion. The senile actually lack reason; children lack the use of reason.

On the other hand, a comparison of the two passages indicates to me that Wolff distinguishes between reason and understanding. In children, their understanding is "very bad" but at least it is present, whereas there is "no use of reason present." Thus reason might be absent in childhood. Similarly, the senile and sick may lose "the sharpness of their under-standing" but not their understanding itself. However, they can indeed lose "their reason." This difference suggests an unexpected conclusion and a perhaps surprising claim about Wolff's metaphysics: he seems to regard understanding as more essential than reason to the human soul. Although this soul may have representational power from its creation on, the superior faculties it expresses (especially reason) may come and go. Even if the loss of reason in old age is temporary (since after death, the distinctness of the soul's cognition is even greater), it strikes me as noteworthy that in section 532, Wolff can imagine the absence of reason in the young and old, but seems unable to imagine the absence of understanding in either case. To put this point strongly: understanding, not reason, distinguishes human from animal. At the very least, this allows us to note that Wolff differs significantly from Leibniz, who regards reason as a divine gift, given at conception, a faculty that marks the transformation of a sensitive soul into an intelligent spirit, that is, into a human being. In terms of his view of the mind, Wolff is, on this one point at least, closer to Locke, whose *Essay* was devoted to human understanding, than to Leibniz. In contrast to the old saw Wolff cites, namely that understanding and reason "doesn't come prematurely" (E 1.2.1:325; sec. 532)—note the singular conjugation, which depicts the faculties as one—Wolff treats these faculties as distinct. However, Wolff does later refer, and in his own voice, to reason and understanding with another singular verb conjugation. (See E 1.5:75, sec. 100.) Perhaps he regarded them as fundamentally one; his text treats understanding as more fundamental than reason.

But reason is crucial for making distinctions *within* the human species: between healthy adults, who express this superior faculty, and inferior humans who fail to do so (children, the senile, the insane). Wolff's works clearly privilege the analysis of the reasonable human mind; they have little to say about humans who only express the inferior faculties. Childhood, senility, and insanity: a deficiency of understanding and lack of (the use of) reason marks all three conditions. These deficient states are opposed to that of the healthy adult, who can fully possess these superior faculties. It may seem odd to twenty-first-century readers that these three conditions would be classified together. Some adults may unfortunately become senile or insane, but all adults were once children. I will hazard the claim that it is generally believed today that children's minds (and bodies) must develop such that their rationality and understanding can be exercised and brought to maturity. In Wolff, the lack of reason in childhood is noted, but left unexplained. An influxionist would certainly argue that the small and weak body of the child actually precludes or limits complex mental operations, but a preestablished harmonist (which I think Wolff here is) would have to argue that the essentially rational soul limits its own mental operations "as long as" the body is small and weak. Created by God at the beginning of time, the soul may limit its own rationality in order to correspond to the deficiencies of the body, but the soul itself is essentially untouched by them. It seems that irrationality corresponds primarily to, though it cannot be said to be caused by, a deficiency of the body. For Wolff, childhood is just such a deficiency.

THE HUMANITY OF
REASONABLE THOUGHTS ON HUMAN ACTIONS

Because they lack the use of reason, children have no proper place in Wolff's moral philosophy, which he first presented in his 1721 *Reasonable Thoughts on Human Actions and Omissions, for the Promotion of Happiness* (referred to in this study as *Ethics*; in German scholarship, this text is usually referred to as his *Moral*).[21] Ethical [*sittlich*] behavior is possible only due to the use of reason, which shows us good and evil. Now, children lack the use of reason, and thus they cannot distinguish between good and evil; accordingly, children are therefore capable of neither virtue nor vice. In addition to this constitutional inability of children to practice virtue, Wolff also blames typical educational patterns: in the preface to the first edition, he laments that future political leaders do not concern themselves with virtue, as though virtue were something they had already learned in their primary education "among unintelligent women or simple tutors" (E 1.4: n. pag.). It seems that virtue can only be taught effectively by a complex intelligent male tutor: hence Wolff's book. More to the point, virtue seems not to be a proper object of primary education at all. Constitutionally, children cannot understand what virtue is. This view informs an insult in Wolff's preface to the second edition (1722), where he derides some readers who misunderstood his work as being "children in understanding" (E 1.4: n. pag.). Despite lacking a *proper* place in Wolff's moral philosophy, children do play a role in *Ethics*. At the outset of the text (in section 1), Wolff makes a binary distinction between actions that are natural and necessary vs. those that are free. Only free actions, those following the dictates of a free conscience, are directly relevant to moral philosophy. Soon thereafter (in section 81), he slightly complicates his distinction by introducing a third category, the hindered conscience (potentially free, but actually enslaved). Children in particular figure largely in such "third categories" Wolff produces to complicate his binary distinctions.

Moral philosophy properly deals with natural obligation. Early on, Wolff explains that this involves being moved by reasons, not by force.

Thus he distinguishes between two types of people and the sorts of obligation that can move them: "Intelligent [*Verständige*] and reasonable people need no more obligation than the natural one: but unintelligent [*unverständige*] and irrational ones need another sort of obligation, and a servile fear of a superior force and power must hold them back from doing what they would like" (E 1.4: n. pag.).[22] Some people can be treated reasonably, as people, while others must be treated as animals. Most children can grow out of this state, but some people of nonmajority status [*Unmündige*], who like children may display a semblance of virtue by just following orders, remain in an animal-like premoral state. Without here explaining the relation between them, Wolff clarifies that there are three laws according to which we must live: the law of nature (treated in *Ethics*), the law of God (on which Wolff was long silent; he wrote no German text on this topic, and while his 1736–37 *Theologia naturalis* is concerned with the existence of God, it is notable that metaphysical matters, rather than religious ones, dominate that text), and the law of people (treated in *Politics*). Whereas revelation plays a role in teaching us of the law of God, reason alone teaches us about the law of nature, and Wolff goes so far as to say that anyone who lives according to the law of nature alone requires no other law. Wolff was able to print this in 1720 and nonetheless avoid being threatened with hanging due to the quick explanation he appended to this claim, namely that God's understanding created nature and its law. In an unconvincing conciliatory move, he claims that those who live according to God's understanding do actually also live according to His will. Wolff's preference for orienting his philosophy around God's understanding vs. His will is, thus far, very much of a piece with Leibniz's philosophy. But there is a perhaps unexpected consequence: this focus on God's understanding corresponds to a focus on human understanding, and thus on the adult human being. Children play no proper role in such a moral philosophy, because they lack the use of reason and a good understanding; children are governed by reward and punishment, not by reflection on the good life. In Wolff's words, children and child-like adults require governance through reward and punishment "because for lack of reason they cannot make room for natural obligation" (E 1.4:29; sec. 39). Although Wolff explicitly says little about the place of children in natural law, the force of most of his statements implicitly suggests that children's primary obligation is to cease being children as early as possible.

Given that Wolff followed Leibniz in identifying God's understanding, rather than God's will, as the ultimate reason for the order of the world, it is fitting that a chapter on the improvement of the human will begins with the statement that one's duty toward the will actually amounts to a duty toward improving the understanding. Thus most of that chapter consists of cognitive therapy, that is, learning to think certain thoughts in order to tame or steer the affects. Wolff contrasts his method to the mistaken one of "keeping youth [*die Jugend*] from evil" (E 1.4:247; sec. 374) by denying them the opportunity or through beatings, neither of which can actually improve the will. Fear leads neither toward good nor away from evil; as soon as the disciplinarian [*Zuchtmeister*] (E 1.4:248; sec. 374) is absent, young people will follow their own inclinations. Thus Wolff would not intervene by directing their bodies (through locking them up or beating them), but rather by directing their minds. The cognitive therapy Wolff suggests can bring youths and others from slavery into complete freedom. Since moral philosophy is concerned with free actions and free conscience, and since children are enslaved, it seems logical to conclude that there can be no theory of moral action in childhood. The closest thing Wolff says on this count is that "as soon as the use of reason expresses itself, one should make the child reasonable regarding the good" (E 1.4:251; sec. 377). Here Wolff implies that sensual childhood is equivalent to slavery; the awakening of reason represents the possibility of freedom and morality.

But what if one cannot "make the child reasonable"? In a later chapter on money, Wolff qualifies his earlier stance that one cannot improve one's charges by denying them opportunities. Wolff now explains that simple people can be tricked into overspending. In such cases, one must indeed keep the simpleton away from bad society. Being simple, the simpleton cannot profit from Wolffian cognitive therapy. And in this context Wolff refers to "young people who are foolish due to their years and the circumstances of their upbringing" (E 1.4:377; sec. 554). Children are similarly seduceable, simple, and incapable of profiting from Wolff's reasonable thoughts on money management. However, Wolff does not exclude children entirely from education. Rather, the cognitive therapy he offers children takes place through the imagination rather than through the understanding. That is to say, it is not exactly a *rational* therapy, and it even involves deception. When writing about getting epicureans to develop a taste for working by removing the distaste attached to work, Wolff notes that one uses precisely this means "with children who are inclined towards sensuality [*Wollust*] and thus prove themselves to be slow [*träge*] in learning" (E 1.4:400; sec. 585). According to this method, one should "make them imagine [*man bildet ihnen ein*] that their industry would be rewarded by an invisible being with sugar and other sweets" (ibid.). This ruse will presumably incline children toward study. As we recall from Wolff's autobiography, he himself required no such childish trickery. As Wolff tells it, his thoughts were always reasonable ones.

Wolff's ternary distinction between humans, children, and animals orients his treatment of conscience. Conscience is the power to judge whether our actions are good or evil. Ideally, this judgment is distinct. It is indistinct when pleasure, pain, or affects mix into our judgments. To the extent this mixture occurs, "man is enslaved and not really free" (E 1.4:50; sec. 81). This explanation allows Wolff to distinguish between a free and a hindered conscience, and it should be immediately clear that children, who are ruled by pleasure, pain, and affects, must by definition lack a free conscience. But children are not at the same level as animals: conscience comes from reason; animals simply lack reason; thus animals simply lack conscience. Children cannot be said to *simply* lack conscience, because they become adults who (ideally) possess it. Perhaps this is why Wolff goes on to write about the sleep of conscience. When the senses dominate, reason and conscience slumber. Wolff exhorts his readers to "seek to become free from the slavery of the senses and affects" (E 1.4:70; sec. 120), which amounts to the conscience awakening from its slumber. One might well think that maturation itself involves such an awakening, but Wolff is not forthcoming in this regard; he does not state whether human conscience started its existence asleep or awake. In a word: Wolff gives no explanation of the development of conscience. He does not clarify whether conscience is present but hindered in children, or whether it is not yet present in children. Instead, near the end of the chapter on conscience, Wolff merely states that "conscience derives [*entspringt*] from reason" (E 1.4:76; sec. 137). It seems that all children and some adults are enslaved, that is, ruled by affects, pleasure and pain, and are thus unconscientious. Wolff does not comment explicitly on children in this chapter, but presumably conscience is sleeping in children, rather than absent. This sleep is an enslavement, from which only reason can free us. As he writes later, when one listens to reason (vs. to the senses, imagination, and passions), one overcomes oneself and becomes "lord over oneself" (E 1.4:113; sec. 185). Now children, lacking reason, are incapable of this mental operation; this is presumably why they need others to be lords over them. Wolff's paternalistic political theory already finds a support in these passages of his moral philosophy.

The duties of "man" toward himself are the subject of the lengthy part 2. At the outset, Wolff states that self-knowledge is necessary to fulfil these duties. Thus one might not expect Wolff to even mention children—who barely have knowledge, much less self-knowledge—in this part of the text. Surprisingly, Wolff does so; a lengthy citation seems appropriate:

> Because children and those equal to them in understanding like to imitate what they see in others, as is sufficiently evident from daily experience (§ 325 Met): thus it would be good if one were to immediately get children used to paying attention to other people's actions and omissions, and if one were to urge them to imitate the good but refrain from the evil that they perceive in others. Even if during childhood and young years, when one does not oneself have enough understanding to distinguish the good according to its correct value, one does many things only due to a prejudice for the regard of others [*Vorurtheile für das Ansehen anderer*]: with increasing understanding, this prejudice can nevertheless be removed quite easily, and since we have not been thereby seduced onto the wrong path, it is just as much, as if we had ourselves perceived [*eingesehen*] the good and oriented our action and omission according to reason (§ 368 Met). (E 1.4:152–53; sec. 238)

Wolff does not explain how this transition (from merely imitating the good, irrationally, to actually following the good, rationally) occurs. A transition is certainly indicated: note that the subject of the quote is initially "children," then "[one] during childhood and young years," and finally "we," the adult Wolff and his reasonable reader. It certainly seems noteworthy that Wolff here depicts children as morally neutral, in that they imitate whatever they encounter. (Later, following Descartes and Leibniz, he deviates from the dominant orthodox Protestant doctrine of inherited depravity, clarifying that we desire evil only due to an intellectual error: see E 1.4:252; sec. 378.) But it hardly seems consistent with his rationalism that he would state that when a child has imitated good examples, this ultimately carries the same moral weight as when we do good out of actual insight, as when we are actually virtuous. Such a view would seem to entail this corollary: that children who follow bad examples, presented to them through no fault of their own, can be judged as though they were actually vicious. Nothing Wolff says here precludes such a conclusion. That he rejected it is clear from a passage much later in the text: "What is said of the godless is not to be interpreted as applying to children, whom one can make pious before they become godless"

(E 1.4:463; sec. 672). Unfortunately, Wolff does not return to this co-nundrum: it seems to be one of the unconsidered issues in his philosophy of childhood.

Interestingly, Wolff does not once mention damnation as the wages of vice. The bad things that happen to us are described as punishments that are designed to improve or warn us. Several times, Wolff describes God as acting "as a loving father" (E 1.4:474; sec. 689), but one who also in-spires fear in his children. The character of this fear is noteworthy: it is not a "servile fear" (E 1.4:483; sec. 705), such as that which servants have toward masters. Rather, God inspires "a childlike fear" (E 1.4:478; sec. 694). In a later chapter on friendship, Wolff identifies the concern we have to ensure that we do not displease our friends as also being a childlike fear. (See E 1.4:552; sec. 786.) Thus, "childlike fear" seems to be what we might call esteem or respect. This is a fear oriented not to-ward reward and punishment, the outcomes of God's will, but rather to-ward God's will per se. It is certainly curious that the sort of fear that leads to virtuous action is called "childlike," when children are incapable of virtuous action. Wolff's uncharacteristically complimentary statement about something childlike marks a contradiction in his moral philosophy.

A salient feature of Wolff's philosophy of childhood is evident in the lengthy passage quoted above, namely that Wolff regards childhood as a period of "not . . . enough" (E 1.4:153; sec. 238)—in this case, not enough understanding to recognize the good as the good. Maturation is here marked as "increasing understanding [*zunehmenden Verstande*]," which recalls the statement in his *Metaphysics* that "the soul increases along with the body" (E 1.2.1:325; sec. 532). But this increase in under-standing is not just a natural fact of development: in *Ethics*, Wolff makes it into a duty. A significant chapter on duties toward the soul relates Wolff's decision to treat the inferior cognitive faculties of sensation and imagination in a later chapter on the body, rather than in the chapter on the soul, where he examines only understanding and reason. (It is deci-sions like this against which the later eighteenth-century discourse on the "whole person" would rebel. Alexander Baumgarten's cautious alignment of the inferior and superior faculties, discussed in my chapter 6, seems all the more heroic when one has read Wolff.) The greatest duty that children and youth have in relation to understanding and rea-son is simply to exercise these faculties ever more. Thus Wolff often in-sists that one should engage in certain practices or get one's pupils to do so "from youth on" and even "from earliest childhood on."[23] The upshot is this: once reason does appear in children, its use should be encouraged. Wolff encourages his adult readers to always ask their children what the reason is for various things; in addition to exercising the child's faculty of reason, Wolff writes in all seriousness that this practice will have the added benefit of getting the child to more quickly memorize the principle of sufficient reason, which will further the child's increasing rationality. (See E 1.4:222; sec. 337.) Whereas children in general have not enough reason and understanding, some lucky ones do at some point have enough of these faculties to begin to profit from Wolff's reasonable thoughts.

Wolff's thoughts on our duties toward God are as reasonable as are his other thoughts; that is, they exclude children. When he states that our main duty is to honor God, he immediately clarifies that this honor is based on recognition [*Erkäntniß*] of God. Luckily, God created the world such that "all reasonable creatures" (E 1.4:457; sec. 662) — thus, not yet children — could recognize God and thus honor Him. Prayer, defined as a cognitive and linguistic act, must involve an active consideration of God's goodness, and must be spoken aloud. Wolff explains that a silent call to God leaves us susceptible to the distracting influence of the imagination and the senses. Speaking aloud helps involve the senses in the rational consideration to be achieved, blocks imagination from operating (since the senses are so occupied), and thus leads to actual devotion. Wolff explains that this cognitive linguistic act is also social. External worship and ceremonial observances (such as congregating in a church at specific times) are important, because solely internal worship runs the same danger of having the senses and imagination captivate the mind and thus lower the clarity and distinctness of the thoughts one should be having during worship. (Here is a good reason that the Pietists of Halle should have taken offence to Wolff; Pietists did not congregate in churches.) One should not miss that the devotion [*Andacht*] of which Wolff writes is first and foremost a cognition [*Denken*]. When a spoken prayer is not wedded to cognition, it amounts to chatter [*plappern*]. A clear implication is that children should not memorize mere words of prayer without having thoughts to support the words. It is important to note Wolff's summary conclusion that "*Man [der Mensch]* is obligated to pray" (my emphasis; E 1.4:527; sec. 748). Understanding is the key to prayer, and yet as Wolff repeatedly observes, children lack a good understanding.[24]

Perhaps the most surprising thing Wolff writes about children in this text is that children are like drunks. A chapter on duties toward the body includes such diverse material as a prohibition against suicide, an

exhortation to walk in such a way that one is not likely to fall, dietary
tips and fashion advice. Eating and drinking are treated in multiple contexts; indeed, Wolff's description of sensuality [*Wollust*] refers rarely to
sexual lust, about which he writes very little, but rather predominantly
to culinary pleasures. Immoderate drinking is his greatest target in this
chapter precisely because it weakens or removes reason, leaving us
under the control of our inferior faculties (memory, imagination, the
senses). Alcohol can make us "like animals" and even "less than animals"
(E 1.4:322; sec. 472). But Wolff's concern is less immediately moralistic
than calculating: it is not the loss of reason per se that he explicitly decries, but the fact that our impairing our faculties through strong drink
can lead us to reveal truths that should remain hidden. Thus, Wolff ad-
vises us not to drink when an enemy is in the company, when one has a
secret, or if one has a bad inclination that one can keep under control
when one is sober. Drunks tell the truth and express who they actually
are because reason is not able to calculate the bad effects and curb them
from doing so. And thus, Wolff continues, "drunks are like children in
this respect: for since children by nature have no complete use of reason,
they also express thoughtlessly [*aus Unbedacht*] what they are thinking
[*gedencken*]" (E 1.4:323; sec. 474). This parallel finds expression in a
common saying Wolff cites: "Children and drunks speak the truth"
(ibid.). Wolff presumes that humans have a free choice to drink or not to
drink, and generally seems to prefer that they do not (lest they turn bes-
tial or worse). But children have no choice about being children. Certainly, childhood cannot be described as a vice, as drinking can, but the
comparison between the age of childhood and the state of intoxication
clearly marks both as undesirable. Though childhood for Wolff may not
be a vice, it is even more clear that for Wolff, truth-telling in childhood
has nothing to do with the good nature of children or their virtue (as the
lexica of a century later would have it). Rather, this behavior derives
from children's thoughtlessness.

Wolff's theory of education, as articulated in his *Ethics*, encounters a
limit in the concept of character. Locke had previously engaged a similar
problem, though his premises are of course different: Locke's educational tract opened with the claim that "of all the men we meet with, nine
parts of ten are what they are, good or evil, useful or not, by their education."[25] But later, Locke seems to concede the power of an innate temper,
"which way the natural make of his mind inclines him. Some men by the
unalterable frame of their constitutions are stout, others timorous, some
confident, others modest, [etc.]."[26] The unalterability of the frame seems

to speak against Locke's opening claim of malleability through education. Wolff's focus on cognitive therapy as a means of self-improvement
has a similar limitation: it only works for honor-respecting characters
[*Gemüthe*]. When such people recognize a good, they strive toward it;
the will follows the understanding. Such characters "make education
[*Auferziehung*] not difficult" (E 1.4:408; sec. 599). Not only do they not
require threats and beatings to motivate them to do good, they may actually not even need instruction, if they are of the type of which one
could rightly say that "they raise [*ziehen*] themselves" (ibid.). By contrast, base [*niederträchtig*] characters make education difficult. They follow inclination and habit, not honor and reason. Such people can be
moved only by force: "Reasonable notions bear no fruit with them—
they have to learn through damage to themselves" (E 1.4:409; sec. 600).
But although Wolff now recognizes that some characters are tractable
and others intractable, he does not revise his rationalist premise: that
whoever recognizes the good inclines to it. A later chapter on friends
and enemies suggests a way of reinstating consistency into this aspect of
his philosophy: he concedes that some people do indeed take pleasure in
evil, which should be inconceivable according to his premises. But note
that he calls such people "inhuman monsters" [*Mißgeburten oder Unmen-
schen*]" (E 1.4:598; sec. 860). This is a tidy way of excluding them from
his moral philosophy, which is concerned with reasonable thoughts on
human [*des Menschen*] action.

Wolff's 1721 *Reasonable Thoughts on Human Social Life, in Particular the
Commonwealth, for the Promotion of Happiness of the Human Race* (referred to
in this study as *Politics*) is known as his "German politics," since 80 percent of it (part 2) pertains to statecraft, civil law, and war.[27] The first political unit, treated in the introductory 20 percent (part 1), is the household, defined as a complex society made up of three simple ones. Hans
Werner Arndt has identified a short text by Leibniz, "On Natural Law,"
as one of Wolff's sources.[28] Indeed, Wolff's text clearly mirrors Leibniz's
identification and sequential treatment of natural societies: "The first
natural society is between man and woman/wife [*Weib*], for this is necessary to maintain the human race. The second one is between parents and
children; it follows from the previous one, for where children have been
conceived or freely adopted, they must be brought up, that is, ruled and
provided for. . . . The third natural society is between master and ser-

vant. . . . The fourth . . . is the household, which is composed of the previously named societies. . . . The fifth . . . is civil society. . . . The sixth
natural society is the church of God."[29] Wolff's text opens with a chapter
considering societies in general, followed by four chapters that correspond to Leibniz's first four societies. The remaining 600 pages of the
Politics examine civil society, the fifth one in Leibniz's list. (At this point
of his career, Wolff is silent on the church of God.) While Wolff clearly
uses Leibniz's essay to orient himself, the relevant passages span ap-
proximately three pages in Leibniz, while Wolff's treatment of the
household approaches 150 pages. The ideas expressed in those pages
concerning children and their upbringing may thus be safely attributed
to Wolff rather than to Leibniz.[30]

An analysis of childhood in part 1 of *Politics* — the focus of the remainder of this chapter — can illuminate aspects of the political theory developed in part 2. For example, the division in civil society between superior
magistrates [*Obrigkeiten*] and inferior subjects [*Unterthanen*] (E 1.5:173–
74; sec. 229) mirrors the hierarchical organization of both the house (in
part 1) and the mental faculties (in the *Metaphysics*). And Wolff's preference for an enlightened monarchy follows from his view that the father is
the natural head of the household. It is appropriate to refer to regents as
"fathers of the country [*Landesväter*]" because a ruler relates to subjects
"like a father to children" (E 1.5:200–201; sec. 264). This simile is supported by chapter 3 of part 1, which examines how fathers (and, to an extent, mothers) and children should relate to each other.

Children are both included in and excluded from Wolff's reasonable
thoughts. The first two sections (in chapter 1) dramatize this ambivalent
status. Wolff's first distinction is that between the solitary animal, whose
actions are completely determined, and the social human, whose actions
are not completely determined and who therefore can improve his or her
welfare by learning from others. Like many natural law theorists before
him, Wolff defines society as a contractual agreement between human
beings to seek a common good. Yet this initial orientation places children in an exceptional position: children are neither animals (since children can imitate and be educated) nor social (since children cannot
make contracts). That is, children fall squarely on the human side of the
distinction animal/human (section 1), but the foundational statement of
politics (section 2) imputes to the human being an ability (making contracts) that Wolff later says children lack.

But children are integral to society. The sole purpose of marriage, the
first simple society Wolff treats (in chapter 2), is the procreation and ed-

ucation of children. Wolff's sexual conservativism, which I will not exfo-
liate here, follows directly from this axiom.[31] Suffice it to say that Wolff
claims that reasonable people are moved to engage in (hetero)sexual intercourse not only because of its sensual pleasures, but in addition "because of a natural inclination to propagate the species, which derives in
part from the pleasure that one has in children who turn out well, in part
from the desire to maintain one's memory in prosperity, in part so that
one has someone to whom one can leave one's possessions after one's
death, in part due to other causes, such as experience can confirm sufficiently; thus nature has attached many reasons to the production of children and obligates us to do so" (E 1.5:10; sec. 17). As Wolff depicts it,
the very first thing that husband and wife do, after uniting in order to
produce children, is to agree to educate them.

The most extensive pedagogical sketch in Wolff's writings is given in
chapter 3, which presents the natural society of parents and children. It
is imperative to note that Wolff depicts this parental society as a paternal
one. Indeed, near the end of the chapter, Wolff observes that children
tend to "think less of their mothers than they do their fathers" (E
1.5:114; sec. 159), and helpfully attempts to explain why this is so: mothers love too much and forget to discipline, or do so incorrectly. Besides,
Wolff adds, mothers do not always know what is best for their sons' upbringing. Sons do indeed appear to be the privileged children of Wolff's
discourse. The absence of the subcategory *daughter* from the category
child at the end of chapter 3 corresponds to the obliteration of the
mother's authority in the definition of the *paternal* society at the beginning of that chapter. There, Wolff blithely defines *paternal* society as "society between *parents* and children for the sake of their upbringing" (E
1.5:57; sec. 80, my emphasis). John Locke, who excoriated Robert
Filmer for confusing these terms (see my chapter 3), was at least aware
that his own thoughts on education were directed to boys rather than to
girls; Wolff did not even mention this issue.

Wolff did admit that his pedagogy was incomplete, but this did not
overly concern him, for two reasons. First, he says, whoever reflects
upon the care of children can apply a general rule (one should care for
children's bodies) and derive its specific applications oneself. "It would
become overly prolix" (E 1.5:60; sec. 85) if Wolff himself had to list
these cases. Second, following this rational explanation for Wolff's
nonexhaustive treatment of pedagogy is an empirical one: "it would be
useful if people would learn well from experience, and state what has
worked and what has not worked; thus one would progress ever further

in the upbringing of children [*Kinder-Zucht*], upon which so much rests" (E 1.5:61; sec. 85). I do not know whether any of Wolff's students heeded his call (repeated at E 1.5:80; sec. 105) to publish such observations. Precisely because of his rationalist premises, Wolff treats children in an incomplete, ambivalent, and sometimes incoherent manner. For example, he quickly dispatches with the feeding and care of children's bodies, even though "initially, one only has to look after [children's] bodies" (E 1.5:62; sec. 87). In his discussion of children's souls, Wolff just as quickly glosses over the inferior faculties such as memory, even though children must initially use their memory, rather than their understanding, to learn truths (see E 1.5:69; sec. 92). Wolff seems anxious to turn his attention to children's reasonable thoughts, rather than to their semirational ones or to their irrational sensations. Nevertheless, Wolff's teleological focus on adult understanding and rationality is tempered by his belief that there are no leaps in nature. This balance between rationalism and continualism results in a number of fascinating passages in which Wolff treats the early education of the understanding.

Wolff's rationalism, which here means his privileging the education of understanding and reason, even in childhood, motivates the extreme brevity of his treatment of the inferior faculties; only one section is devoted to them, and all Wolff says there is that "one should determine, either through experience or reason, what impedes the senses, memory, and the imagination" (E 1.5:62; sec. 86) in order to know what to avoid.[32] (That he accords equal weight to experience and reason as a source of knowledge indicates that his approach to pedagogy is eclectic.) Since children operate largely according to precisely these faculties, one might well have expected Wolff to write more about them. A curious feature of this short section is that it is flanked by sections explicitly about the body (83–85) and about the soul (87). It seems Wolff cannot decide in section 86 whether the inferior faculties belong to the body or to the soul. (In his *Metaphysics*, he attributed them to the soul, but recognized that some readers might be inclined to attribute them to the body. See E 1.2.1:123; sec. 222.) I submit that this interstitial position results from Wolff's view that the soul's superior faculties distinguish humans from animals. No wonder the inferior faculties, which Wolff and his contemporaries agreed dominate childhood, receive such short shrift. Even in his discussion of children's education, Wolff's energies are devoted to the superior faculties.

From section 87 on, Wolff describes the education of children's understanding. Recall Wolff's view in *Metaphysics* that children's understanding is "very bad" and that they "show no use of reason" (E 1.2.1:325; sec. 532). It seems that in *Politics*, Wolff regards this deficiency as a contingency, rather than as a necessity: "one has to look after the improvement of understanding and of will earlier than people typically tend to think" (E 1.5:62–63; sec. 87). Wolff argues that early intellectual education is both possible and desirable. It was against such a view that Rousseau later argued for delaying intellectual education until the inferior faculties could be adequately exercised. Obliquely referring to this slow developmental view, Rousseau stated that he was gaining time by losing time.[33] By contrast, Wolff is quite simply concerned about losing time. Perhaps one could say that Wolff's *Cartesian* commitments (to the superior faculties, with a concomitant distrust of the inferior ones) led him to downplay his *Leibnizian* commitments (to continualism).

But Wolff does attempt (in sections 88–90) to depict the transition from immaturity (clear but indistinct cognition) to maturity (distinct cognition) as a process less abrupt than Descartes's conversion-like meditations would have it. Because children are "initially unsuited for that sort of attention and consideration" (E 1.5:63; sec. 88), they initially can only acquire indistinct concepts. But so that they may come to acquire distinct concepts, one should "bring all sorts of things before their eyes and get them used to looking at them [*darauf zu sehen*]" (E 1.5:64; sec. 88). And once children learn to speak, one should get them used "to asking what this or that is called" (ibid.). The more clear concepts the child can thus acquire, the better. Relying on his continualist dictum, "nature makes no leaps," Wolff states in the intermediate section 89 that one should not immediately stride [*schreiten*] from one cognitive level to another, but rather get one's standing [*zu Stande kommen*] in the earlier level first, to prepare well for progress to the next level. This continualism has an interesting effect: although Wolff posits a two-sided distinction (clear but indistinct cognition/distinct cognition), he ends up discussing a third, intermediate state as well. To advance the child from this intermediate state toward the distinct one, Wolff looks to the adult to conclude what the child needs. "For our part [*von Seiten unser*]" (E 1.5:64; sec. 89), distinct concepts require that we attend to the parts of things and then to their connection and order. And what is epistemologically good for adults must also be good for children. Thus through further "show and tell," one can train children to become aware of the different parts of objects, and to begin naming them. It seems children can be just as reasonable as adults, but Wolff's conclusion reminds us that children have not yet made a complete transition to the other side of his distinction: "Through this, children learn without noticing [*unvermerckt*] that many things appear in an object and that one should not attend to it superficially [*obenhin ansehen*] if one wants to really know it"(E 1.5:65–66; sec. 89). Although the subject of education is learning an adult capacity (distinct cognition), it does so in an indistinct (childlike) manner, that is, without noticing. This paradoxical language continues into the next section (90), which marks the period where children can be trained to think distinctly. (Wolff does not say at what age this might occur. He merely states that one should begin training in distinct cognition as soon as it can be done.) The strategy here is to place objects before them of which they already have clear concepts, then show them "the various things that are notable [*anzumercken*] in them" (E 1.5:66; sec. 90). With small children, this can be done with playthings; with children who have begun to learn, one can use geometrical figures and numbers. "Thus children realize without noticing [*unvermerckt*]" (E 1.5:67; sec. 90) that even in a thing one thinks one knows well, one can find much to examine more carefully. In sum, Wolff says that children learn, without noticing, to notice things. He continues by stating that whoever wants to know how to continue in such exercises should refer to his *Logic*. The latter text, entitled *Reasonable Thoughts on the Powers of Human Understanding*, is evidently suitable for making children reasonable.

Wolff often appears to be oriented toward the goal of rationality, such that he omits observing the state of the children who should attain that goal; however, he does make two distinctions that depict children as having qualities of their own, rather than merely lacking what adults have. First, Wolff states that he is here only concerned with children exercising the facility of understanding, vs. acquiring actual knowledge of things per se. By implication, actual knowledge is an adult concern. Childhood is an age of exercise. (My chapter 6 examines Baumgarten's similar assessment.) Second, children can use any number of objects in such exercise because they are "not yet spoiled by prejudices" (E 1.5:68; sec. 90). This claim is completely alien to Descartes's view of childhood as precisely the period in which all human beings are spoiled by prejudices. But one should not hyperinflate this contrast: immediately after stating this, Wolff claims that making children quick-witted [*witzig*] not only prepares them for later cognition in adulthood, but also helps them overcome their otherwise childish ways now: "Yes, since children, lacking reason, have to base their actions on the expectation of similar cases, thus in this respect they act in a manner more according with reason" (E

1.5:68; sec. 91). The goal of "making children reasonable," a phrase Wolff often repeats, amounts to making them less like children.

Wolff's liberal intellectual pedagogy conflicts with his conservative moral philosophy on at least one significant point. In sections on the education of the understanding, he says that children "become reasonable when they get used to always asking the reason why something is, and why they should do this or that" (E 1.5:69–70; sec. 93). This habit leads to intellectual independence, including the recognition that "something is not true because another says that it is" (E 1.5:69; sec. 92). But in sections on the education of the will, he says that children should obey their parents' orders because they are their parents' orders (see E 1.5:90–91; sec. 120). If a child asked for the principle of sufficient reason for being obligated to perform some task, this would be impertinent, against the law of nature, and thus irrational. Parents have the power to give orders to their children, and as long as the orders do not go against the law of nature, children must oblige them. This discrepancy need not be regarded as a logical contradiction. One might say that intellectual independence is appropriate for responding to propositions (i.e., judging their truth content) whereas filial dependence is appropriate for responding to parental orders (i.e., obeying them). Still, this very different emphasis points to a division in Wolff's system: in *Politics*, his statements on parental authority are supported by references to his *Ethics*, while his antiauthoritarian statements on distinct cognition are supported by references to his *Logic* and *Metaphysics*.

As he begins to discuss the improvement of the will, Wolff abandons his former language of "making children reasonable." Since children are unreasonable (he now writes instead), natural obligation cannot move them. Parents must obligate them in another way, namely through reward and punishment. Parents thus become less like teachers and more like gardeners: they should "implant" love of virtue and hatred of vice early on and "extirpate" all desires for evil and antipathy for good (E 1.5:71; sec. 95). (Desire for fame and love for other people should also be "implanted": see E 1.5:87; sec. 112.) But direction through reward and punishment obtains only for very young children. Although the moral direction of children begins with parental/paternal authority, Wolff adds that "as soon as understanding and the use of reason shows itself [the singular conjugation is Wolff's], one should see to it that children do not remain slaves in the good, but rather do good out of complete freedom" (E 1.5:75; sec. 100). That is, children should learn to do good for its intrinsic value, not due to external rewards and punishments. But before the superior faculties are operational, children begin as slaves, and reasonable parents should actually participate in making them slaves to the good. These same parents should later also lead those children out of this slavery into freedom. Perhaps this paradox motivated Wolff to drop the subject. He excuses himself by referring the reader to his "prolix" (ibid.) notes on the improvement of the will in his *Ethics* (sections 373–436), but states that he does not want to discuss how these notes should be adapted to children, as that would lead him into "further prolixity" (E 1.5:75; sec. 100). He does recognize the task of improving children's wills to be of a different sort than improving adults' wills, but he omits exploring this difference himself.

Several notes indicate that Wolff's philosophy of childhood is primarily a philosophy of preadulthood. Thus children play because they are "*not yet* suited to working" (E 1.5:78; sec. 104, my emphasis). But Wolff urges that they should always be playing, lest they become idlers; and they should play in an orderly manner, as orderliness will serve them well later in life. Play is good because it prepares children for work, and through play, children should "impress useful truths into their minds" (E 1.5:79; sec. 105). A note on filial piety is also instructive, and not only to further document Wolff's well-established sinophilia. (Wolff here remarks that in Chinese culture, all young people honor all old people.) Children should learn to honor adults *as such*, Wolff writes, because "adults and especially old people have much good about them that [children] are still lacking" (E 1.5:88; sec. 113). Wolff regarded childhood as a period in which one lacks the goods of adulthood. No wonder he aimed to help accelerate the maturational process.

One of the goods of adulthood, in most cases, is self-rule.[34] Children are ruled by others, in particular their fathers. This is why, as mentioned earlier, children are not allowed to make their own contracts. As long as children are children, they are obligated to display obedience, thankfulness, and "childlike fear" to their parents. Here Wolff's explanation is intellectualist: if children recognize the good (for example, the good that their parents do for them), then they can only be thankful. Some children of course fail to do this: these are "wicked" and "degenerate characters [who] have little or no reason" (E 1.5:96; sec. 128). He also blames ingratitude on the "weakness of their understanding" (E 1.5:98; sec. 131). Recall that the childlike fear of parents is rational, based on recognition of obligation, while servile fear is irrational, based on anticipation of punishment. Wolff applies this distinction here to explain the difference between good vs. wicked children. Yet he stated earlier that *all* children (thus good *and* wicked) are enslaved to the senses and thus display only servile fear. It seems that only those children who become reasonable also become unenslaved, and can thus display obedience, thankfulness, and childlike fear. It is curious that small children as a class cannot display childlike fear. Here as elsewhere, Wolff's concepts bracket all young children from view.

Wolff's "house"—the union of three simple societies (between husband and wife, parents and children, masters and servants)—is a complex society headed by a "housefather" and a "housemother" (E 1.5:135–36; sec. 192), but this parallel status is only apparent. Her orders must be extensions of his, approved by him in advance, or at least must be in line with his wishes. And where she in fact knows best—a possibility Wolff does entertain—her duty is to advise the housefather, but nonetheless to follow his orders (see E 1.5:137; sec. 195). I underscore this view, not atypical for the period, because Wolff's justification of the mother's subjection to paternal power turns entirely on the fate of children she might be carrying. She should not be the one to scold or punish the servants, because her getting angry might be harmful to her unborn child, should she be carrying one. Such anger can harm her health and often makes for a difficult birth that can endanger her life (see E 1.5:138; sec. 196). And if the child survives, it might receive a natural inclination toward anger. It is precisely due to concern for the children that Wolff believes the housemother should be subject to the housefather. We are certainly far from the children's room at the center of the nineteenth-century bourgeois house.[35] But in its own way, Wolff's early modern house is organized around its children.

Ternary distinctions and "third categories" produced some disturbance in Wolff's discussions of childhood; in the magnum opus of his most famous student, such distinctions proved to be most fruitful, but as the following chapter shows, they also entailed a thorough revision of Wolffian rationalism.

6

Baumgarten:
Childhood and the
Analogue of Reason

Twenty-one years old, Baumgarten opened his dissertation by reflecting on his childhood. The title of his 1735 *Meditationes philosophicae de nonnullis ad poema pertinentibus*, laconically rendered in an English translation as *Reflections on Poetry*, signals a reliance upon Descartes and implies an allegiance to rationalism.[1] In this text, Baumgarten does utilize the "geometric mode" of presentation, following the deductive style of Descartes's *Principles*, some of Leibniz's essays, and most of Wolff's books. But Baumgarten's meditations owe nothing to Descartes's similarly titled anxious explorations of radical doubt. It is rather the autobiographical portion of Descartes's *Discourse* that Baumgarten's preface echoes:

> From my earliest boyhood [*ab ineunte pueritia*] a certain branch of study attracted me very much. . . . Since the time when . . . Christgau . . . adroitly guided my first steps in the study of the humanities, scarcely a day has passed for me without verse. As I grew older [*Succrescente paullatim aetate*], my attention turned more and more to the sterner studies appropriate to the upper forms at school, until at length the academic life seemed to require other labors and other interests. Nevertheless I addressed myself to the necessary studies in such a way that I never entirely renounced poetry, which I valued highly. . . . Meanwhile . . . it happened that duty required me to tutor young men preparing for the university, in poetics, along with so-called Rational Philosophy [*philosophia, quam vocant, rationali*]. What in such a situation was more reasonable than, at the first opportunity, to translate our philosophical precepts into practice? What, indeed, is more unworthy of, or more difficult for, a

164

philosopher than to swear allegiance to another man's formulas, to de-
claim in ringing tones the precepts of one's teachers? By way of prepara-
tion I set to work to reconsider [*ad meditationem*] all those things which I
had learned in the usual way and by the traditional method.[2]

In this one respect, Descartes's spirit is evident: the way Baumgarten
had been taught was all wrong, and so he would have to reinvent a new
method, drawing on his own resources through meditation. But where
Descartes had called for a turn away from the senses, which dominate
and contaminate all judgments made in childhood, Baumgarten turns
precisely toward sensate knowledge. Thus Baumgarten's Cartesian gesture (setting all previous experience aside as potentially prejudiced) in-
augurates meditations on a non-Cartesian (perhaps even anti-Cartesian)
topic.

Noting that the demands of a school life could have led him to either
renounce his childhood interest in poetry or else teach poetics as
though it were not philosophically relevant, Baumgarten suggests that
such a school is mistaken. It is precisely his combination of poetics and
so-called rational philosophy for which Baumgarten is still remembered, but that combination has also raised questions about Baumgarten's allegiance to Leibnizian-Wolffian thought.[3] Baumgarten pro-
moted a more capacious rationalism than he knew from his schooling;
he likely intended to reform Wolffian rationalism from within. One
should not overlook the distancing effect of Baumgarten's reference to
"so-called" rationalist philosophy. In my estimation, Baumgarten intended to make philosophy more deserving of the name by exploring
hitherto unexamined fields. By expanding so-called rationalism to include poetics and "aesthetics" (a term Baumgarten coins for the first
time in noun form, thus creating the discipline of philosophical aesthetics) along with logic, by expanding so-called reason to include sensate
knowledge along with intellectual knowledge, Baumgarten clearly sig-
naled and helped effect a transformation of rationalist discourse.[4]
Raised in a school that called him to turn away from the inferior faculties and toward the superior ones, Baumgarten had the audacity to try
and remain true to both inferior and superior, both poetry and philosophy. Although he wrote a book on logic, which describes the functioning of the superior faculties, i.e., adult reason, Baumgarten's innovation
is to have written a book (though incomplete) on aesthetics, which describes the functioning of logic-like knowing, or in his terms, reason-
analogous knowing.

Baumgarten's definition of aesthetics as *ars analogi rationis*, an *art of reason's analogue*, has left commentators unsure of his rationalism. Benedetto Croce interpreted this analogy as unproblematic evidence of Baumgarten's rationalism. By contrast, Leonard P. Wessell, Jr. interpreted this analogy as evidence of an internal resistance to rationalism: "Rationalists, such as Descartes, clearly maintained that the same epistemological method was unequivocally to be applied to different fields without any diminution of the method. The term *analogy* shows Baumgarten's break with rationalism. Analogy implies that there is something the same and something different in the sciences of logic and aesthetics."[5] But despite using the strong term "break," Wessell later states equally strongly: "Baumgarten was a rationalist."[6] And between these two opposed assertions, one can read the nuanced claim that Baumgarten has "roots in rationalism" but "widened the concept of knowledge" to include an aesthetic type that is irreducible to the logical type.[7] The knowing that aesthetics takes as its object is reason-analogous, but is never ultimately reducible to reason. These two types of knowing, rational and sensate, make up two separate halves of a combined whole. But given that Wolff had referred to "that which is similar to reason [*das Aehnliche der Vernunft*]" (E 1.2.2.229, 230; secs. 374, 377) in his German and Latin psychologies to describe the empirical manner in which *animals* think —"*Bruta habent analogum rationis*" (E 2.6.678; sec. 765) —it is not surprising that Baumgarten's adoption of the term to describe a *human* capacity has raised some eyebrows.[8]

Many scholars view Baumgarten as prefiguring the concept of "the whole person," famously championed in German letters by Johann Gottfried Herder.[9] Rationalist thought before Baumgarten had intended to make universal claims, but critics such as Terry Eagleton (whom I discuss in the conclusion to this chapter) have charged European rationalism with being secretly particular, that is, with taking the reason of (white European) man to be the measure of all things. While Baumgarten does not venture to think beyond Europe or beyond the male sex, his focus on the boy's reason-analogous knowing indicates that Baumgarten does think beyond the "reason" of "man." Baumgarten scholarship has long held that including poetics and aesthetics in rationalist philosophy transformed rationalist philosophy. I believe it would be worth considering whether Baumgarten's inclusion of childhood in discussions of reason-analogous thinking helped transform discussions of reason in the second half of the eighteenth century. This chapter focuses on Baumgarten's particular insistence upon including infants and children (or at least boys) in the concept of the whole person. In the previous chapter, I highlighted Wolff's disinterest in tracing mental development. Although Baumgarten uses Wolff's terminology, the opening sections of *Aesthetica* may be considered a foray into developmental psychology. By opening up the field of aesthetics in this manner, that is, by characterizing it as the analogue of reason, Baumgarten thereby drew attention to reason's childhood.

BAUMGARTEN'S ARISTOTELIAN SUPPLEMENT TO WOLFFIAN PSYCHOLOGY

In his *Poetics*, Aristotle states that poetry was engendered by two natural causes: first, it is an instinct of human beings "from childhood [*ek paidōn*]" to engage in mimesis; second, everyone enjoys mimetic objects.[10] In the 1750 installment of his *Aesthetica*, Baumgarten recalls the first half of this statement to chide those who seem to remember only the second half.[11] That is, those who merely appreciate art, who merely exclaim "beautiful, good, well done," who merely savor the artwork, as it were, miss the point. And the point is that we all can and should be inspired by artworks to engage in "the art of knowing beautifully [*ars pulcre cogitandi*]" (*A* 1) or *thinking finely*, as one could also render the phrase in English. (In this chapter, I generally translate *pulcre* as *beautiful*, rather than *fine* or *excellent*, despite the occasional strangeness of resulting phrases.)[12] To deliver this lesson to those who believe art to be merely a matter of appreciation, Baumgarten refers to the figure of a playing child. Early passages of *Aesthetica* highlight the child's propensity to imitate and improvise, to play games with total seriousness. This positive assessment of children's self-generated activity distinguishes Baumgarten from his rationalist teachers, especially Wolff, who had almost nothing good to say about childhood. Where Wolff had written most often of the weakness that characterizes childhood cognition, Baumgarten states that the child who imitates beauty (vs. merely appreciating it) engages in beautiful knowing. At this moment of Baumgarten's text, the child has the correct aesthetic response. Admittedly, Baumgarten's primary focus is on culture, an adult realm. But it seems noteworthy that Baumgarten does not begin his text with the fully-formed adult who is ready to learn the rules of artistic production. Instead, Baumgarten traces the development of beautiful knowing *ab ovo*, beginning with the infant's spontaneous productions and the child's improvisations.

Baumgarten follows Aristotle (particularly chapter 4 of *Poetics*) in describing a parallel development between the individual and the species; having posited a natural origin of poetry in mimesis, Aristotle posits a historical origin as well: "in the earliest times [*ex arkhēs*] those with special natural talents for these things gradually progressed and brought poetry into being from improvisations [*ek tōn autoskhedias-matōn*]."[13] According to this conjectural history, poetry branched into two, underwent gradual changes, and ultimately settled into the genres of comedy and tragedy. The latter are the main focus of Aristotle's interest: *Poetics* is devoted to a consideration of tragedy, and another book, lost to us, is devoted to a consideration of comedy. But at this point of the text, Aristotle is interested in poetry *before* it settled into the genres of comedy or tragedy. In this prehistory, poetry "came into being from an improvisatory origin [*ap' arkhēs autoskhediastikēs*]."[14] Let us call this origin phase one. In phase two, poetry was "gradually enhanced;" in phase three, "after going through many changes, tragedy ceased to evolve, since it had achieved its own nature."[15] Below, I discuss how Baumgarten adapts Aristotle's three-part history—first, natural improvisations; second, gradual enhancement of potential; third, actualization of potential in the nature of a genre—in the early sections of his *Aesthetica*.

Baumgarten's transformation of rationalist philosophy is well documented in some respects: using Wolffian terms, he supplemented logic with aesthetics, the art not of reason per se but of "the analogue of reason" (*A* 1). His taking this "inferior" faculty seriously enabled later Enlightenment thinkers to further explore sensate knowing. This much has been widely proclaimed and generally celebrated.[16] In this chapter, I highlight a specific manner in which *Aesthetica* deviates from rationalist faculty psychology: Baumgarten begins to offer a developmental psychology *avant la lettre*. Both Wolff and Baumgarten divide the human being into quadrants of faculties: superior, inferior, cognitive, and desiring. Thus, both thinkers engaged a similar question: how to represent the unity of the so-divided human being. Their answers to this question differ significantly. Recalling Leibniz's monadology, Wolff grounds this unity in the soul's essential, God-given power. Although the faculties appear to us as a multiplex, this apparent variety has no metaphysical reality. In *Aesthetica*, Baumgarten omits discussion of extraexperiential, extratemporal realms.[17] His field there is, after all, the logic of sensate experience. Thus, he searches for the unity of the human being in this world and in time. But experience presents disjunctions, rather than unity: the human is a desiring but also a thinking being; some of our thoughts and desires are base, others elevated; the human is a natural being, but also a cultural one. So formulated, the unity of the human being can seem paradoxical: the human is a sensual-cognitive, rude-erudite, natural-cultural being. As Niklas Luhmann has discussed, one way to escape the impasse of a paradox is to temporalize it.[18] By *plotting* the two terms, one can remove the irritating simultaneity of the paradoxical formulation. Thus, one may take a static distinction (nature/culture), begin with one side (nature), and narrate the transition to the other side (culture). The two terms are no longer simultaneous, but rather sequential. As I argue below, Baumgarten aims to represent the unity of the human being, which obtains across the variety of realms (nature and culture), by tracing human development from infancy to adulthood.

By organizing his narrative around maturation, Baumgarten smooths out the difference between nature and culture by showing a gradual transition from the one to the other. This narrative strategy—the assertion of a gradual development of one quality (culture) out of its opposite (nature)—was utilized by other midcentury writers, but was questioned in the later Enlightenment.[19] Discussing Étienne Bonnot de Condillac and Moses Mendelssohn, David Wellbery writes: "The passage from nature to culture . . . implies a radical transformation which to many appeared paradoxical. . . . To solve the problem, a number of gradualist accounts attempted—in lieu of appeal to a more or less fictional hypothesis of divine instruction—to interpolate transitional stages between the radically opposed poles of nature and culture, sensation and thought, dependence and freedom."[20] In *Émile*, Rousseau also charted transitional stages between the natural infant and a utopic culture to come (a citizenry of natural men). As I mentioned in chapter 5 (note 33), Rousseau openly admitted the paradoxical nature of this endeavor: "Common readers, pardon me my paradoxes. When one reflects, they are necessary."[21] Because Rousseau's assessment of modern European culture is so much bleaker than is Baumgarten's, one might be surprised to learn of this affinity between the two thinkers: in order to trace the successful unfolding of natural talent into culture, they both begin their analysis with the spontaneous activities of the infant and the young boy.[22] Baumgarten was ultimately less provocative than was Rousseau, but the attention Baumgarten gave to childhood nevertheless represented an innovation within the rationalism that dominated German thought around 1750.

A DISTINCTION (NATURE/CULTURE) BECOMES
A NARRATIVE (FROM NATURE TO CULTURE)

In the Prolegomena, which scholars have examined in detail, Baumgarten justifies his endeavor and responds to potential criticisms it could occasion.[23] Devoting attention to obscure or confused knowing is worthwhile, he argues, since the clear and distinct knowing of the superior faculties does not come from nowhere, but rather depends upon prior inferior knowing. We are reminded that "nature does not leap from obscurity to distinction. Midday emerges from night through dawn" (*A 7*). For Wolff, as we saw in the previous chapter, this claim represented little more than lip service to a commonplace. But for Baumgarten, this claim motivates his writing sections 2 and 3, which I discuss below. Early on, Baumgarten indicates what he will examine in those sections: "The natural stage of the inferior cognitive faculties, increased solely through application, without cultivated discipline, may be called *natural aesthetics*, and this may be distinguished as is natural logic, namely into innate, that is a beautiful native intelligence, and acquired; the latter, in turn, can be divided into taught and employed" (*A 2*). The very next paragraph already indicates that artificial aesthetics will supplement (and even supplant) natural aesthetics: "Natural aesthetics is succeeded by artificial aesthetics" (*A 3*). And this artificial aesthetics will be Baumgarten's greatest focus. But before there can be discipline, there must be a natural talent that makes its own autonomous progress.

Section 1, "PVLCRITVDO COGNITIONIS" (*A 14–27*), discusses the "beauty of knowing" in general. In the concluding paragraph of this section, Baumgarten announces his plan to examine the origin and development of aesthetic character: "Before all else, let us delineate to some extent the generation and idea of the beautiful knower, the *character of the successful aesthetician*" (*A 27*). He does so in section 2, which treats the innate part of natural aesthetics, and in section 3, which treats the acquired part of natural aesthetics. In section 4, he goes on to examine the young aesthetician's arrival into culture. In my view, the movement from section 2 to section 4 represents the cultivation of nature. But my hypothesis is that this narrative (from nature to culture) not only takes place in the progression from section 2 to section 4, but that it is also recapitulated *within* sections 2 and 3. At the beginning of his text, Baumgarten draws the distinction nature/culture, then examines first one side (nature) and then the other (culture). As he does so, he reapplies the distinction on each side of the distinction, thus producing further differentiation. This operation enables Baumgarten to get from one side to the other, that is, to narrate cultivation.

"Aesthetic nature" is the state in which the faculties develop "exclusively through exercise" and not through "cultural discipline" (*A* 2). This nature is subdivided into "connatal" and "acquired." Since only section 2, which treats the connatal, is titled "AESTHETICA NATVRALIS," I shall follow suit and refer to this section alone as treating natural aesthetics. The title of section 4, "DISCIPLINA AESTHETICA," clearly recalls the cultural discipline marked from the outset as absent from natural aesthetics. Baumgarten closes section 4 with reference to all that he postulates as necessary for any general aesthetic theory: "nature, native intelligence, talent, exercises, cultivation of native intelligence" (*A* 77). This list reviews all that Baumgarten has treated up to that point, in the order of presentation, and it summarizes the transition from nature to culture. *Natura*, treated in section 2, encompasses *ingenium* (native intelligence) and *indoles* (talent). *Exercitia* was treated in section 3, EXERCITATIO AESTHETICA, and so aesthetic discipline, treated in section 4, must be what Baumgarten identifies in this list as *cultura*. The realms of aesthetic nature (section 2) and aesthetic culture (section 4) are linked by an intermediary realm, that of aesthetic exercise (section 3).[24] In Baumgarten's section titles, then, we are confronted with two opposed realms, nature and discipline (culture), and an intermediate realm that links them: exercise. And yet one does not sense that Baumgarten makes paradoxical claims. I discern two operations that are designed to minimize what could easily appear to be a conflictual relationship.

First, Baumgarten moves away from the sharp distinction between nature and culture to other, less troubling distinctions. Section 3, for example, discusses "1) improvisations [*autoskhediasmata*]" (*A* 52) and "2) erudite art [*ars erudita*]" (*A* 58). I am suggesting in this overview (and in the close reading below I will attempt to show) that these "new" distinctions amount in fact to reapplications of the first distinction (between nature and culture). Thus, one might conclude that Baumgarten has not solved the problem of representing the unity of the human being: whatever terms he may generate, they are always as foreign to one another as are nature and culture, the terms with which he began. The first distinction would be covertly omnipresent; it would seem there has been no progress. But Baumgarten's second operation is a response to this dilemma and reveals his cunning. Without fail, every pair of terms he considers is plotted, temporalized, made part of a narrative. He considers these terms sequentially, rather than simultaneously. The term that takes the value of "nature" is always marked as preexisting and preparing the way for the term that takes the value of "culture." For example, in section 2 he discusses several connatal faculties that humans (children and adults) share with animals, such as sensation and memory, before discussing other connatal faculties peculiar to (mature) humans, such as poetic ability and good taste. Although this discussion takes place in section 2, thus under the heading "nature," the latter faculties *anticipate* culture. A further example of Baumgarten's narrative construction pertains to the history of poetry. Homer and Pindar may have written "before erudite arts" (*A* 52) were developed, but these poets precede as "archetypes" of erudite arts, thus *anticipating* these later "manifestations [*ectypa*]" (*A* 53) of erudition.

Terms Baumgarten used to describe the process of cultivation suggest a unity underlying the three fields of nature, exercise, and culture. Left to its own devices, spirit "remains rude, uncultivated [*rudi relicto*]" (*A* 51) and cannot bring about an aesthetic representation. With assistance, however, spirit may be cultivated, and acquire erudition; Baumgarten speaks of "the cultivation of mental powers, which can hardly be sufficiently achieved now without some sort of erudition [*eruditione*]" (*A* 77). Between the rude and the erudite states lies the *inerudite*. Where spontaneous aesthetic representations occur, namely in improvisations, we may already distinguish between "a crude mind [*ingenium rude*]" and "an uneducated one [*ineruditum*]" (*A* 53). Baumgarten is consistent in his usage of these three terms, two of which are opposites, one of which mediates between the opposites. The intermediate term, "inerudite," corresponds to the transitional activity of exercise, which cultivates natural talent. What best summarizes his text is not the statement: the human is a natural-cultural being, which is a static claim that underscores distinctions, but rather this developmental narrative: the human being begins as a natural, *rude* infant, passes through an apprenticeship as an exercising, *inerudite* child, and finally emerges as a cultured, *erudite* adult; this narrative emphasizes the *unity* of the human being beneath the changes it undergoes.

DEVELOPMENT FROM INFANCY TO MANHOOD

In eight paragraphs (*A* 30–37) of section 2, "AESTHETICA NATVRALIS" (*A* 28–46), Baumgarten discusses these inferior cognitive faculties: a) acute sensation, b) the natural disposition of imagination, c) the natural disposition of perspicacity, d) the natural disposition of recognition and memory, e) poetic disposition, f) disposition of beautiful, not common, taste, g) disposition of foresight, and h) disposition of expressing one's perceptions [*a) acute sentiendi, b) dispositio naturalis ad imaginandum, c) dispositio naturalis ad perspicaciam, d) dispositio naturalis ad recognoscendum et memoria, e) dispositio poëtica, f) dispositio ad saporem non publicum, immo delicatum, g) dispositio ad praeuidendum et praesagiendum, h) dispositio ad significandas perceptiones suas*].[25] I contend that what Baumgarten presents is not simply a list of faculties in which the ordering is unimportant. Rather, he suggests a gradual unfolding of the successful aesthetician's nature in the direction of culture. The first hint of such a developmental logic is the marking of the second, third, and fourth dispositions listed (imagination, perspicacity, and recognition/memory, faculties the human being shares with animals) as natural, while the following four dispositions listed, beginning with "poetic disposition," are not so marked, and by this omission appear to be "cultural." Thus, Baumgarten shows how each faculty functions as a *conditio sine qua non* for the next. First, one must sense things acutely, that is, receive information from the outside. If, however, this acute sensation has no complement, then information from the inside could be overshadowed. Thus, Baumgarten discusses the second faculty, imagination, whose information emerges from within. If this faculty is not balanced in turn, then information from the outside could be overshadowed. To achieve this balance, the third faculty, perspicacity, works as a corrective for both the senses and the imagination: it "refines [*poliantur*]" (*A* 32) the information brought from the outside and the inside. Thus far, we have been concerned with information that is *present* to the faculties. With memory, the next faculty discussed, past events (whether real or imagined) can now be represented as well. In order to organize all of this information, which originates from the real and from the imaginary, from without and from within, from the present and from the past, the poetic faculty now appears. Its function is to form relationships that organize this information. The next faculty listed, good taste, then serves as a judge of the efficacy of these relationships.

With the latter four faculties, I suggest, the natural aesthetician is viewed as in transit toward cultural activity. That is, within a section ostensibly treating aesthetic nature, Baumgarten anticipates aesthetic culture. The faculty psychology Baumgarten inherited from Wolff and Leibniz was situated within an episteme of continuity, a worldview according to which all differences are incremental.[26] For Baumgarten in 1750, the difference between nature and culture seems to be no exception. I suggest that the fine gradations Baumgarten explored in the list above serve to make this leap from nature to culture as gradual as possible. The leap is, in fact, only visible in the disappearance of the term "naturalis" as the development of human faculties progresses.

Section 3, "EXERCITATIO AESTHETICA" (*A* 47–61), charts an interstitial space between nature and culture. Here, Baumgarten examines the preconditions for the more perfect cultivation discussed in section 4. He begins by distinguishing natural talent on its own from nature combined with exercise. The latter is superior, because "unless continuous exercise augments dispositions or constitution (§ 47), [natural talent] decreases" (*A* 48). Exercise augments nature. Having distinguished exercise from innate nature on the one hand, Baumgarten quickly moves to further distinguish exercise from serious discipline on the other hand, by contrasting military maneuvers to an actual battle. This double delimitation of exercise indicates that Baumgarten is drawing not a *line* between nature and culture but rather an interstitial *space*. The field he explores in section 3 is bordered on the one side by nature and on the other by culture. This interstitial field of exercise is itself bifurcated, consisting of (1) undirected improvisations [*autoskhediasmata*] and (2) erudite arts [*ars erudita*]. Baumgarten treats the latter quite cursorily, in a single paragraph (*A* 58) that fails to clarify what he means by the term; but other passages, such as the following, may disclose its significance.

Where the first exercises occur, one may already distinguish between "crude [*rude*] and uneducated [*ineruditum*] mental powers" (*A* 53). What was mere nature, rude or raw, has begun to cook, but here nature generates its own sparks: "Here belongs the manifestation of humanity's beautiful knowing before the invention of the erudite arts; here belong anyone's first sparks [*primi igniculi*] of a more beautiful nature, which precede all art" (*A* 52). Baumgarten carefully defines this rudimentary self-instruction as "prior to any direction in erudite arts" (*A* 52). This autodidactic process describes the development of the species as well as that of the individual. Initially, it seems that Baumgarten uses two examples to illustrate the same notion, namely that culture originates from nature such that we can retrace the steps of origination. At the species level, one can link Homer's and Pindar's poetry to later, erudite productions, of which the former is the archetype (see *A* 53). At the individual level, one can link the infant's cognitive exercises (see *A* 54) and the child's games (see *A* 55) to the adult's disciplined studies. In both cases, the chronologically prior position contains the seeds of the later formation. From the later position (that of the cultured, erudite adult), one

may turn one's gaze to the past (that is, to inerudite childhood) for instruction.

In paragraphs 54 to 56, Baumgarten touches in turn on the infant,
the child, and the adult. Although infants and children may be unaware
of what they are doing, they nonetheless do engage in beautiful knowing: "Just as Leibniz calls music an arithmetic exercise in which the
mind counts without being aware of it: in just this way, through the expectation of similar cases and from this just as the first innate imitation,
not yet nearly aware that it knows, much less that it knows beautifully,
now the infant exercises [*exercetur infans*], if by good fortune it falls into
the hands of a master of an art who teaches, who shapes the boy's tender, stammering mouth" (*A* 54).[27] Natural production and cultural correction meet one another halfway in this scene. The first poets, by contrast, had no educators. Homer and Pindar are rather the *teachers* of all
later poets, one might say. As natural geniuses, they are the archetypes
of erudite art. Ontogeny seems here to recapitulate phylogeny: as
Homer and Pindar once did, the infant improvises its way into culture as
it matures.

The autonomous, still unconscious self-exercising of natural talent is
particularly evident in childhood: "The native intelligence further exercises its beautiful nature, whenever it openly exercises of its own accord
(§ 54), even if it does not know what it is doing, as when the boy [*puer*]
tells stories, or plays, especially where he invents games, or directs his
young comrades with thorough zeal, and now wholly intent he sweats,
and produces many things, makes many things, when he sees, hears,
reads, he thinks beautifully, if only he directs all of these things according to §§ 49–51 such that the exercises are aesthetic (§ 47)" (*A* 55).[28] As
I mentioned at the outset of this chapter, Baumgarten refers to childhood play in order to teach the flighty adult a lesson about culture: "We
adults err [*Fallimur adulti*] not seldomly, when reading or hearing a
beautiful speech or writing, etc., we think something to be beautiful, by
contemplating the beautiful thing and, as it were, tasting it (§ 35), and
indeed expressing approval: 'beautiful! good! right,' we silently acclaim
within, though nevertheless we rarely ourselves at the same time sufficiently turn our minds to imitating the beautiful knowing" (*A* 56). In this
paragraph, and in the whole of section 3, the child is valued for his natural imitative drive and for his playful inventions. The child may remind
the adult to rediscover this activity, aesthetic knowing, beneath the judgments of mere taste that obscure this activity. The child's mimetic activity is viewed here as nothing less than the *source* of culture. In this realm

of exercise, midway between nature and culture, infants and children unwittingly become the teachers of their teachers. This "primitivist" tone is all the more noteworthy because Baumgarten soon abandons it: in section 4, "DISCIPLINA AESTHETICA" (*A* 62–77), which is located square-ly on the side of culture, Baumgarten's evaluation of adults vis-à-vis in-fants and children reverses.

Baumgarten predicts that one day, liberal studies "will appear to be worthy not just of boys, but also of men [*non puerilia tantum, sed et viris*] of intelligence" (*A* 76). As Baumgarten opens section 4, he looks back to the rudimentary cultivation treated in section 3, which involved infants and children, and states that aesthetic discipline provides a more perfect insight into beauty than nature and exercises alone can provide. The lat-ter are necessary, but not sufficient for the full realization of aesthetic culture. Baumgarten requires of the mature aesthetician that he have knowledge of God, the universe, man, history, the classics, and the sci-ences of expression. This list recalls the title of Wolff's German meta-physics: *Reasonable Thoughts on God, the World, and the Soul of Man, and all Things in General*. Clearly, such instruction is not child's play: "Here we refer not to any sort of children's [*pueriles*] education (§ 54) nor to hur-ried acquaintance gained from performing lessons, practice, aimless reading, or lectures indiscriminately combined, as treated in section 3, but rather to methodical and manly [*virilem*] skill, howsoever perfect" (*A* 66). I discern three positions in Baumgarten's educational system, as presented in the paragraph above. First is the infant or young child (*in-fans*), whose spontaneous games or improvisations provide the basis for education. Second is the youth (*puer*) who reads indiscriminately and at-tends seminars irregularly — one wonders whether Baumgarten had in mind here some of his own university students — that is, who moves be-yond natural ability, but not yet methodically. Third is the man (*vir*), whose knowledge is more perfect than that of the infant, child or youth, because that knowledge is disciplined, methodically acquired. In this passage, the man occupies the envied position. All that precedes the man is (now) marked by imperfection or deficiency.

THE AMBIVALENT STATUS OF CHILDHOOD

Baumgarten's 1735 *Reflections on Poetry* opened by professing allegiance to his childhood interest in poetry. But in the very first paragraph of that text, following the preface, Baumgarten also illustrated a deficiency of understanding by offering children as a prime example of the "unguided mind" (37). This fluctuation from a positive to a negative evaluation of childhood occurs in the 1750 *Aesthetica* as well.

Two components of the word *autoskhediasmata* (improvisations) deserve comment here. *Auto-* indicates that improvisations are self-generated; a *skhedia* is a raft or a float.[29] It is presumably with reference to this part of the word that Baumgarten compares the improviser with one who has learned "to swim without a cork [*sine cortice natare*]" (*A* 57).[30] This developmental accomplishment, though important, is not simply celebrated. Initially, the child may educate himself; he has need of neither authority, teachers, nor instruction for his initial, natural productions. But this is no *Sturm und Drang* text. Thus, negatively put, the young swimmer may also be seen to "move uncertainly to and fro, sway, rock; to lack firmness . . . to be at a loss, be unstable, waver."[31] (These are all meanings of *nato*.) These negative connotations document the need for aesthetic discipline, above and beyond one's autonomous natural ability to improvise. The ambivalence of improvisation shows that Baumgarten values the position of childhood, but only as a developmental stage in a progressive narrative. The full paragraph reads as follows: "In themselves, greater powers now offer greater exercises, giving and invoking heuristic improvisations [*autoskhediasmata eurisikha* (sic)], which act independently and automatically [*automatōs*] from the bottom of the soul, when now it can swim without a cork, whether this has been taught (§§ 54–56) or is innate (§ 53)" (*A* 57). The paragraph numbers to which Baumgarten refers indicate that "innate [*natus*]" marks the species-level analysis, i.e. the natural talent of Homer and Pindar, while "taught [*doctus*]" marks the three subject positions (infant, child, adult) of the individual-level analysis. Thus the modern individual is always described as having an educator. Still, Baumgarten's focus on the autonomy of *autoskhediasmata* is designed to show that erudition is not acquired by simply learning knowledge imparted by an instructor. The infant or child must produce something, automatically and autonomously, that can then be corrected by an adult critic.

But it would be preferable to *be* that adult. Baumgarten's understanding of childhood seems ultimately Aristotelian, in that he regards adulthood as the proper telos of human development and ceases to value the impromptu games of childhood as he traces cultivation into adulthood (in section 4, and in the hundreds of pages that follow). And yet, I would like to underscore that Baumgarten's suggestion (in section 3) that the child has a more adequate, full reaction to aesthetic objects than do many adults has no parallel in Aristotle.[32] In section 4, Baumgarten's

semantics of childhood agree with those of his teacher, Christian Wolff.
But before this return to the rationalist fold, Baumgarten has shown
himself to value the infant and the child in a manner not to be found in
Wolff. Indeed, Baumgarten's emphasis in section 3 on the autonomy of
the playing child seems to prefigure several reevaluations of childhood
in German letters around 1800. If one considers Herder's attention to infant cognition, Goethe's discussion of childhood play—and his naming
Wilhelm Meister's child Felix, which might well be an echo of Baumgarten's ideal of the successful aesthetician (*felix aestheticus*)—or Schiller's famous elaborations of the play drive (*Spieltrieb*), it seems plausible
to suggest that an examination of Baumgarten's brief passages on childhood may improve our understanding of the extended passages on
childhood written during the Age of Goethe.

But how are we to understand Baumgarten? What should we make
of his transient primitivism, ultimately left behind as he considers the
adult? Recall Aristotle's statement that "after going through many
changes, tragedy ceased to evolve, since it had achieved its own nature."[33] It seems that for Baumgarten, the human being achieves its own
nature when it becomes an adult. Does this endpoint give Baumgarten's
argument a teleology (for better or for worse) such that the final stage
replaces or displaces the earlier stages? This sort of question, which I
pose regarding childhood, has been considered with respect to Baumgarten's entire project, which might be summarized as trying to find
something that is both sensation (the lowest faculty) and reason (the
highest). Terry Eagleton concludes that *Aesthetica* "opens up in an inno-
vative gesture the whole terrain of sensation, [but] what it opens it up to
is in effect the colonization of reason."[34] Eagleton argues that the autonomy of the inferior faculties, often celebrated in Baumgarten scholarship, is only a *relative* autonomy. That is, the dominion of reason over the
senses in Baumgarten may not be tyrannical, but it is still hegemonic. I
find Eagleton's argument worth considering, but it is marred by an error
in reading: he suggests that logic is like a domineering older brother to
aesthetics: "Aesthetics, Baumgarten writes, is the 'sister' of logic, a kind
of *ratio inferior* or feminine analogue of reason at the lower level of sensa-
tional life. . . . It is born as a woman, subordinate to man but with her
own humble, necessary tasks to perform."[35] In fact, Baumgarten writes
that logic is the older sister of aesthetics: "Our aesthetics (§ 1) is like
logic, its older sister [*soror eius natu maior*]" (*A* 13). My correction does
not negate all concerns about the dominion of logic and reason over aesthetics and sensation, but it certainly does qualify Eagleton's insinuation

that patriarchy explains this particular difference of power. Baumgarten explicitly presents these philosophical disciplines as a sorority; in the relationship between logic and aesthetics, age, rather than gender, is the operant distinction.[36] Certainly, Baumgarten aims to do justice to both the older and the younger sister. (Whether he succeeds is an open question.) Similarly, Baumgarten praises the boy's aesthetic activities—which are appropriate in their own realm, namely childhood—but finally, his *felix aestheticus* is undoubtedly a man. Although Baumgarten values the accomplishments of the young improviser, they are ultimately overshadowed by those of the aestheticological adult.

Afterword

"ON NE CONNOIT POINT L'ENFANCE."[1] WITH THIS SENTENCE, LOCATED in the preface to his 1762 *Émile*, Jean-Jacques Rousseau effectively terminated the early modern discussion of childhood, part of which I have reconstructed in the preceding chapters. Allan Bloom translates thus: "Childhood is unknown."[2] In Barbara Foxley's rendering: "We know nothing of childhood."[3] Many readers in Europe and beyond were convinced that until Rousseau, they had known nothing of childhood, but that after Rousseau, they were in a position to begin reforming early child care and education. Numerous endeavors, including the creation of new pedagogical institutions, based themselves on the new knowledge of childhood provided by Rousseau.

We know little of childhood in the early modern period. Intellectual historians have justly devoted much attention to both Locke and Rousseau; in recent years, scholars who have overcome the thrall of these twin peaks of eighteenth-century childhood discourse have begun to survey other features of this terrain. In this study, I have examined a sample of what early modern philosophers before Rousseau believed they knew about prematurity. Because my chapter 1 ends at 1650 and chapter 2 begins around 1700, I should like to at least mention three avenues of research, involving that time span, that would further enhance our understanding of the history of ideas of childhood. Since I have focused largely on early modern rationalism, the most significant lacuna is an examination of the works of Baruch Spinoza, who is widely regarded as one of the triumvirate, along with Descartes and Leibniz, of the great early modern rationalists. (I plan to research this topic as soon as possible.) Second, I believe that an examination of natural law theory, in particular that of Samuel Pufendorf, could be very fruitful for the intellectual history of childhood.[4] (I plan to leave this task to others.) Third, it seems to me that further study is needed of seventeenth-century religious discourse, Jansenism in particular. Calvinism has received much more scholarly attention, perhaps because of its strong influence on British colonies in America. Although my chapter 4 and appendix document Nicole's statements on children and original sin, I believe that a treatment of Jansen's 1640 *Augustinus* and its effect on childhood in subsequent theological discourse would be most instructive. Having named these lacunae, I would like to sketch two lines of inquiry, pertinent to the understanding of childhood after Rousseau, that can build upon the results of the present study.

Histories of aesthetics have observed that Schiller's "play drive" was elaborated based on a study of Kant's third critique. The German idealist notion of *play* as a signal of freedom from determination was crucial for the development of aesthetic theory in the nineteenth century and beyond, up to Hans-Georg Gadamer.[5] Although Baumgarten is recognized as the creator of the noun form of the word aesthetics, it seems to me that a closer examination of Baumgarten's influence on Kant and Schiller is warranted. A hindrance to this examination has been the lack of a translation of Baumgarten's full text. Now that *Aesthetica* has been fully translated into German, such research can be more easily undertaken.

In this study, I began to discuss Leibniz's *New Essays* in relation to Locke. I have come to suspect that Leibniz's text had a subcutaneous but significant influence on the development of childhood concepts in the long nineteenth century. It is known that Herder and Kant studied the *New Essays* carefully after its publication in 1765. The fact that its reception history begins soon after the publication of Rousseau's *Émile* seems to me worth considering. After Rousseau shook up European discourses regarding childhood, it could not be possible for readers of *Émile* (such as Herder and Kant) to examine Leibniz's reply to Locke without being sensitized to the childhood concepts put forth in their respective texts. Herder, who was also a careful reader of Baumgarten, went on to write a short world history involving concepts like "the human race in its childhood," a metaphor that Georg Friedrich Hegel later adapted as "the child-age of history" in his lectures on the philosophy of history.[6] Friedrich Froebel, inventor of the *Kindergarten*, borrowed heavily from German idealist thought in general and Hegel in particular as he formulated his vision of holistic development. Thus I suspect that an intellectual history connecting Leibniz to Froebel through these intermediaries remains to be written. A further chapter of such a history might examine the transplanting of kindergarten from Europe to the American midwest in the later nineteenth century. In St. Louis, Hegelian "kindergartners"

such as Susan Blow developed variations on Froebel's particular application of German idealism; while in Chicago, the young John Dewey
and others of the new "child study" movement labored to develop less
mystical, more scientific views of childhood and of early childhood education. Dewey's second book publication, incidentally, was a treatment
of Leibniz's *New Essays*. A study that would trace German and American
understandings of childhood from the 1760s to the 1890s, using Leibniz's *New Essays* as a touchstone, could build upon the present book. I
hope to write this study and thereby contribute further to the intellectual history of childhood, from Kant to kindergarten and beyond.

Appendix

PIERRE BAYLE, *RESPONSE TO THE*
QUESTIONS OF A PROVINCIAL, CHAPTERS 177–78

THE FOLLOWING IS A TRANSLATION OF PIERRE BAYLE, *REPONSE AUX Questions d'un Provincial*, vol. 3 (1706), 1197–1234. Earlier chapters to which Bayle refers are contained in vol. 1 (1704) or vol. 2 (1706) of this work. For several passages in which Bayle cites authors other than Jurieu or Nicole, I have cited existing translations. Otherwise, all translations are mine.

Bayle's marginal notes (which he marked with letters, numbers, and asterisks, resetting to "1" or "a" on each new page) are rendered here as serially numbered endnotes. Bayle placed his notes at the beginning of citations; following modern practice, I have placed them at the end of citations. Text in the endnotes enclosed in brackets is mine.

To indicate citations, Bayle alternates between double quotation marks and italics. I have used double quotation marks to indicate citations, single quotation marks to indicate citations in citations. For example, when Bayle cites Nicole citing Jurieu, Nicole's words are here enclosed in double quotes, and Jurieu's words are enclosed in single quotes.

I have been unable to consult either Jurieu's original texts or the first edition of Nicole's *De l'unite de l'Eglise* (1687), the edition Bayle used, but retain page references given by Bayle or Nicole. I have been able to consult the second edition (1709) of Nicole's text; in the notes, I give in brackets the corresponding page number in the second edition, along with occasional comments on elisions in Bayle's citation of Nicole.

In cases where it seemed informative, I have given the original French terms in brackets.

CHAPTER 177

CONCERNING THAT WHICH TRANSPIRED BETWEEN
MR. JURIEU AND MR. NICOLLE ON THE SUBJECT OF
THE CRUELTY OF HYPOTHESES, OR ON THE SUBJECT
OF SYSTEMS THAT DAMN AN INFINITY OF PEOPLE.

While I am on this topic, it seems relevant to finally respond to a question that I have already started to address,[1] and to give you the detail that I led you to expect.[2]

It is a Papist dogma that all children who die before having received Baptism are damned, and that all adults who die in heresy or in schism, that is, separated internally or externally from the Communion of Rome, go to Hell.[3] "This doctrine is so odious" to Mr. Jurieu (I am using Mr. Nicolle's words) "that when he thinks about it, he loses his composure and he cannot speak of it except with great emotion and convulsions.[4] In one passage, he says: 'When one begins to speak to us of similar things, we shudder [*nous frémissons*] and we deplore the blindness of those who, instead of drawing a veil over the passages of ancient writers, spread them and glorify them. These are amazing cruelties which we can never believe that a single person of good sense could digest [*digérer*] today.'[5] In another passage, he says: 'It is this question that I have said is the most cruel, and most absurd one ever asked, and so absurd that one can never persuade me that those who defend it actually believe it.'[6] This is what makes him say in the same passage that 'supporting this doctrine without believing it must be political and a demonic ruse.' Elsewhere, he says: 'I will say once more that imagination is the most foolish thing installed in the human spirit.' Finally, he is so outraged by this point that he declares 'that it is one of those things that even if one swears a thousand times that one believes them, one could never persuade people of good sense.'"[7]

It was not possible to more skillfully take advantage of [*profiter de*] Mr. Jurieu's thought than Mr. Nicolle has, but I must warn you that this moderation, this honesty that has been praised so much,[7] and of which one finds many indications in his book, hardly appears in this passage: here, he employs harsh and injurious terms that he certainly could have omitted. His response could be just as strong and brilliant without them.

I. The first thing he did was to claim that his adversary copied the Socinians, and he gave this evidence: "What is more universally accepted and believed in all of Christianity than the eternity of suffering with which reprobates are menaced? Nevertheless, an author who recently published a detestable book with the title, *The Peaceful Protestant* [*Protestant pacifique*], pretends that no one has ever believed nor today believes this doctrine."[8]

II. In the second place, he depicted the horrible precipices to which this accusation of cruelty, which Mr. Jurieu forms against the doctrine of the Roman Church, is capable of leading people. "For if it is permitted to reject dogmas accepted by the entire Church based on the fact that the human spirit unilluminated by faith finds there something shocking and harsh, what doors will not be opened to the Socinians to shake up and reverse the foundations of Christianity? What could appear more harsh than the condemnation of all infants for the crime of a single man, when they had no part in it with their own wills? And if one gives human reason liberty to rise up against the authority of the Church and against Scripture as interpreted by the Church, how much will reason strongly counter this article, as well as countering the judgment held by the Roman Church concerning the state of heretic and schismatic sects, and concerning the damnation of the unbaptized children of the faithful? What is less in keeping with ordinary human understanding [*lumiéres*], with which men judge of justice and mercy, than St. Paul's pronouncement against all those who commit crimes, which he enumerates in his letter to the Galatians, whereby he excludes them from the kingdom of God, which includes damnation in eternal flames, according to the knowledge and belief of the entire Church, and also that of the Protestants? Similarly, the Socinians do not protest any less against this article than against original sin, and they depict it no less as an excess of cruelty."[9]

III. In the third place, he accused his antagonist of inconsistency: "At the same time that Mr. Jurieu accepts and embraces the two dogmas of original sin and the eternity of suffering, maintained by the Church against the Socinians, which are like the triumph of God's authority[10] over human reason; at the same time that he renounces his feeble understanding to adore the incomprehensible judgments of God's justice: he is not aware [*il ne prend pas garde*] that his animosity against the Roman Church leads him to form reckless accusations against two parts of these dogmas which he professes to believe as a whole. For what is the doctrine of the Church, which teaches that the children of the faithful who die without baptism are excluded from the kingdom of God and punished by eternal damnation; what, I say, is this doctrine other than a small part of the general doctrine of original sin which condemns to eternal damnation all unbaptized children? And what is it that the same

Church teaches regarding heretics and schismatics, that those who die in schism and in heresy will never enter the kingdom of Heaven, but will share the fate of hypocrites and reprobates, other than a small part[11] of that which is contained in the letter of St. Paul, which excludes from the kingdom of God all crimes, explicitly including schisms and heresies? What harshness, what cruelty is there in these two particular dogmas that is not contained in the general dogmas? The children of the faithful, when they have never received baptism, are they not guilty of original sin? . . . How is it that Mr. Jurieu and the ministers dare to thus remove a part of the general dogma of original sin? . . . Why are the same heresy and schism, which all tradition represents to us as being among the number of the greatest crimes that one can commit, excepted by Mr. Jurieu's imagination [*la phantaisie*] from the letter of St. Paul, who excludes those who commit these crimes from possessing the kingdom of God, and who condemns them to eternal torment?"[12]

IV. In the fourth place, he claimed "that there was something less absurd in the procedure of the Socinians than in that of Mr. Jurieu. The Socinians, in denying original sin and the eternity of suffering for crimes, distance themselves from faith; but that is in order to favor reason. On the contrary, Mr. Jurieu, in accepting the two dogmas as being true and certain, and thus as neither harsh nor cruel, and rejecting at the same time two small parts of these dogmas based on a vain reproach of cruelty, distances himself equally from faith and from reason."[13]

V. He remarked in the fifth place that there is no cruelty at all "in that which the ancient Church decided regarding the state of unbaptized infants, even those born of the faithful, supposing, as faith obliges us to believe, that God justly treats all infants whom he has not graced with baptism in a similar manner?"[14]

VI. He went on to draw this conclusion: "Let Mr. Jurieu therefore learn that it is by the truth of dogmas that one must judge whether they are cruel, and not by the vain ideas of a so-called cruelty that one is to judge their truth. Everything that God does can not be cruel, since he is sovereign justice itself. We must therefore limit all our research to that, and not pretend to judge[15] whether he has done or has not done something, according to the feeble ideas we have of justice and of cruelty."[16]

VII. Then he negated Mr. Jurieu's supposition that a schismatic can be "full of faith, charity, and zeal for the true Gospel."[17] He demonstrated through the doctrine of the Church fathers that charity and zeal for Jesus Christ cannot be found outside of the unity of the Church, and he refuted that which one would like to infer "from the quantity of apparent good works performed by heretics and schismatics."[18] Let Mr. Jurieu therefore, he concluded, "not make these fantastic hypotheses" of a heretic "or a schismatic, full" of charity, "who suffers martyrdom" for Jesus Christ;[19] for he must know that the Church denies them this possibility; that the Church recognizes nothing in the so-called martyr other than a human steadfastness that may excite pity in the senses, due to our small understanding, but which God counts for nothing, because he sees the evil foundation which is its source. It is thus necessary that, without help from these vain hypotheses, he attaches this amazing cruelty of which he accuses the Roman Church to this sole point: that the Church regards schism and heresy as a moral sin which God will punish with exclusion from his kingdom. But what is the Church doing here other than following the doctrine of St. Paul, who expressly places heresies and divisions among the crimes of which he said that those who commit them will never inherit the Kingdom of God?[20]

VIII. Finally, he articulated the crimes that accompany heresy and schism, and refuted the excuses that one might like to ground based on heretics and schismatics, as those who do not sin at all "from cupidity or passion" or against the illumination of conscience, but "in good faith and from a simple lack of illumination."[21] This, he said, may at best diminish the enormity of their crime, but he denied that they are exempt from passion. "There is always some secret cupidity, some hidden pride, some temerity that grows from presumption, which incites people to hastily form criminal judgments about the Church of Jesus Christ."[22]

Mr. Jurieu replied in a manner that may show that he became even angrier than usual. I will take from his reply only what is essential to our subject.

I. He began with the syllogism: "every religion that makes it an article of faith to damn millions upon millions of Christians, without basis, without reason, and without charity, is an anti-Christian religion, an enemy of God, opposed to Jesus Christ, and is even the path to damnation. Now the Roman Church does this: thus it is a Church without charity, without reason, without humanity, without mercy, and which should not expect any in return."[23] In the true Church, he added, "mercy is glorified over judgment; in the false Church, judgment and cruelty rise up above mercy."

II. In a second passage he declared "that reason must never be the judge of the cruelty and the severity of God's ways, when God himself proclaims certain articles that seem harsh to the human mind [*l'esprit*]. It is absolutely the same with these as with articles of faith.[24] Where God speaks, reason should fall silent. But as it is not permitted, and is also a great crime to unnecessarily accuse religion of having false, harsh, and unbelievable mysteries, it is likewise a great crime to blame God's ways; odious things that are capable of giving an untoward idea and distancing men from true religion."[25]

III. Applying this remark furthermore, he guaranteed "that it would be enough for the Christian religion to have to propose the adorable mystery of the Trinity of persons in a single divine essence, and the incarnation of one of these persons, the mystery of the satisfaction of Jesus Christ and that of the resurrection of the flesh. That would be enough, I say, to exercise the humility of faith and there would be no need to add on false mysteries to the divine mysteries to render the Christian religion inaccessible to the human mind. Regarding the ways of God the wonderful adorable mysteries of predestination, the depths of his providence which permits so many evils, which allows so many Saints to suffer, and allows so many criminals to triumph would suffice to keep the human heart in humility and oblige it to cry out upon the edge of these abysses: *O what depths*, etc. And it would not be necessary to accuse God's merciful ways of a dispensation just as odious as this one would be: to render to eternal flames an infinity of Christians who follow a rabble-rouser or a fanatic, who follow him, I say, in the simplicity of their heart and otherwise retain Christian faith and the cult of Jesus Christ. Nevertheless, if this odious dogma were in Scripture, or if one saw it in experience, as I see the impenetrable depths of God's providence, I would place my finger on my lips, I would adore in silence that which I could not comprehend. . . . But concerning an odious dogma of which one cannot bring a single bit of proof other than the equivocal testimonials of men, and not a single word either from Scripture or from reason: concerning such a dogma, I say, I can make no other judgment than that it is false, and being false, that it is not bad in a mediocre way, but rather is entirely abominable."[26]

IV. In a fourth passage he maintained that the doctrine of original sin is supported by "evident proofs in Scripture, in reason, in experience," but that the Roman dogma that he accuses of cruelty "has no bit of proof either from Scripture or from reason."[27]

V. In a fifth passage he examined that which his opponent cited of St. Paul. The sinners, he wrote, "of which St. Paul makes a list in his letter to the Galatians, and in that to the Corinthians:"[28] These are the fornicators, the idolaters, the adulterers, the effeminate, those who live with males, the thieves, the drunkards, the slanderers, the robbers. Do not be deceived: such people will never inherit the Kingdom of God.[29] The works of the flesh are adultery, fornication, impurity, disobedience, idolatry, poisoning, hostility, strife, spite, wrath, schism, heresy, envy, murder, drunkenness. All those who commit these things will not inherit the Kingdom of Heaven.[30] "The above is rewritten by Mr. Nicole:" what conforms less to ordinary human understanding "than that God excludes from the Kingdom of heaven, and condemns to eternal flames the parricides, the murderers, the poisoners, the Sodomites, and the adulterers? In truth it seems that Mr. Nicole has divorced from reason on purpose. If this judgment of Saint Paul conforms so little to human understanding, I ask you, whence did it come among the nations who are governed only by human understanding? Whence come the wheels of Ixion, the stones[31] of Sisyphus, the barrels of the Danaides, the Minos, the Radamanthes, the Styx, the Cocytus, the rivers of hell, the fires, and the flames that pagan theology has built, kindled and prepared for the wicked?"

VI. After this he anticipated a certain response from Mr. Nicolle. "He may say that it is not the chagrin of the crimes that causes the spirit to suffer, but rather that it is the eternity of sufferings. I would respond that reason, custom, and all the laws of the world respond to his difficulty. Reason tells us that a creature that cannot cease to be criminal also cannot cease to be miserable: that men inflict eternal pain without being accused of injustice. I would rather like to know if when a counterfeiter's hand is cut off, it is not an eternal punishment received from those who order the punishment? Do they assign a time after which they will return his hand to him? When a criminal is executed, is that not an eternal punishment? Does the judge order that the sepulcher be raised and that he be resuscitated at the end of a year? It is therefore a mockery of religion to seriously propose this as a dogma that seems to oppose natural understanding."[32]

VII. Then he proceeded to the parallel of original sin and treated it "in an irrational manner [d'un égarement d'esprit]. This is to reason just like a man who believes that up to today, all men are damned without exception, that is to say," that this doctrine is something other than part of a general judgment which has been pronounced since the beginning of the world, namely that on the day that you sin, you will suffer death. "Are the general rules violated by the exceptions that God has himself set? What follows from this? All children are deserving of death; thus children who are born in the alliance of grace must be damned. Is this what follows?"[33]

VIII. He agreed with all that Mr. Nicolle "said about heretics and schismatics, in the sense of St. Paul," and he wanted that the heretics of whom St. Paul speaks, "impious people who deny the immortality of the soul and the resurrection of the body," whether magicians or adversaries "of the divinity of Jesus Christ," and all those who resemble them, would be "delivered over into the hands of Mr. Nicolle," who would do whatever he deemed right, but he did not consent to the damnation of those whom the Council of Gangres anathematized for having cut "their hair too long or too short," nor of those who deny purgatory, or the authority of the Pope.[34]

IX. Finally, he recognized this thesis as sound, "that outside of the Church there is neither grace nor virtue," but he cited one of his works, where he proved that the characters of the true martyr can be found among the Calvinist martyrs.[35]

You may remark, if you like, that he kept profoundly silent regarding Mr. Nicolle's first observation. It may well have been odious: it was a shot at point-blank range [*un coup à brûle-pourpoint*].

CHAPTER 178

REFLECTIONS ON THAT WHICH MR. JURIEU
REPLIED TO MR. NICOLLE ON THE SUBJECT OF
THE DISPUTE RELATED IN THE PRECEDING CHAPTER.

There are Protestants who, before having attentively examined Mr. Nicolle's response to this accusation of cruelty, said that Mr. Jurieu had embarked without provisions [*sans biscuit*] and that he was dazzled by a thought that appeared to him to be new,[36] one which he indulged himself in repeating from time to time, that he never considered the bad passages, never foresaw the false consequences that one might thus be introducing. They believed that his replies would not be at all good, and that in them he would convey only pride and a scornful, insulting attitude. Several of these gentlemen changed their minds after reading them, and were very content with them, almost to the point of enchantment. Others became upset for having been good Prophets, that is, they judged that these replies were just as they had expected. The reflections that I have made may help you in taking part in this discussion.

I. First I must tell you that one is taken aback when one sees the syllogism that heads Mr. Jurieu's replies. The triumphant attitude with which he availed himself of the accusation of cruelty, the vivid manner in which he noted several times the impression that it made on him, would be able to persuade one that he had found a simple and infallible method to put an end to controversies, a new character of truth, *criterium veritatis*, a new touchstone, much more manageable than previous ones, for distinguishing between the true and the false Church. Indeed, if the cruelty of a hypothesis were a certain sign of error, and if it consisted in excluding from salvation all Christians other than those who form a certain community, one could instantly conclude with certainty that the Communion of Rome is false, since it makes a syllogism of which the major premise is evident, and of which the minor premise is a fact confessed by Roman Catholics. What a let-down, what surprise for those who had counted on this new touchstone, to see that Mr. Jurieu took away all its virtue in reducing it to a syllogism of which the minor premise is denied by his adversaries! For they would have no defense in confessing that they damn "without basis, without reason, and without charity" many millions of Christians. This minor premise revives all the controversies; we thus reembark once again on the Ocean of disputes, and the most troubling thing is that the first controversy that comes up, namely that concerning the unity and the authority of the Church, is a place where the enemy can lay traps in the terrain much better than anywhere else. Our reason prefers [*goûteroit mieux*] the ideas the Roman Catholics give to the Church less than those Mr. Jurieu forms of it; our reason, I say, will go there on sure footing, even if history or an event or experience shows us the too great obstacles, and in the end one cannot deny that the nature of a Church[37] composed of several societies that anathematize each other is not a shocking thing. Be this as it may, this accusation of cruelty that promises such marvelous advantages finds itself reduced to nothing: it does not spare us any sort of discussion; it is no less necessary to examine whether previously all the members of the true Church had to recognize each other as brothers, if it is permitted to some to break with the union, etc.

Mr. Nicolle's chapter was able to make people fear the unfortunate success of the accusation of cruelty, for he showed that it proved too much, and that it entailed, along with the condemnation of Papism, that of the whole Christian Church, which confesses original sin and the eternity of suffering, and which damns all pagans, all Jews, and all Muhammadans and almost all Christians.[38] Is this a true Church, is the character of a true Church, as Mr. Jurieu contends, "to glorify mercy above judgment"?[39] So much for what I had to tell you regarding his first remark.

II. The second remark is just as discomforting as the one I have already discussed. It presupposes that which is in question, and thus spares us no dispute. It wants without reason to connect to the other difficulties of the Gospel that of the damnation of sects. But we can deny to Mr. Jurieu that this connection has been made unnecessarily. We return thus to begin examining the controversy concerning the authority of the Church, that of its unity, that of the nature of schism, etc. I would say the same thing concerning the third and fourth remarks. But in addition, they contain a particular subject of criticism.

III. For as much as Mr. Jurieu is well founded in maintaining that Scripture and experience prove original sin, he is just as mistaken to allege that "reason establishes it in an invincible manner. Reason says," he alleges, "that the effects are, or must be, similar to their causes; that an evil cause can never produce a good effect, that a corrupt man must produce a corrupt son: that children follow the condition of their fathers, that an enslaved father cannot beget a free child, and thus that men subject to the curse can only beget children likewise subject to the curse."[40] If we didn't have better proofs of the existence of original sin, we would manage very badly in a dispute on this material. For the same reasons that we have just seen used to assail this dogma, that since Adam was reconciled with God before he begot children, one must say that they are born reconciled with God, if it is true that children must "follow the condition of their fathers." The amnesty that one grants to criminals extends to all of their posterity. Where would one find thus the children of Adam subject to the curse, having been delivered by divine mercy? Aren't the children of the predestined also predestined? I pass in silence over the fact that Mr. Jurieu's reasons prove too much: they prove that a father and a mother who are intelligent and beautiful, or who have certain virtues, or certain particular faults, always produce children who resemble them in this respect; this is contrary to experience. What are we to say about the idea that fathers and mothers in no way produce the souls of their children and nonetheless that the soul is susceptible to the corruption of sin? How would we reply to those who depict for us that according to the lights of reason[41] the suffering of a crime must tend toward curing the inclination toward the same crime, as long as it involves an invincible inclination[42] toward that crime? Does reason approve of monarchs who, in order to castigate a rebel, condemn him and all his descendants for being inclined to rebel? I am surprised that Mr. Jurieu has said nothing to us about the law of certain peoples[43] who condemn to ultimate torment all the relatives of a man guilty of crimes against the throne [*leze-Majesté*]. Perhaps he knew that an infinity of great men have condemned[44] such a jurisprudence that has almost no place among Christians, and that after all does not merit being excused, when the public good demands that one show more regard for utility than for justice. This always presumes in the person of the legislator an absolute incapacity to otherwise remedy the evils that one dreads: but there is no evil that God cannot prevent through an infinity of means. This is why it is necessary that our reason sacrifice here its understanding to divine authority. Zanchius sincerely avows that one cannot give another reason for original sin than the will of God.[45]

IV. The fifth remark of Mr. Jurieu will occupy us for a longer time. You must primarily keep in mind that Mr. Nicolle's objection consists in effect in posing that nothing "less conforms to ordinary human understanding according to which men JUDGE OF JUSTICE AND MERCY than does the pronouncement made by St. Paul against all those who commit the crimes that he lists."[46] Mr. Jurieu never shortened these words, he reported them with a complete fidelity, and he accepts the list in question. This is a point where the strifeful, the hostile, the spiteful, the wrathful, the contentious, the envious, drunkenness, insolence, slander, and avarice have their place along with fornication, adultery, sodomy, idolatry, poisoning, theft and murder.[47] Nonetheless Mr. Jurieu supposed that Mr. Nicolle only had in mind parricides, murderers, poisoners, sodomites, and adulterers, and that he paid no attention to this main point, "according to which" (ordinary human understanding) "MEN JUDGE OF JUSTICE AND MERCY."[48] This false supposition and this omission were the bases of his reply; this is what he wanted to pass off to you as a malicious fraud,[49] and what I prefer to treat as an illusion.[50]

Be this as it may, he succeeds badly in refuting Mr. Nicolle's objection, since there is an extreme difference between his proposition, and what was said to him of the Ixions and the Danaides. He may be right that the pagan doctrine on the pains of Hell derives from "natural sources and natural understanding,"[51] without Mr. Nicolle's proposition losing any of its truth. For those among the pagans who had the greatest belief in the dogma of eternal suffering had no scruple in confessing that it does not conform to ordinary human understanding, according to which they judge of justice and mercy. And if they had difficulty in confessing this, they had to be forced, by asking them how they would judge a Prince who would condemn all of the inhabitants of a rebellious country, not to death, but to a long life in which he kept them alive in torments.

Were they able to get off responding that he showed no sign of mercy, and that instead of exercising justice, he got carried away in the greatest excess of cruelty? Then why weren't they asked beforehand whether they teach that the judges of Hell condemn all the guilty without excepting anyone from eternal suffering? Weren't they constrained to respond that these judges did not at all follow this ordinary understanding according to which we judge of justice and mercy, that divine laws are superior to those of Monarchs, *sunt superis sua jura*, and that whatever is bad in the human tribunal can be good in the tribunal of Pluto? If one had thus questioned Virgil about the dreadful description he made,[52] whether about the multitude of the damned or about the eternal rigor of their torments, don't doubt that he would only have responded that the principles according to which we judge of human virtues are in no way applicable to the conduct of the Gods. He could never have found another view than this one in order to remove himself from the difficulties with which he could have been confronted. He would have been primarily troubled if the state of the question had been put to him according to the points of Mr. Nicolle's argument [*endroits du plan*], which had been eclipsed and refuted [*mis à quartier*] by Mr. Jurieu. For according to that state, not only Medea who killed her brother and his children, or Tully who dethroned his own father, and who vented his anger on the dead corpse of the good Prince, would have been sentenced to eternal suffering, but also all the slanderous, greedy, insolent, envious, argumentative women, and in general all people of one or the other sex who have participated in the pleasures of love outside of marriage, or those who have gotten drunk, or those who have subjected themselves to any of the other faults specified by St. Paul.[53]

It is clearly known that it does not at all conform to ordinary human understanding according to which men judge of justice and mercy, that those could not be excused who so obviously stray from the path. Nonetheless, this is what Mr. Jurieu has done: he lost his route as though he had been walking in shadow. We see plainly that a Sovereign who wants to exercise both justice and clemency, when a city has risen up in rebellion, must content himself with punishing a small number of the mutineers, and pardoning all the rest, for if the number of those who are castigated is a thousand to one in comparison with those who are pardoned, he cannot be considered kind, but rather as cruel. He will ultimately be considered an abominable tyrant if he chooses torments of long duration[54] and if he does not spare the blood when he could be persuaded that death would be preferable to a miserable life, and finally if his desire to avenge himself carries more weight than his desire to serve the public good regarding the punishment he would mete out upon nearly all the rebels.

The malefactors who are executed are considered to fully expiate their crimes by their loss of life, and the public demands no more than that, becoming indignant if the executioners are not skillful. They would be stoned if people thought that they intentionally gave several axe-blows: and the judges attending the execution would not be out of peril if people believed that they enjoyed this evil game of the executioners, and that they had been told secretly to engage in it.[55]

Finally, it is of unequaled notoriety that these Sovereigns who regulate matters based on St. Paul, that is to say, those who condemn to ultimate punishment all those whom he condemns to eternal death, are considered enemies of the human race and destroyers of society. It is incontestable that their laws are far from being proper, according to the aim of legislators, which is to maintain society, when they ruin it entirely.[56]

The first thing that Solon did once the Athenians granted him stewardship of the police was to repeal "all Draco's laws, except those concerning homicide, because they were too severe, and the punishment too great; for death was appointed for almost all offences, insomuch that those that were convicted of idleness were to die, and those that stole a cabbage or an apple to suffer even as villains that committed sacrilege or murder. So that Demades, in after time, was thought to have said very happily, that Draco's laws were written not with ink but blood; and he himself, being once asked why he made death the punishment of most offences, replied, 'Small ones deserve that, and I have no higher for the greater crimes.'"[57]

V. Let us see whether Mr. Jurieu was more successful in responding to an objection which he supposed Mr. Nicolle could raise to him. You will find this response in the sixth remark.[58] His claim goes to the point that if it conforms to our manners of judging justice and mercy that counterfeiters' hands are cut off, and that murderers are hanged, then it conforms to the same manners that the wicked are punished eternally in Hell. His reason is that our judges do not trouble themselves to reattach that hand, do not resuscitate a hanged man, and thus the suffering they inflict is eternal. But this reason proves even more that according to common notions there would be nothing to reconsider in the annihilation of reprobates. Thus it is not a question of this, but of a sensation of pain that is never interrupted, and which will endure eternally. The sentence of our judges is quite different. They do not prevent the counterfeiter from promptly having his arm bandaged, and if he finds a way to assuage his pain, and become as happy as before, they do not take any action against him, they do not return to the charge.[59] The ultimate punishment is generally a very short pain and that is where the suffering inflicted by the Magistrates ends, who elsewhere give the criminal all the help at their disposal so that in losing a life that the course of nature would have taken from him perhaps the very next day, and certainly after several years, he might enjoy a happiness that will never end. I have already observed[60] that the public does not approve if those condemned to death are made to suffer a long time, they complain about the executioner who cannot cut off a head except in three or four swings. If cruel torments are approved,[61] this is because the society's public good demands in certain places and at certain times that evildoers are intimidated by the fear of suffering the torment of hanging. In a word, our natural understanding approves of the castigation of malefactors because it is necessary to the public good, and because the sovereign power is not at all capable of bending the wills of individuals, and because it has no other resource for restraining the wicked, other than punishing them. Here then, are the differences[62] between the things that Mr. Jurieu compares together as if they resembled one another. There is such error in his remark on liberty where he says that the Judges refrain from returning an amputated hand and do not resuscitate a hanged man! Could they do such things, which are impossible for them? Does he know what they would do if it were up to them? Is it improbable that after a certain time they would, if they could, return the hand, the life, to those from whom they had cut them away? Didn't the laws establish a statute of limitations of twenty years in favor of criminals? Doesn't a sentence made in absentia and executed in effigy become null and void after thirty years? Is there nothing there that is contrary to Mr. Jurieu's remark?

"Reason tells us," he adds, "that a creature that cannot cease to be criminal also cannot cease to be miserable."[63] He doesn't know the language of reason at all, since he conveys it so badly. Reason says that creatures may always cease being criminal, since they can be destroyed or converted at any moment.[64] Reason also says that once creatures could not cease being criminal, they would cease to be so, as a frenetic and a maniac cease to sin as soon as it is impossible for them to avoid that which they do and that which they feel.

VI. On Mr. Jurieu's seventh remark I only have to make the same reflection that I did on the first four remarks. He leaves us all the burden of examining whether it is correct or incorrect to place in the same class all children who die before baptism. He wants that those who are born within Christianity should be saved, even if their fathers and mothers are not married, have committed incest, and are destined to eternal damnation. He has his reasons, but they have been disputed; this is a very complicated controversy.

VII. His eighth remark serves to open a vast field of dispute on the authority of Councils: I will not give much pause to this. I will only say that if the Council of Gangres was wrong to fulminate anathemas concerning haircuts, the Ecclesiastics who did not conform to the Canons of that assembly are just as culpable. What would Mr. Jurieu say if the Walloon Synod had ordained that all Ministers with long hair be deposed, and two or three Ministers mocked this ordinance and incited their flock to make a schism? Wouldn't he find them more criminal than he would the Synod that had abused its power? He should recall the Liturgy which is solemnly read to the people in the reformed Churches on all Communion days. This Liturgy places schismatics in the category of sinners who are unworthy of approaching the holy Table. "We have heard, my brothers," these are the words of the Liturgy, "how our Lord had his Last Supper among his disciples: and thereby he shows us that strangers, that is, those who are not in the company of the faithful, may never be admitted. Thus, following this rule, in the Name and with the authority of our Lord Jesus Christ, I excommunicate all idolaters, blasphemers, those contemptuous of God, heretics, AND ALL PEOPLE WHO FORM SEPARATE SECTS IN ORDER TO BREAK THE UNITY OF THE CHURCH, all perjurers, all those who rebel against their fathers and mothers and their superiors, all the seditious, rebellious, batterers [bateurs], riotous, adulterers, promiscuous, thieves, the greedy, usurers, abductors [ravisseurs], drunkards, gluttonous, and all those who live a scandalous life: they are denounced in that they must abstain from this holy table, for fear that they will pollute and contaminate the sacred meats that our Lord Jesus Christ gives only to his servants and faithful."[65] If Mr. Jurieu follows his method regarding persecutions, alleging that the Protestants, given that they are orthodox, are right to thus treat their schismatics, but that the Roman Church is wrong to mistreat their schismatics in this way,[66] then he does not deserve to be heard.

VIII. His last remark is a new field of dispute where one can combat him with his own weapons, for he said on the virtues of the Socinians[67] the same things that his adversary touched on regarding the virtues of the schismatics and heretics, and if he places almost no difference between the Socinians and those who find Socinianism tolerable,[68] he must believe the Remonstrants, the Anabaptists, etc., to be beyond the path of salvation, he who judges thus of this sect. He must therefore judge of the virtue of the Anabaptists and the Remonstrants, and of the disposition that they display as martyrs,[69] if the occasion presents itself, that which Mr. Nicolle similarly judges of the sectarians separated from Catholicism. If one asked him what he judges of the devoted Papists, the Missionaries of the Pope who suffered martyrdom in the Orient and elsewhere, and of the austerity of the Trappist monks, he would no doubt respond that these are the depths of Satan,[70] and he would copy Mr. Nicolle word for word. Add to this the fact that he argued[71] that the good faith that heretics may have cannot consist in anything other than this: that they do not want to formally persevere in a known error, but that nonetheless their error is an effect of sin and of some malignant passion, and consequently that their ignorance does not exculpate them at all. This is copying Mr. Nicolle.

You will conclude from all this whatever you like, Sir, but for me my conclusion is that no attack is more vain, more false, more badly supported, than the accusation of cruelty which Mr. Jurieu brought with so much noise and so much presumption against Papism. Nothing would be more fitting than contempt and even mockery from the Roman Catholics, for if their definition of the Church appears to them to be based in reason, it would be absurd to abandon it under the pretext that it results in this consequence, that one is off the path of salvation in all heretical and schismatic sects. It wouldn't be necessary that, under the same pretext, they would abandon the doctrine of original sin and the eternity of infernal suffering, against which the objection of cruelty would be much more plausible than against the doctrine that Mr. Jurieu attacks. Wouldn't they be straining out the gnat after having swallowed the camel if they admitted original sin and the eternity of suffering, but raised scruples about damning heretics and schismatics?[72] But into what abysses are they not hurling themselves if they have no other reason to change the definition of the Church, than for fear of the consequence that Mr. Jurieu disagrees with them? Wouldn't it be necessary, then, following the example of the Socinians, to save all children and annihilate all reprobates? Could they accordingly recognize that Judaism, which damns all the rest of the world, was a true religion up until the coming of JESUS CHRIST? Could they believe that the Gospel announced by the Apostles as the sole and unique path to salvation was a true religion? For if it is a cruelty to damn heretics and schismatics, it would be the height of ferocity to damn all non-Christians.

I have always been surprised that Mr. Nicolle did not find it advisable to retort to this argument, for he could have shown that Mr. Jurieu completely ruined the Protestant hypothesis: that since the introduction of idolatry and the reign of the beast, that is to say, since the fourth or the fifth century, there has never been a true Church visible beyond the small troops of the faithful, who appeared from time to time like lightning in the Alpine valleys, in Languedoc, in Bohemia, etc. This damns incomparably more people than does the Roman Church. If you want to see this objection of Mr. Jurieu turned in ways contrary to his doctrines, consult a book that was printed in 1692.[73]

Abbreviations

AG   G. W. Leibniz, *Philosophical Essays*, ed. and trans. Roger Ariew and Daniel Garber (Indianapolis, IN: Hackett, 1989); parenthetical citations in the text refer to page numbers.

AT   *Œuvres de Descartes*, 11 vols., ed. C. Adam and P. Tannery (Paris: Vrin, 1964–1976); parenthetical citations in the text refer to volume and page numbers.

CSM   *The Philosophical Writings of Descartes*, 2 vols., ed. and trans. John Cottingham, Robert Stoothoff, and Dugald Murdoch (Cambridge: Cambridge University Press, 1984–1985); parenthetical citations in the text refer to volume and page numbers.

CSMK   *The Philosophical Writings of Descartes*, vol. 3, ed. and trans. John Cottingham, Robert Stoothoff, Dugald Murdoch, and Anthony Kenny (Cambridge: Cambridge University Press, 1991); parenthetical citations in the text refer to page numbers.

E   Christian Wolff, *Gesammelte Werke*, ed. Jean Ecole et al., 150 vols. to date (Hildesheim: Olms, 1962–); parenthetical citations in the text refer to division, volume, page, and (where applicable) section numbers.

G   *Die philosophischen Schriften von Gottfried Wilhelm Leibniz*, 7 vols., ed. C. J. Gerhardt (1885; Hildesheim: Olms, 1961); parenthetical citations in the text refer to volume and page numbers.

INDIVIDUAL WORKS

A   Alexander Gottlieb Baumgarten, *Aesthetica* (Hildesheim: Georg Olms, 1986); parenthetical citations in the text refer to section numbers.

Essay   John Locke, *An Essay concerning Human Understanding*, ed. Peter H. Nidditch (Oxford: Clarendon Press, 1975); parenthetical citations in the text without the abbreviation refer to book, chapter and section numbers; parenthetical citations in the text with the abbreviation refer to page numbers.

NE   G. W. Leibniz, *New Essays on Human Understanding*, ed. and trans. Peter Remnant and Jonathan Bennett (Cambridge: Cambridge University Press, 1996); parenthetical citations in the text refer to page numbers.

RQP   Pierre Bayle, *Reponse aux Questions d'un Provincial*, 4 vols. (Rotterdam, 1704–1707); parenthetical citations in the text are from vol. 3 (1706) and refer to page numbers.

T   G. W. Leibniz, *Theodicy*, ed. Austin Farrer, trans. E. M. Huggard (Chicago: Open Court, 1985); parenthetical citations in the text with this abbreviation refer to section numbers; parenthetical citations in the text with the abbreviation *Theodicy* refer to page numbers.

Notes

INTRODUCTION

1. Susan M. Turner and Gareth B. Matthews, eds., *The Philosopher's Child. Critical Essays in the Western Tradition* (Rochester, NY: University of Rochester Press, 1998).

2. Ibid., 1.

3. See Arnulf Zweig, "Immanuel Kant's Children," in ibid., 121–35. Zweig's essay is devoted to concepts of the family; the concept of childhood actually receives only brief treatment. For a recent essay on Kant that does make childhood central to its argument, see Edgar Landgraf, "The Education of Humankind: Perfectibility and Discipline in Kant's Lectures *Über Pädagogik*," *Goethe Yearbook* 14 (2007): 39-60.

4. For just one example, see John Cleverley and D. C. Phillips, *Visions of Childhood. Influential Models from Locke to Spock* (New York: Teachers College Press, 1986). As the title suggests, Locke is taken as the starting point for significant discussions of childhood in the seventeenth and eighteenth centuries. See also Colin Heywood, *A History of Childhood: Children and Childhood in the West from Medieval to Modern Times* (Cambridge: Polity Press, 2001), 23–27. Heywood's brief discussion of the eighteenth century also centers on Locke and Rousseau, before turning to Romanticism.

5. A number of recent works in German literary studies draw inspiration from Friedrich Kittler, *Discourse Networks 1800/1900* (Stanford: Stanford University Press, 1990), originally *Aufschreibesysteme* (München: Fink, 1985). On childhood in novels around 1800, see Annette Simonis, *Kindheit in Romanen um 1800* (Bielefeld: Aisthesis, 1993) and Stephan Schindler, *Das Subjekt als Kind: die Erfindung der Kindheit im Roman des 18. Jahrhunderts* (Berlin: Schmidt, 1994). The best study of childhood in German literature just after Rousseau remains Hans-Heino Ewers, *Kindheit als poetische Daseinsform. Studien zur Entstehung der romantischen Kindheitsutopie im 18. Jahrhundert: Herder, Jean Paul, Novalis und Tieck* (München: Fink, 1989).

6. Antoine Furetière, *Le Dictionnaire universel*, ed. Alain Rey, vol. 2 (1690; Paris: Le Robert, 1978), n. pag. Translations of this and the following definitions are mine.

7. Johann Georg Walch, *Philosophisches Lexicon*, 1775 ed. (1726; Hildesheim: Georg Olms, 1968), 1550.

8. Johann Heinrich Zedler, *Grosses vollständiges Universal Lexicon aller Wissenschaften und Künste*, vol. 15 (1744; Graz: Akademische Druck- und Verlagsanstalt, 1961), 640.

9. Denis Diderot and Jean LeRond D'Alembert, *L'encylopédie ou dictionnaire raisonné des sciences des arts et des métiers*, vol. 1 (1760; New York: Readex, 1969), 651–52.

10. Johann Christoph Adelung, *Versuch eines vollständigen grammatisch-kritischen Wörterbuches der hochdeutschen Mundart, mit beständiger Vergleichung der übrigen Mundarten, besonders aber der oberdeutschen*, vol. 2 (Leipzig, 1775), 1580.

11. Johann Christian August Heyse and Karl Wilhelm Ludwig Heyse, *Handwörter-buch der deutschen Sprache*, vol. 1 (Magdeburg, 1833), 858.

12. See Avital Ronell, "On the Unrelenting Creepiness of Childhood: Lyotard, Kid-Tested," lecture, The European Graduate School, New York, 2001, www.egs.edu/faculty/ronell/ronell-unrelenting-creepiness-of-childhood-2001.html.

13. The "philosophy for children" movement began with Matthew Lipman's attempts to introduce philosophy to grade-school curricula. See Michael Pritchard, "Philosophy for Children," *Stanford Encyclopedia of Philosophy*, http://plato.stanford.edu/entries/children/.

14. Arthur O. Lovejoy and George Boas, *Primitivism and Related Ideas in Antiquity* (Baltimore, MD: Johns Hopkins University Press, 1935), x.

15. Turner and Matthews, *Philosopher's Child*, 1.

16. See the valuable collection of essays in Marcia J. Bunge, ed., *The Child in Christian Thought* (Grand Rapids, MI: Eerdmans, 2001). Although the focus of this volume is theological rather than philosophical, it does treat several figures sometimes referred to as philosophers, such as Thomas Aquinas and Friedrich Schleiermacher.

17. Philippe Ariès, *Centuries of Childhood: A Social History of Family Life*, trans. Robert Baldick (New York: Vintage, 1962). Originally *L'Enfant et la vie familiale sous l'ancien régime* (Paris: Plon, 1960).

18. J. H. van den Berg, *The Changing Nature of Man: Introduction to a Historical Psychology* (New York: Norton, 1961, 20–114. Originally *Metabletica; of, Leer der veranderingen; beginselen van een historische psychologie* (Nijkerk: Callenbach, 1956).

19. George Boas, *The Cult of Childhood* (Dallas, TX: Spring, 1966). In this slender volume, Boas surveyed concepts of childhood from Plato to the Christian fathers (in ten pages), as well as in the literature, art, and philosophy of the sixteenth through twentieth centuries. This gem of a study deserves to be consulted more often, but in the present context one should note that Boas's examination of pedagogical theory jumps from Montaigne to Rousseau, thus eliding 1580 to 1762, precisely the period on which I focus.

20. For an illuminating critical discussion of Ariès, including a critique of his "presentist" methodology, see Adrian Wilson, "The Infancy of the History of Childhood: an Appraisal of Philippe Ariès," *History and Theory* 19.2 (1980): 132–53.

21. See the excellent study by James A. Schultz, *The Knowledge of Childhood in the German Middle Ages, 1100–1350* (Philadelphia: University of Pennsylvania Press, 1995).

22. See Lloyd de Mause, "The Evolution of Childhood," in *The History of Childhood* (New York: Harper, 1974), 1–73.

23. See John Higham, "American Intellectual History: A Critical Appraisal," *American Quarterly* 13.2.2 (1961): 219–33; here 220.

24. See Anja Müller, ed., *Fashioning Childhood in the Eighteenth Century: Age and Identity* (Aldershot: Ashgate, 2006), 4.

25. Turner and Matthews, *Philosopher's Child*, 3.

26. Ibid.

27. Schultz, *Knowledge of Childhood*, 11.

28. Schultz's study seems designed to defamiliarize the use of the verb "to know." For example: "Most North Americans . . . know that a child's early experiences determine her subsequent development. . . . The writers of texts in M[iddle] H[igh] G[erman] can ignore the first years of life because they know that the course of the individual life is determined not by early experience but by inherent nature" (ibid., 1–2). While such an in-

distinction between knowing and believing might seem indicative of relativism, I believe that Schultz's study can encourage his readers to question what they have believed they have *known* about children, precisely in order to recognize the presence of (contingent, culturally specific) beliefs in what has hitherto passed as *knowledge*. Schultz's project is one of enlightenment, or in a phrase he cites from Michel Foucault, a project of "free[ing] thought from what it silently thinks" (13).

29. Ibid.

30. Descartes had one child; although he was not married to her mother, Helena Jansdr vander Strom, the child was legitimate, since Descartes identified himself as the father in a Reformed Church baptism. Her name was Francine (Fransintge in the baptismal registry); after she was born, Descartes published his *Discourse* in the French language. It seems Descartes wanted his works to be accessible to women, who would not have had the opportunity to learn Latin. (Evidence suggests that vander Strom could read and write, presumably in Dutch.) It is unclear how much time Descartes spent with his child and her mother, though some evidence suggests he strove to keep them near or in his own places of residence during Francine's short life. She died at age five, in September 1640 (the year before *Meditations* was published). A number of biographies lose sight of vander Strom afterward. As late as 2005, A. C. Grayling speculated that she might have succumbed to the same fever that ended Francine's life. See A. C. Grayling, *Descartes: The Life and Times of a Genius* (New York: Walker, 2005), 153. A more recent biography dispels this speculation: Desmond M. Clarke documents Descartes's assistance to vander Strom at her wedding to one Jan Jansz van Wel in 1644. Descartes may have even donated a substantial amount of money to help her transition into a respectable life. (She had four further children and eventually inherited an inn.) See Desmond M. Clarke, *Descartes: A Biography* (Cambridge: Cambridge University Press, 2006), 131–36. Richard Watson has posed an interesting question about Francine's brief childhood: if Descartes as a young child was likely swaddled, stuck in walkers, often beaten, and slightly starved (as was typical of seventeenth-century French childhoods), did his daughter receive similar treatment? Or did the more lenient Dutch upbringing that vander Strom would have experienced trump Descartes's French upbringing? See Richard Watson, *Cogito, Ergo Sum: The Life of René Descartes* (Boston: Godine, 2002), 41–64.

Locke had no children, but took interest in the education of Benjamin Furly's and Edward Clarke's children. He was personally involved in the education of Francis Masham, the son of his former love interest, Damaris Masham. See Roger Woolhouse, *Locke: A Biography* (Cambridge: Cambridge University Press, 2007).

Neither Bayle, Leibniz, nor Wolff appear to have fathered any children, and I am not familiar with any evidence to suggest they spent significant time with any children.

Baumgarten seems to have had four children with his second wife, Justina Elisabeth née Albinus; two of these children survived infancy. Three of them (Eleonora Juliana, Carl Gottlieb, and Gottlieb Wilhelm, the last of whom was born several months after Baumgarten's death and lived only several days) are mentioned in Georg Friedrich Meier, *Alexander Gottlieb Baumgartens Leben* (Halle, 1763), 21. A fourth child, Eleonora Wilhelmina, who lived between October 1749 and September 1750 (the year part one of *Aesthetica* was published), is documented in a Baumgarten family genealogy: see Jan Lekschas, *Alexander Gottlieb Baumgarten*, http://www.jan.lekschas.de/.

31. Higham, "American Intellectual History," 232.

32. See Lloyd DeMause, "The Childhood Origins of the Holocaust," lecture, Klagenfurt University, 2005, http://www.psychohistory.com/htm/childhoodHolocaust.html.

33. For a graphic depiction of the six stages of child-rearing modes, see de Mause, "Evolution of Childhood," 53.

34. Müller, *Fashioning Childhood*, 3.

Chapter 1. Descartes

1. Paul's term is *nēpios*, which signifies a very young child, or a toddler, as opposed to the more general term, *pais*, the root of words such as pediatrics and pedagogy.

2. *A Greek-English Lexicon*, comp. Henry George Liddell et al. (Oxford: Clarendon Press, 1996), 908.

3. J. F. Niermeyer and C. van de Kieft, *Mediae Latinitatis Lexicon Minus: A-L* (Leiden: Brill, 2002), 503.

4. *Oxford Latin Dictionary*, ed. P. G. W. Glare (Oxford: Clarendon Press, 1982), 624.

5. Augustine, *On the Trinity. Books 8–15*, ed. Gareth B. Matthews, trans. Stephen McKenna (Cambridge: Cambridge University Press, 2002), 144.

6. Ibid., 143.

7. Henri Gouhier, *La pensée métaphysique de Descartes*, 4th ed. (Paris: Librairie philosophique J. Vrin, 1999). Translations of Gouhier are mine.

8. Ibid., 52.

9. Cardinal of Bérulle, cited in ibid., 51.

10. Ibid., 52.

11. Ibid., 58.

12. Descartes's understanding of maturation as a purgation of childish things is clearly indebted to Bonaventure. (Thanks to Horst Lange for pointing this out to me.) The first of three ways toward spiritual advancement discussed by Bonaventure is the *via purgativa*, in which one recognizes one's ignorance and attempts to rid oneself of knowledge gained through imagination and the senses. On Descartes's debts to such devotional exercises, see Bradley Rubidge, "Descartes's *Meditations* and Devotional Meditiations," *Journal of the History of Ideas* 51.1 (1990): 27–49.

13. Daniel Garber, *Descartes Embodied: Reading Cartesian Philosophy through Cartesian Science* (Cambridge: Cambridge University Press, 2001).

14. Ibid., 231.

15. Ibid., 249.

16. Ibid., 254.

17. Ibid., 256.

18. The claim that Descartes was a dualist is correct in that he holds that only two types of substance exist: material (extended things) and intellectual (thinking things). But this claim must be nuanced, given that Descartes also sometimes spoke of the intermingling and even union of body and mind, in particular in his 1649 *The Passions of the Soul*. Given this hybrid third realm of inquiry, some have argued that Descartes might be more accurately called a "trialist." See John Cottingham, "Cartesian Trialism," *Mind* 94 (1985): 218–30.

19. For an excellent discussion of Descartes's *Search*, see Saskia Brown, "The Childhood of Reason: Pedagogical Strategies in Descartes's *La recherche de la vérité par la lumière naturelle*," *Romanic Review* 87.4 (1996): 465–80. This article, in particular its glosses on

childhood in other works by Descartes, was quite helpful to me at an early stage of research. Brown concludes by stating that a longer study would be necessary to substantiate the argument that in Descartes, "childhood is *in fact* the starting-point of existence . . . but reason is nevertheless *in essence* timeless, always already mature and at work in an essentially rational humankind" (479). I submit that my chapter provides material in support of precisely this argument.

20. Many biographies identify the German city of Ulm or its environs as the location of Descartes's *poêle*. Reasons to identify Neuburg instead as the locale of Descartes's meditations are outlined in Geneviève Rodis-Lewis, *Descartes: His Life and Thought*, trans. Jane Marie Todd (Ithaca, NY: Cornell University Press, 1999), xiii–xiv and 35–37. Note that the index refers to Neuberg (261), while Rodis-Lewis refers to Neuburg, in both the English translation (xiii, 36) and the original French edition: Geneviève Rodis-Lewis, *Descartes: Biographie* (N.p.: Calmann-Lévy, 1995), 13 and 54. On the current lack of consensus regarding where Descartes meditated, see Richard Watson, *Cogito, Ergo Sum*, 104–7. Note that Watson also refers to Neuberg (106–7), as does Grayling, *Descartes: Life and Times*, 57. Clarke locates Descartes at Neuburg. See Clarke, *Descartes: A Biography*, 58.

21. I have underscored the vocabulary of solitude in Descartes's description of the ideal architect and of his own life because in both cases, such solitary existence appears to be possible only in adulthood. For initial orientation on the large topic of privacy and solitude in Cartesian philosophy, see Kevin Dunn, "'A Great City is a Great Solitude': Descartes's Urban Pastoral," *Yale French Studies* 80 (1991): 93–107.

22. While I focus on age as that which made Descartes's meditations possible, I fully appreciate that location (in Holland) is another. For an excellent discussion of the role of the Dutch Republic in the emergence and dissemination of Cartesian thought, see Jonathan I. Israel, *Radical Enlightenment: Philosophy and the Making of Modernity, 1650–1750* (Oxford: Oxford University Press, 2002), esp. 23–58.

23. Nancy Yousef suggests that Descartes's ideal of solitary maturity must be seen as a *retreat* from sociality and dependence. See her excellent study, *Isolated Cases: The Anxieties of Autonomy in Enlightenment Philosophy and Romantic Literature* (Ithaca, NY: Cornell University Press, 2004), 4–5.

24. This phrase titles a section of Garber's analysis. See Garber, *Descartes Embodied*, 235–42.

25. Descartes reiterates this declaration of independence from his parents in a letter to Claude Clerselier of April 23, 1649: "That is to say, even though everything we are accustomed to believe of them is perhaps true, that is, that they begat our bodies [*ils ont engendré nos cors*], still I cannot imagine that they made me, in so far as I consider myself only as a thing which thinks, because I see no relation between the physical act by which I am accustomed to believe they begat me [*ils m'ont engendré*], and the production of a substance which thinks" (CSMK 378, AT 5:357).

26. I will not speculate on Descartes's piety, but note that Arnauld was convinced of it. As Elmar J. Kremer discusses, Arnauld's writings were not consistently Cartesian, either departing from Descartes's positions on various points whenever religious orthodoxy required it, or else incorrectly interpreting Descartes as continuous with Augustine and Aquinas where Descartes in fact had broken from the traditions they engendered. See "Arnauld's Interpretation of Descartes as a Christian philosopher," in *Interpreting Arnauld*, ed. Elmar J. Kremer (Toronto: University of Toronto Press, 1996), 76–90. Steven

Nadler similarly notes that Arnauld could only be an orthodox Cartesian because he failed to detect anti-Augustinian principles in Descartes's philosophy. See Steven Nadler, *Arnauld and the Cartesian Philosophy of Ideas* (Princeton, NJ: Princeton University Press, 1989), 15ff.

27. After completing this analysis, I read Alan Nelson, "The Falsity in Sensory Ideas," in Kremer, *Interpreting Arnauld*, 13–32. Nelson argues that Descartes's theory of materially false ideas should be understood as a theory of habits of judgment, against what Nelson calls the widely accepted picture, according to which Descartes believed there was an "intrinsic deceptiveness in the phenomenological contents of false ideas" (14). My analysis supports Nelson's view of Descartes's theory of false ideas. Yet I should like to emphasize that this *became* Descartes's theory around 1642, and that this happened due to his discussions with Arnauld and Gassendi concerning infancy.

28. In CSMK, this clause is incorrectly placed.

29. This notion of the body as a prison figures prominently in the second set of replies. Mersenne had asked Descartes to consider whether a body might be capable of thought. Descartes claims that this erroneous view arises only because no one has ever been without a body, and the body has in fact impeded our mental operations; but it does not follow that the body is necessary for thought. "It is just as if someone had had his legs permanently shackled from infancy: he would think that the shackles were part of his body and that he needed them for walking" (CSM 2:96). Now, Descartes is in a curious position, since his "legs" had also been "shackled" from infancy; that is, he has also always been embodied. The liberation Descartes arrogates to himself consists in a consciousness of bodily impediment, which frees the mind, if not from the body, then at least from philosophical materialism.

30. Garber's contrast of the two models contains an inaccuracy: "[The general overthrow of opinions] is to be accomplished not by eliminating them one by one, as his later metaphor of the apple basket suggests, but by eliminating the foundations on which all those prejudices rest" (*Descartes Embodied*, 237). But Descartes did not speak of *removing* the "apples" one by one: the basket is tipped over and emptied just as suddenly as the "beams" of the "house" come crashing down once the "foundation" is removed. And in *Meditations* as well as here, beliefs are added back one by one, as they pass inspection. So there is no difference between the models in terms of sudden elimination and additive reinclusion of beliefs. The difference between the two kinds of elimination concerns anxiety level: an imploding building is certainly more alarming to a human being in the vicinity than is a basket overturning.

31. We cannot avoid having been infants; only Adam and Eve appear to have been so lucky. Principle 45 of part 3 of Descartes's *Principles* notes that "Adam and Eve were not born as babies but were created as fully grown people. This is the doctrine of the Christian faith, and our natural reason convinces us that it was so. For if we consider the infinite power of God, we cannot think that he ever created anything that was not wholly perfect [*absolutum*] of its kind" (CSM 1:256; AT 8A:100). It should be evident that Descartes means here to underscore that babies are not wholly perfect of their kind. One might also recall the passage in *Discourse* where Descartes "reflected that we were all children before being men and had to be governed for some time by our appetites and our teachers . . . hence I thought it virtually impossible that our judgements should be as unclouded and firm as they would have been if we had had the full use of our reason from the moment of our birth, and if we had always been guided by it alone" (CSM

1:117). Citing this passage, Gouhier says that these "strange regrets" are quite integral to a philosophy that regards the necessity of being a child before becoming an adult as "a fundamental obstacle to any search for truth. . . . The age of reason arrives too late" (49). But then the continuation of Descartes's principle is all the more interesting: "Nevertheless, if we want to understand the nature of plants or of men, it is much better to consider how they can gradually grow from seeds than to consider how they were created by God at the very beginning of the world" (CSM 1:256). That is, having made a nod toward creation, as told in the book of Genesis, Descartes says we will understand better if we examine beings in their genesis. Though this general viewpoint would support the study of something like developmental psychology, Descartes's principles focus on the development of planets and living beings. As a physical scientist, Descartes certainly worked to liberate science from theological commitments. But regarding the mind, he seems to have always remained enthralled by the ideal of the adult mind, here depicted by God's finest creations, the adults Adam and Eve.

32. Note that Arnauld bases his theory of ideas in the Port-Royal *Logic* on precisely this notion in Descartes: "Because we were children before we became adults, and because external things acted upon us, causing various sensations in the soul by the impressions they made on the body, the soul saw that these sensations were not caused in it at will, but only on the occasion of certain bodies, for example, when it sensed heat in approaching the fire. But it was not content to judge merely that there was something outside it that caused its sensations, in which case it would not have been mistaken. It went further, believing that what was in these objects was exactly like the sensations or ideas it had on these occasions. From these judgments the soul formed ideas of these things, transporting the sensations of heat, color, and so on, to the things themselves outside the soul. These are the obscure and confused ideas we have of sensible qualities, the soul adding its false judgments to what nature caused it to know." See Antoine Arnauld and Pierre Nicole, *Logic or the Art of Thinking*, ed. Jill Vance Buroker (Cambridge: Cambridge University Press, 1996), 49–50. But for Arnauld and Nicole, there is another source of epistemic trouble than childhood, namely the Fall: "For, as St. Augustine often remarks, since the Fall we have been so accustomed to thinking only about corporeal things, whose images enter the brain by the senses, that the majority believe themselves unable to conceive something if they cannot imagine it, that is, represent it under a corporeal image. It is as if this were the only way we had of thinking and conceiving" (25). Of course Arnauld and Nicole do not believe this is the only way we have of thinking, and they go on to use Descartes's example of conceiving a chiliagon (which cannot be properly imagined) to make this point. Still, as they say, the Fall tends to make us empiricists. I have not observed Arnauld and Nicole to make an explicit connection between their Augustine view of the Fall and their Cartesian view of childhood; this topic would be worth exploring.

33. Gouhier, *La pensée métaphysique*, 50.

34. Arnauld regarded similar statements by Descartes as a sign of his submission before Catholic church authority, rather than as a cautious bow to its temporal power. See Aloyse-Raymond Ndiaye, "The Status of Eternal Truths," in *Interpreting Arnauld*, ed. Kremer, 64–75. Ndiaye makes this interesting summary statement: "What [Arnauld] always liked in Descartes was his submission to the church and his constant care not to meddle in theology, that is, in the theology that arises from Revelation. Because he recognized his incompetence in the area of theology, Descartes was assured of an ally of

great authority in Antoine Arnauld" (74). However, this incompetence could also be regarded as indifference, if not hostility. Cf. Peter A. Schouls, "Arnauld and the Modern
Mind," in *Interpreting Arnauld*, ed. Kremer, 33–50. Underscoring that Arnauld failed to
see Descartes's modernity, Schouls describes Cartesian method as "an emancipation
which firmly launches Western philosophy on the adventure later named 'the Enlightenment'" (42). I cannot quite accept Schouls's claim that "counterbalancing a 'supremely
good' God with a 'malicious demon of the utmost power and cunning (*summe potentem &
callidum*)' has the effect of freeing the thinker from both. Here is the typically modern
mind" (44). Descartes's reliance upon Anselm's ontological proof of God's existence
early in *Meditations*, it seems to me, belies the claim that Descartes has freed the thinker
from God. The thinker can only recognize itself as such because of the meditation-won
conviction that God exists and is good. Of course there is reason to regard Descartes as
an important figure in a tradition of thought that has freed many thinkers from the
power of religious institutions. But I have not seen evidence to suggest that he has freed
thinkers from God, as Schouls suggests. One would have to discuss what sort of God is
in question (Christian, deist, Spinozist, etc.), which topic lies far afield of my present
subject.

35. The Latin term *species* and the French term *espece* have several meanings, including form, impression, image, and representation. In the passages I cite, "impression"
seems to be the best translation. For a discussion of the scholastic doctrine of species, see
New Advent Catholic Encyclopedia, art. "species": http://www.newadvent.org/cathen/14210a.
htm.

36. Typically, tracks that appear not to be human are attributed to animals. Parallels
between children and animals have a long history, and they appear in Descartes's correspondence with Henry More as well. In his letter to More of February 5, 1649, Descartes explains that appearances might lead one to believe that animals have sensations as
we humans do, and thus that they have thoughts of a sort. But he concludes that it is
more likely that animals act as though they were machines, than that they have thoughts.
The crucial point of this argument is that animals have not been observed to use human
speech. In his letter to Descartes of March 5, 1649, More wrote: "You could say the like
about infants" (AT 5:311, quoted in CSMK 374). To this Descartes replied, in a letter of
April 15, 1649: "Infants are in a different case from animals [*Dispar est ratio infantum &
brutorum*]: I should not judge that infants were endowed with minds unless I saw that
they were of the same nature as adults; but animals never develop to a point where any
certain sign of thought can be detected in them" (CSMK 374, AT 5:345). Looked at empirically, minded infants and unminded animals seem indistinguishable. Given that Descartes believes that mind is present and active in infants, this apparent equation of infants and animals seems rather startling. But of course, we should not trust what we see
when we look at infants empirically; we should rather examine them rationally. And then
we recognize that infants partake of human nature, despite appearances to the contrary.

37. See Ralph Heyndels, "*Camera obscura* de la mémoire: Descartes," *Biblio* 17 (1993):
259–66. (Translations of Heyndels are mine.) Heyndels observes in Descartes "the obligation to remember to forget (or if one prefers, not forgetting to forget)" (260), specifically "not forgetting to forget received opinions" (263). See also Timothy J. Reiss,
"Denying the Body? Memory and the Dilemmas of History in Descartes," *Journal of the
History of Ideas* 57.4 (1996): 587–607. Reiss initially follows Heyndels in discussing Descartes's "*will to forget*" (595) his books, histories, and experiences of body. However, Reiss

goes on to note that method is not a matter of forgetting prejudice; rather, method is about opposing prejudice with counter-prejudice, the point being "to render this physical history inoperative" (ibid.).

38. Reiss notes that Descartes took from Aristotle the idea of memory as a wax imprint, but also "the thought that memory came both from the external and the internal world" (Reiss, "Denying the Body?" 596), which may have been the source of Descartes's distinction between physical and intellectual memory. See the thought-provoking essay by Neil Hertz, "Dr. Johnson's Forgetfulness, Descartes' Piece of Wax," *Eighteenth Century Life* 16.3 (1992): 167–81. Hertz explains that Descartes's choice of wax as an object to manipulate in the second meditation derives in part from its having been commonly used in the seventeenth century to seal letters, that is, to receive the imprint of the sender's signet ring. This use of wax has been, since Aristotle, "the privileged figure for the receptivity of the senses, or of the memory, or of the imagination or, more vaguely, of the mind" (175). In Hertz's view, this sense of receptivity is disavowed in *Meditations*, in which Descartes's mind "suppress[es] at once the figurative nature of its operations and the fact that its meditative progress is inseparable from writing" (178). See also the excellent essay by Margreta de Grazia, "Imprints: Shakespeare, Gutenberg, and Descartes," in *Printing and Parenting in Early Modern England*, ed. Douglas A. Brooks (Hampshire: Ashgate, 2005), 29–58. Following Hertz, de Grazia emphasizes that Descartes's "choice of wax was a choice of wax-without-signet" (30). That is, Descartes's refiguration of this figure from Plato and Aristotle signals his desire to dismantle this traditional epistemology and metaphysics.

39. Reiss, "Denying the Body?" 600–601.

40. On the absence of memory from Descartes's list of the mental faculties in *Principles*, see Heyndels, "*Camera obscura*," 261.

41. Heyndels regards Descartes's failure to explicate the difference between the two forms of memory as no biographical contingency, but as necessary for his philosophy, "an essential caesura" (ibid., 264) between a traceable physical memory and an intellectual or metaphysical memory that "has no proper place" (ibid.). In Heyndels's view, precisely this impropriety allows radical doubt to function. The result of subsequent meditation is that "intellectual memory effectively invents the moment of a fictive anteriority" (265) in which certain knowledge of God and geometry will have resided. It is because its function is to form a foundation myth (that of reason) that the precise place of intellectual memory is inscrutable in Descartes.

42. Gareth Matthews has shown that Plato wavered on the question whether children can be suitable philosophers. See Gareth Matthews, "Socrates's Children," in *Philosopher's Child*, ed. Turner and Matthews, 11–18.

43. Augustine writes that perhaps we should believe of the infant mind that it too "knows itself, but is too intent on those things through which it begins to experience pleasure through the senses of the body. . . . So too with the other senses of the body: the souls of children so confine themselves, as it were, by their concentration upon them, insofar as that age permits any concentration at all, that they either intensely abhor or else desire nothing else except that which harms or entices them through the flesh. They have no thought of their inner self" (Augustine, *On the Trinity*, 143–44).

44. Heyndels, "*Camera obscura*," 262.

45. Support for this notion of epistemological adult baptism is given in Descartes's image at the outset of meditation two: "So serious are the doubts into which I have been

thrown as a result of yesterday's meditation that I can neither put them out of my mind nor see any way of resolving them. It feels as if I have fallen unexpectedly into a deep whirlpool which tumbles me around so that I can neither stand on the bottom nor swim up to the top" (CSM 2:16). For a discussion of this passage in relation to Descartes's usual images of pathways and roads, see Georges Van Den Abbeele, *Travel as Metaphor: From Montaigne to Rousseau* (Minneapolis: University of Minnesota Press, 1992), 41–48.

46. As Nelson explicates, the bad habits of judgment that Descartes opposes "serve well in childhood, and even in everyday life, but not when doing philosophy" (Nelson, "Falsity in Sensory Ideas," 14). Indeed, obscure and confused sensory ideas are quite useful in preserving life, and thus Descartes does not seem to lament them per se. They "can be disastrous, however, for anyone embarking on a philosophical or scientific project" (ibid., 26).

Chapter 2. Locke and Leibniz

1. John Locke, *An Essay concerning Human Understanding*, ed. Peter H. Nidditch (Oxford: Clarendon Press, 1975). This modern edition is based on the fourth edition of 1700, the last one in which Locke made substantial changes. Subsequent references to this work are cited parenthetically in the text by book, chapter, and section numbers; references to Locke's prefatory material are given by the abbreviation "*Essay*" and page numbers in Nidditch's edition.

My research indicates that most histories of childhood that involve Locke refer only to his *Some Thoughts*. See John Locke, *Some Thoughts Concerning Education and Of the Conduct of the Understanding*, ed. Ruth W. Grant and Nathan Tarcov (Indianapolis: Hackett, 1996). Some refer to the *Essay* as well, but do so quite generally and restrict their claims to summaries of book 1. For example, C. John Sommerville, in *The Rise and Fall of Childhood* (Beverly Hills: Sage, 1982) simply identifies Locke's *Essay* as an "attack on innate ideas" (121). Hugh Cunningham, in *Children and Childhood in Western Society Since 1500* (Harlow: Pearson Education Limited, 2005) states that the *Essay* regards the child as a blank slate in ideas, if not in temperament (60). Steven Mintz, in *Huck's Raft. A History of American Childhood* (Cambridge: Harvard University Press, 2004) actually misidentifies Locke's *Essay* as a childrearing tract (51); perhaps this was a slip. Mintz's other references to Locke simply mention the doctrine of malleability. A slightly more comprehensive view of childhood in Locke and in the *Essay* is given in David Archard, *Children. Rights and Childhood* (Oxon: Routledge, 2004), 1–11. Archard recognizes that Locke writes different things about children in different contexts; Archard discusses not only Locke's *Some Thoughts* and *Of the Conduct of the Understanding* but also the political *Treatises*. Still, his comments on the *Essay* are restricted to the topic of empiricism and the white paper thesis. Thus, Archard's presentation of the *Essay* concentrates on book 1 and gets no further than 2.2.24. For another version of his presentation, which however says little more of the *Essay*, see David Archard, "John Locke's Children," in *Philosopher's Child*, ed. Turner and Matthews, 85–103.

2. See John W. Yolton, *A Locke Dictionary* (Cambridge: Blackwell, 1993), 37.

3. On the Descartes-Locke relationship, see Peter A. Schouls, *Reasoned Freedom: John Locke and the Enlightenment* (Ithaca, NY: Cornell University Press, 1992), esp. 1–37.

4. Cf. Nicholas Jolley, *Locke: His Philosophical Thought* (Oxford: Oxford University Press, 1999). Jolley notes that recent scholars have "sought to throw off the shackles of

a historiography inspired by German idealism" (2), which regarded the *Essay* as primarily concerned with promoting the doctrine of empiricism. Reading Locke more carefully has allowed recent scholars to depict him less as "a philosopher obsessed with the problem of breaking out of the circle of ideas" (ibid.) and more as "a scientific realist" (ibid., 3). But this advance has still resulted in a one-sided view of Locke, such that "it comes as something of a shock and surprise to discover that the original impetus to the writing of the *Essay* came, not from the natural sciences, but from a discussion of the principles of morality and revealed religion" (ibid.). Jolley recognizes that this religious concern is also central to Locke's chapter on personal identity; see 100–103. Jolley's study, which touches on many aspects of the *Essay*, considers neither the personhood of infants nor the fate of infants and changelings on Judgment Day. On changelings, see my chapter 4.

5. G. W. Leibniz, *New Essays on Human Understanding*, ed. and trans. Peter Remnant and Jonathan Bennett (Cambridge: Cambridge University Press, 1996). Subsequent references to this work are cited parenthetically in the text as the abbreviation *"NE"* with page numbers.

6. See Bertrand Russell, *The Philosophy of Leibniz* (New York: Routledge, 1997), 163–64.

7. Turner and Matthews explain "the often cursory and sometimes unphilosophical manner in which . . . philosophers present their views about children and childhood" by noting that most of their claims about children and childhood "fall into the category of the *obvious*" (Turner and Matthews, *Philosopher's Child*, 1).

8. Remnant and Bennett render "ce que j'appelle des pensées sourdes en partie" as "partly of the kind I call *blind*" (*NE* 254, G 5:236; my emphasis), rather than *deaf*. The difference between the ocular and acoustic register is not crucial for my argument, but it seems worth noting that Leibniz chose the latter. Remnant and Bennett's translation choice seems all the more regrettable if one recalls Leibniz's exemplification of minute perceptions in the inability to distinguish the sounds of individual waves as one listens at shore to the roaring of the sea. (See *NE* 54–55.)

9. See William Walker, "Locke Minding Women: Literary History, Gender, and the *Essay*," *Eighteenth-Century Studies* 23.3 (1990): 245–68. My own sentence is a modification of Walker's: "In the *Essay*, woman is before the beginning" (249). Walker argues interestingly and often convincingly that women have an important presence (and absence) in Locke's *Essay*. I engage some of Walker's arguments in several notes following.

10. On the classical epigraph, see Stephen Buckle, "British Sceptical Realism: A Fresh Look at the British Tradition," *European Journal of Philosophy* 7.1 (1999): 1–29. Since this epigraph urges us to admit our ignorance rather than to speak about what we do not know, it seems reasonable to assume that it announces Locke's attack on doctrines of substance. On a surprising aspect of the quote's context in Cicero—it marks an academic criticism of epicureans, who are closest in doctrine to the corpuscularians Locke supported—see ibid., 4.

The biblical epigraph indicates the influence of embryology on Locke's thinking. Locke had been exposed to and took interest in the work of Jan Swammerdam and Antoni van Leeuwenhock. See Peter Walmsley, *Locke's* Essay *and the Rhetoric of Science* (Lewisburg, PA: Bucknell University Press, 2003). By 1700, embryology had developed sufficiently such that the natural historian "could no longer simply describe the mature specimen, but was compelled, more and more, to plot out stories of generation, growth, and decay" (60). Locke's interest in the *Essay* is generally mental rather than material, but similarities between the *Essay* and embryology obtain, such as "the impulse to search out origins, a conviction of the explanatory powers of narratives of beginnings, and a recognition of the remarkable transformations that time effects on living beings" (63).

11. Buckle, "British Sceptical Realism," 4.

12. Ibid.

13. Walker suggests that Locke does more than sound a note of epistemological modesty: "The possible analogy between God/works and woman/child is stifled by a grammar that grants 'her' not a way or activity of making, but only the status of the site of a mysterious growth" (Walker, "Locke Minding Women," 249). That is, Walker reads gender bias in this passage. This conclusion fails to persuade, if one recalls that in section 53 of the *First Discourse*, Locke argued that *neither* the father *nor* the mother should be regarded as the proper makers of their children, since neither can account for how children are made. Children are, rather, made by God, and no parents can pretend to be their children's creators. See John Locke, *Two Treatises of Government and A Letter Concerning Toleration*, ed. Ian Shapiro (New Haven: Yale University Press, 2003), 36. I certainly do not wish to argue that Locke has no bias against women—indeed, I think that Locke's bias has been minimized in a number of scholarly treatments, including feminist ones—but rather that this bias is not on display in this epigraph.

14. On natural law theory, see J. B. Schneewind, "Locke's Moral Philosophy," in *The Cambridge Companion to Locke*, ed. Vere Chappell (Cambridge: Cambridge University Press, 1994), 199–225. Given Leibniz's citation of Paul, it is worth noting that Locke himself cites Paul in section 19 of *The Reasonableness of Christianity*, arguing precisely as Leibniz did in the *New Essays*. It is all the more a pity that Locke did not engage Leibniz in dialogue. See John Locke, *The Reasonableness of Christianity*, ed. George W. Ewing (Washington, DC: Regnery, 1997), 9.

15. In another context, Locke approvingly cites the same verse from Paul. (See Locke, *Reasonableness*, 9). But he underscores that although the law of nature (part of the law of works, distinguished from the law of faith) is knowable by reason, it is not easily knowable. If Locke had encountered Leibniz's defense of innate ideas as being like veins in marble, he might well have replied with this statement from his *Essays on the Laws of Nature*: "Concealed in the bowels of the earth lie veins richly provided with gold and silver; human beings besides are possessed with arms and hands with which they can dig these out, and of reason which invents machines. Yet from this we do not conclude that all men are wealthy" (qtd. in Locke, *Reasonableness*, 162).

16. Understanding is for Locke a matter of kind (either/or), for Leibniz a matter of degree (more/less). But Locke and Leibniz differ in the opposite way regarding reason. For Leibniz, reason is a matter of kind, whereas Locke held that one can have more or less reason, and that "one" need not even be human.

17. See Nicholas Jolley, *Leibniz and Locke: A Study of the* New Essays on Human Understanding (Oxford: Clarendon Press, 1984). Jolley has argued, in my opinion convincingly, that Leibniz's reply reads coherently when read as a refutation of the materialism that Locke's account either maintained or at least held open as a possibility. "From a Leibnizian perspective, the central issue between Locke and himself is not epistemological at all; it is metaphysical. The chief focus of Leibniz's hostility to Locke's philosophy is what he takes to be its pervasively materialist tendency" (6–7).

18. The reason we can trust this candle light becomes clear in book 4, where we learn that it is "the Candle of the Lord set up by himself in Men's minds" (4.3.20).

19. Leibniz's concession that "it is true that explicit knowledge of truths is subsequent (in temporal or natural order) to the explicit knowledge of ideas" (*NE* 81) is immediately followed by the claim that neither intellectual ideas nor truths "originate in the senses; though it is true that without the senses we would never think of them" (ibid.). That is, our knowledge begins with but does not originate in the senses. Cf. Immanuel Kant, *Critique of Pure Reason*, trans. Norman Kemp Smith (New York: St. Martin's Press, 1965). The claim with which Kant opened his first critique echoes Leibniz: "There can be no doubt that all our knowledge begins with experience. . . . In the order of time, therefore, we have no knowledge antecedent to experience, and with experience all our knowledge begins" (41). A new paragraph then starts: "But though all our knowledge begins with experience, it does not follow that it all arises out of experience" (ibid.).

20. See *G. W. Leibniz's* Monadology: *An Edition for Students*, ed. Nicholas Rescher (Pittsburgh: University of Pittsburgh Press, 1991). In section 56, Leibniz writes: "Now this interlinkage or accommodation of all created things to each other, and of each to all the others, brings it about that each simple substance has relations that express all the others, and is in consequence a perpetual living mirror of the universe" (24; see also 198–200).

21. Jolley states that the monad is confusedly omniscient, though subject to time (Jolley, *Leibniz and Locke*, 29). Compare Leibniz in section 13 of the *Principles of Nature and Grace*: Each soul knows the infinite—knows all—but confusedly (AG 211).

22. It is not conclusive whether Leibniz argues the strong version of innate ideas (that all ideas are innate) or the weak one (that some ideas are innate); there seems to be evidence for both positions. On the difference between dispositional, implicit, and unconscious knowledge in Leibniz, see Jolley, *Leibniz and Locke*, 170–75.

23. Jolley argues that the textbook distinction between rationalism and empiricism is of limited use in helping one understand seventeenth-century philosophers in general, Locke and Leibniz in particular. See ibid., 4–6.

24. See Henri Ellenberger, *The Discovery of the Unconscious: The History and Evolution of Dynamic Psychiatry* (n.p.: Basic, 1970). Ellenberger traces Leibniz's influence on Freud via Herbart, who "took the concept of small perceptions and the threshold from Leibniz, but introduced a dynamic viewpoint" (312). It is relevant to Herbart's supposed innovation that, as Ellenberger himself points out, "Leibniz is generally credited with having coined the word 'dynamic'" (289). Cf. Paul Ricoeur, *Freud and Philosophy: An Essay on Interpretation*, trans. Denis Savage (New Haven: Yale University Press, 1970). Ricoeur considers Nietzsche, Schopenhauer, and Spinoza as Freud's forerunners, but states that "perhaps the one who most clearly prefigures Freud is Leibniz" (455). After comparing Leibniz on appetites as perceptions and Freud on affects as instinctual representatives, Ricoeur asks "What is an existent that has an archaeology?" then comments that "the answer seemed easy prior to Freud: it is a being who was a child before being a man. But we still do not know what that means" (457).

25. See Douglas Greenlee, "Locke and the Controversy over Innate Ideas," *Journal of the History of Ideas* 33.2 (1972): 251–64. Greenlee notes that "the bulk of Book I turns out upon examination to consist in an attack upon innate principles rather than innate ideas" (251). Explaining the difference, he distinguishes between meaning and truth, "for ideas merely are, whereas principles are true (or false)" (258). The question motivating

Locke's attack is what gives us purchase on truth: supposed innate principles implanted by the divine understanding, as Locke's unnamed opponents would have it, or the activity of human understanding, as Locke held.

26. See Boas, *Cult of Childhood*. Boas describes the cult of childhood as one part of a general history of cultural primitivism, defined as the belief that contemporary culture is degenerate compared to an earlier manifestation of culture. This earlier manifestation may be represented by a chronological or a cultural archetype, and the most likely candidates at various times were "Woman, the Child, the Folk (rural), and later the Irrational or Neurotic, and the Collective Unconscious" (8). All of these candidates inherited qualities previously attributed to the noble savage.

27. The ultimate aim of this and the following chapter is to sketch Locke's uses of the term "child." I take Locke's "idiot" to signify a human being with life but little or no understanding. For an excellent discussion of how the idiot became a category problem for postrestoration dissenters, see C. F. Goodey and Tim Stainton, "Intellectual Disability and the Myth of the Changeling Myth," *Journal of the History of Behavioral Sciences* 37.3 (2001): 223–40.

28. Contemporary dictionaries and encyclopedias regularly depict children as lacking intelligence and reason. For several examples, see the introduction to this study.

29. Locke's influence on Rousseau is here particularly evident. In his preface to *Émile*, Rousseau states: "We know nothing of infancy." Jean-Jacques Rousseau, *Œuvres complètes*, vol. 4 (n.p.: Gallimard, 1969), 241, my translation. In Allan Bloom's translation: Rousseau, *Emile or On Education* (n.p.: Basic, 1979), the sentence reads: "Childhood is unknown" (33). Barbara Foxley's translation: Rousseau, *Émile* (London: Everyman, 1993) renders it "We know nothing of childhood" (1). This is not the place to do so, but I would argue that books 2 through 4 of *Émile* do indeed purport to express a knowledge of childhood, whereas book 1 tends to emphasize our nonunderstanding of infancy; hence my translation. Caveat lector: Foxley's translation is abridged, though the edition nowhere states this fact.

30. Leibniz's statement that "it is appropriate that children should attend more to the notions of the senses, because attention is governed by need" (*NE* 86) recalls Descartes's view that sensate knowledge is useful for preserving life, if an impediment to science and philosophy.

31. Locke says that the intellectual activity of counting requires having the concept of "one," as well as a functioning memory, but an important second requirement is having names. "This, I think, to be the reason why some *Americans*, I have spoken with, (who were otherwise of quick and rational Parts enough,) could not, as we do, by any means count to 1000; nor had any distinct *Idea* of that Number, though they could reckon very well to 20. Because their Language being scanty . . . the *Tououpinambos* had no Names for Numbers above 5" (2.16.6). The question is whether children lack counting skills for the same reason (lack of names) as the Americans and Tououpinambos, or whether a deficit of memory, a general cognitive deficit, or a lack of knowledge of unity is to blame. "Thus Children either for want of Names to mark the several Progressions of Numbers, or not yet having the faculty to collect scattered *Ideas* into complex ones, and range them in a regular Order, and so retain them in their Memories, as is necessary to reckoning, do not begin to number very early, nor proceed in it very far or steadily, till a good while after they are well furnished with good store of other Ideas . . . before they can tell 20" (2.16.7). Locke concludes this chapter with two prerequisites to reckoning right: distin-

guishing ideas and retaining names in memory. In the case of Americans and Tououpinambos, lack of names in their languages is to blame. In the case of English children
who have sufficiently mastered their native language, a deficit of memory or of distinguishing ideas must be to blame. The proximity of children and savages is certainly
worth noting, but here I am struck by the difference between the categories. That is,
Americans have a deficient language but are of rational Parts; children are not of rational
Parts. To use Boas's terms: Locke does not here conflate cultural and chronological primitivism. (Leibniz is silent on Americans, Toupinambi, and children's counting abilities.)

32. One can see exactly this program being followed in the work of Dietrich Tiedemann, who is known as one of the first developmental psychologists. See Dietrich Tiedemann, "Beobachtungen über die Entwickelung der Seelenfähigkeiten bei Kindern," *Hessische Beiträge zur Gelehrsamkeit und Kunst* 2.2 (Frankfurt am Main, 1787), 313–33 and
486–502; translations mine. Tiedemann sought to further the nascent study of "the development of human mental powers" (502) and he attributed the lack of progress in the
field to the paucity of "precise and sufficiently numerous observations of children's
minds" (313). Thus he published notes on his son's development from birth to two and
one half years of age. A partial translation is available as "Tiedemann's observations on
the development of the mental faculties of children," *Pedagogical Seminary* 34 (1927):
205–60. For a discussion of Tiedemann's place in the history of psychology, see Siegfried
Jaeger, "The Origin of the Diary Method in Developmental Psychology," in *Contributions to a History of Developmental Psychology*, ed. Georg Eckardt et al. (Berlin: Mouton,
1985), 63–74.

33. Boas traces the concept of the child as *speculum naturae* to Cicero, who attributes
this notion to Epicurus, but the concept seems to extend far into Greek antiquity. See
Boas, *Cult of Childhood*, 14–15.

34. Here the idiot takes the role of the cretin, a term deriving from *chrétien*, the good
Christian, and pointing toward the doctrine of the holy innocent. See Goodey and Stainton, "Intellectual Disability," 225.

35. Leibniz has often been referred to as a cosmopolitan thinker, and his writings on
the natural wisdom of the Chinese are often cited as unusual among his eurocentric contemporaries. In the *New Essays*, at least, Leibniz states that "nations which have cultivated their minds have some grounds with crediting themselves with using good sense
and savages with not doing so" (*NE* 98) but also that "savages surpass us in some important ways, especially in bodily vigour. Even with regard to the soul, their practical
morality can be said to be in some respects better than ours" (*NE* 99). The conclusion of
this passage calls for a certain hybridity: "There is, however, nothing to prevent men
from combining the advantages which nature gives to these people with those which reason gives to us" (ibid.). Whether this call to mix the old and new worlds amounts to cos-
mopolitanism is another question. There seems to be ample evidence that in some respects, Leibniz was happy to be a European. His antipathy to Islam has been recently
discussed in Ian Almond, "Leibniz, Historicism, and the 'Plague of Islam,'" *Eighteenth-
Century Studies* 39.4 (2006): 463–83.

36. Pierre Bayle cited atrocities quite similar to Locke's in order to dispute the possibility of *rationally* comprehending God's goodness: according to reason, Bayle argues,
God is a monster. Leibniz's response to Locke here is similar to his later response to
Bayle: Leibniz defends God with the concept of an optimal world. On Bayle and Leibniz, see my chapter 4.

37. Locke, *Two Treatises*, 38.

38. Schouls argues that "Locke rejects all but one of the forms of the doctrine of original sin" (Schouls, *Freedom*, 193), putting in its place a doctrine "of original neutrality" (ibid.). This view of the noncorrupted state of the intellect and will does seem to follow from Locke's *Reasonableness*, but I am unsure how *original neutrality* can explain passages like those of 1.3.13 in the *Essay*. In any case, Schouls chooses this term over alternatives such as *original innocence*, explaining that "no human beings start out from either innocence or guilt but from a position which, once left, will place them in the camp of the innocent or the guilty" (ibid., 197). Schouls does not explain when this position is left, nor what God decides about those who never had a chance to choose one or the other camp.

39. One might well ask whether there is a contradiction between Locke's denial of original sin in *The Reasonableness of Christianity* and his affirmation in the *Essay* that our appetites are disordered. (In orthodox Christian theology, disordered appetites are the result of original sin.) An excellent study examining Locke's relation to the Broad Church movement is provided by W. M. Spellman, *John Locke and the Problem of Depravity* (Oxford: Clarendon Press, 1988).

40. Locke's conclusion here echoes Descartes's criticism of sensate knowledge. In both cases, we are said to have forgotten what really happened in childhood.

41. Cf. Schouls, who underscores "Locke's anti-trust stance" (Schouls, *Freedom*, 26). Even children should only accept as true that which they clearly and distinctly perceive to be true. While I agree on the importance of this stance for Locke, it seems nonetheless to follow that if young children, according to Locke's presentation, cannot perceive things distinctly, then the anti-trust stance cannot hold for early childhood.

42. Greenlee, "Locke and the Controversy," 264.

43. Ibid.

44. Walker, "Locke Minding Women," 251.

45. Leibniz says very little about Locke's discussion of principling children other than to "acknowledge that the distinguished author . . . says some very fine things on that score" (*NE* 100).

46. Schouls, *Freedom*, 25–27.

47. Ibid., 93, my emphasis.

48. Ibid., 93–94.

49. Cf. Yolton, *A Locke Dictionary*, 30–33. The mental faculties of young children and animals seem to overlap until children are capable of abstraction.

50. Schouls notes the similarity of Cartesian and Lockean method, and recalls that Locke invites us to "dare shake the foundations of all [our] past Thoughts and Actions" (1.3.25) in "one of the most revolutionary passages of the *Essay*" (Schouls, *Freedom*, 26). Earlier, Schouls noted that "Locke was a revolutionary because he accepted Descartes's method" (ibid., 9).

51. Locke says that children's minds "may be disposed to consent to nothing but what may be suitable to the dignity and excellency of a rational creature" (Locke, *Some Thoughts*, 25; sec. 31). He is aware that most readers will raise an objection to regarding children as rational creatures: "It will perhaps be wondered that I mention *reasoning* with children; and yet I cannot but think that the true way of dealing with them" (58; sec. 81). His ensuing discussion clarifies that one reasons with children differently than one does with adults, but it is still remarkable that he retains the term.

52. Touching obliquely on theological debates about free vs. enslaved will, Locke says the question is badly posed: liberty belongs to the man, not to the will. Locke holds that talk about an enslaved will is motivated by a desire to shift personal guilt off from oneself (2.21.22). It seems that for Locke, there is no guilt that is not personal. Of course this conclusion entails that beings that are not persons cannot be guilty of anything. As I go on to show, infants and changelings are just such beings.

53. Locke's example of the animal's inability to discern is relevant not only to intellectual life, but to emotional life as well: dogs that have multiple puppies in a litter seem not to notice when one or two are removed surreptitiously. (See 2.11.7.) Presumably, this oversight would be unthinkable with human parents. Here, one might recall Locke's single viable candidate for an innate practical idea (could one exist): "Parents, preserve and cherish your children." Lacking discernment, animals are even less capable than humans of following this command.

54. See Kathryn J. Ready, "Damaris Cudworth Masham, Catharine Trotter Cockburn, and the Feminist Legacy of Locke's Theory of Personal Identity," *Eighteenth-Century Studies* 35.4 (2002): 563–76. However, it seems to me that a feminist appropriation of Locke would have to adequately explain his several explicit statements about the fair sex's lack of intellectual abilities in general, whatever he may have thought of Damaris Masham in particular. For a start, see the recent collection by Nancy J. Hirschmann and Kirstie M. McClure, *Feminist Interpretations of John Locke* (University Park: Pennsylvania State University Press, 2007).

55. Locke, *Reasonableness*, 3.

56. Ibid., 6.

57. See Derek Parfit, "Personal Identity," *The Philosophical Review* (1971): 34–47 and *Reasons and Persons* (Oxford: Clarendon Press, 1984). See also Harold W. Noonan, *Personal Identity* (London: Routledge, 1989), 163–77.

58. In the first section of *The Reasonableness of Christianity*, Locke referred to the Augustinians as representing one bad theological extreme: "Some men would have all Adam's posterity doomed to eternal infinite punishment for the transgression of Adam (whom millions had never heard of, and no one had authorized to transact for him or to be his representative)" (Locke, *Reasonableness*, 1). In the ensuing pages, Locke concludes that "everyone's sin is charged upon himself only" (ibid., 4). Although Locke agrees that in Adam we all die, Locke takes death to signify eternal nonexistence rather than eternal punishment. Since existence was God's gift, not owed to us, nonexistence cannot be interpreted as a punishment. This is how Locke can conclude that "therefore, though all die in Adam, yet none are truly punished but for their own deeds" (ibid., 5).

59. Locke states that "the sentence of condemnation passes only upon the workers of iniquity" (Locke, *Reasonableness*, 5), whereas those who work obediently "might have a title" or even "a claim of right to eternal life" (6). This binary view leaves unexplained what fate will befall human beings as yet incapable of "work." Locke does not provide clarity on this point as he goes on to discuss the law of faith (as opposed to the law of works). He explains that according to this new law, "faith is allowed to supply the defect of full obedience; and so the believers are admitted to life and immortality as if they were righteous" (10). The Protestant notion of "baby faith" (about which see my chapter 4, note 10) would have allowed him to include baptized infants into this class, but Locke says nothing about this. And his comments on baptism omit mention of children or in-

fants. Given Locke's fame as the first philosopher of childhood, it is striking that children form a category error in his discussions of God's justice.

60. For an overview of the reception of Locke as a simple memory theorist, see Raymond Martin and John Barresi, *Naturalization of the Soul: Self and Personal Identity in the Eighteenth Century* (London: Routledge, 2000), 16–17.

61. Ibid., 20.

62. Ibid., 20–21.

63. Ibid., 21.

64. I take the view expressed in Leibniz's 1710 *Theodicy*, that identity is located in spermatozoa, to be his settled one. Around 1705, it seems Leibniz was still considering the possibility of ovism, though his preference for spermism is also obvious: "we do not know for sure with animals whether it is the male or the female, or both, or neither, which mainly determines the species. The theory of the female ovum . . . seemed to reduce males to a position like that of moist air in relation to plants. . . . But M. Leeuwenhoek has restored the male kind to its eminence, and the other sex has been lowered accordingly and regarded as having only the function which earth has with respect to seeds, namely providing them with lodging and nourishment. That could be the case even if we still accepted the theory of ova" (*NE* 316). For a presentation of contemporary discussions of biological preformation, relevant to Leibniz's ultimate choice of the sperm as the vehicle for the soul, see Clara Pinto-Correia, *The Ovary of Eve: Egg and Sperm and Preformation* (Chicago: University of Chicago Press, 1997), 83 and 92–94.

65. In the *Second Treatise*, Locke states that children "are not born in this state of equality, though they are born to it" (Locke, *Two Treatises*, 123; sec. 55). Meanwhile, the law of nature requires all parents to care for their children until they become reasonable. But does this ward status begin with birth? Since Locke named abortion an atrocity, it seems one could rephrase the statement and conclude that Locke held that children are not conceived in this state of equality, though they are conceived to it.

Chapter 3. Locke

1. Leibniz noticed this discrepancy between Locke's eloquence and his denunciation of eloquence as well: "sir, you seem to be fighting eloquence with its own weapons, having at your command an eloquence which is superior to the deceptive kind you are attacking. . . . But that very fact proves that your thesis needs to be moderated and that certain devices of eloquence are like the Egyptian vases which could be used in the worship of the true God" (*NE* 350).

2. Susan Haack, "'Dry Truth and Real Knowledge': Epistemologies of Metaphor and Metaphors of Epistemology," in *Manifesto of a Passionate Moderate: Unfashionable Essays* (Chicago: University of Chicago Press, 1998), 69–89; here 69.

3. Ibid., 78.

4. Ibid., 88.

5. Haack cheerfully states that "Locke's position is mistaken; metaphor may be a very useful device of instructive discourse" (ibid., 78). If this is so, then Locke's use of metaphor in the *Essay* would not preclude one from regarding the *Essay* as philosophy, according to the distinction between the civil/philosophical use of words: it just means that Locke was wrong about the usefulness of his own metaphors in his instructive discourse.

6. Paul de Man, "The Epistemology of Metaphor," *Critical Inquiry* 5.1 (1978): 13–30; here 15.

7. Ibid., 14.

8. Ibid.

9. Ibid., 21.

10. Ibid.

11. Here I allude to Friedrich Schlegel's essay on incomprehensibility. For a thoroughly intelligible discussion of Schlegel as an important influence on de Man, see Avital Ronell, *Stupidity* (Urbana: University of Illinois Press, 2002), 110–61.

12. Haack, "Dry Truth," 72.

13. In a first move, de Man says that "in fact, we discourse a great deal about simple ideas" (de Man, "Epistemology of Metaphor," 17). Locke himself showed the absurdity of such discourse at 3.4.9 with the example of defining motion as passage (when passage means motion anyway). De Man continues Locke's demonstration of absurdity by showing that the phrase *to understand the idea of light* ends up meaning *to light the light of light*. Though Locke decries the failure to define in one place (*passage* fails to define *motion*), he is guilty, according to de Man, of failing to define in other crucial places: Locke's *idea* fails to translate *light* and even worse, *understand* fails to translate *understanding*. The simple idea, in de Man's reading, is anything but simple: it is rather a "delusion of light, of understanding, or of definition. This complication of the simple will run through the entire argument" (18). In drawing this conclusion, de Man makes a small error in saying that Locke's simple ideas are "simpleminded; they are not the objects of understanding" (17). De Man here confuses understanding and reason as Locke uses the terms. That is, simple ideas may be nondiscursive, but they are most certainly in the understanding, that is, in the mind. The problem de Man underscores (the discursive deployment of that which is supposedly nondiscursive) is certainly a problem in Locke, but I believe it is not where de Man located it, that is, in the discussion of simple ideas. Rather, the problem is located in the movement from simple ideas (which are given in the understanding directly by the senses) to complex ideas (which are formed in the understanding by the understanding, in comparing and contrasting simple ideas, or by reason, which examines the connections between ideas). De Man is correct to think of the child, who apprehends simple ideas, as "a stuttering idiot but, at least from an epistemological point of view, a happy one" (18). The happiness derives from children's perceiving particulars. (Recall that Locke stated that particulars are the only true existents.) Although we do need general concepts to do more than stammer, these general concepts are never adequate to the particularity of the world. Thus one might say that children are happy understanding idiots, whereas adults are unhappy reasoners. In a second move, de Man follows Locke's discussion of complex ideas of substances (that of *Man* in particular) to one of its category problems (how can we distinguish between the changeling, which de Man took to be the simpleminded child, and an animal?). Where Locke here invites us to "quit the common notion of species and essences" (4.4.16), de Man concludes that "this would reduce us to the mindless stammer of simple ideas and make us into a philosophical 'changeling'" (de Man, "Epistemology of Metaphor," 20). It rather seems to me that Locke's urging us to "quit the common notion of species and essences" is part of his call for a nominalist taxonomy, against the received scholastic one, which believed it had access to real essences. It is not evident to me how this call reduces our discussions of the

complex idea of Man to a simpleminded chatter. This is neither Locke's conclusion, nor does de Man convincingly prove it. (Also, de Man here conflates the changeling and the idiot.) Thus, in my estimation, de Man shows the complication of the simple, but fails to show the simplification of the complex.

14. De Man, "Epistemology of Metaphor," 17.

15. Ibid., 20.

16. Ibid., 19.

17. Ibid., 18.

18. A later passage in chapter 4.6 specifies why we have so little knowledge and certainty concerning substances. Most of the chapter concerns gold (4.6.4–10), with the occasional pansy (4.6.5), turning in 4.6.11 toward vegetables and animals. Locke argues there that much of what makes any substance have its particular qualities depends upon external factors, as opposed to internal ones. Part of what makes an animal have motion is the fact that it can breathe air. Remove the air, and you remove the animal's motion. Move the sun a few miles toward or away from the earth, and you similarly affect the lives of most plants and animals on Earth. So not only do we have to understand the state of the universe in order to understand one vegetable or animal substance (which exceeds human abilities), but also our thinking that the animal is determined by *internal* springs (a *substantia*) only is simply *wrong*.

19. Other than to say that he does "not believe that it is fair to mock philosophers," as Locke does here, Leibniz provides here no cogent reply to Locke's ridicule. Leibniz merely asserts that "this conception of substance, for all its apparent thinness, is less empty and sterile than it is thought to be" (*NE* 218).

20. A useful summary of the Locke-Stillingfleet debate on substance is given in Edwin McCann, "Locke's Philosophy of Body," in *Cambridge Companion to Locke*, ed. Chappell, 56–88; see 78–79.

21. On Locke's aim and targets, see Greenlee. Also see McCann: "We have seen that one of Locke's main aims in the *Essay* was to promote the corpuscularian version of mechanism over the Cartesian one, and to eliminate the Aristotelian-Scholastic obstacles to the acceptance of mechanism. We have also noted how each of these rival views makes central use of the doctrine of substance. Now we have Locke arguing that this notion is irredeemably obscure and confused, and of little use in philosophy. . . . If this pulls the rug out from under Aristotelianism and Cartesianism, then so much the worse for these views and so much better for mechanistic corpuscularianism" (McCann, "Locke's philosophy of body," 85).

22. W. L. Uzgalis convincingly shows that essentialist readings of Locke, such as those of Arthur Lovejoy, David Wiggins, and J. L. Mackie, fail to recognize that Locke regards classes as nominal rather than real. See W. L. Uzgalis, "The Anti-Essential Locke and Natural Kinds," *The Philosophical Quarterly* 38.152 (July 1988): 330–39.

23. Leibniz's comments on chapter 3.6 end with section 42; he thus omits all discussion of Locke on Adam's children.

24. For an excellent summary of Adamic language theory and its reception in seventeenth-century England, see Hans Aarsleff, *From Locke to Saussure: Essays on the Study of Language and Intellectual History* (Minneapolis: University of Minnesota Press, 1982), 42–83.

25. "The word comes from the French *essai*, and means a trial, or an attempt, or even an experiment. (The French meaning is preserved in the English *assay*: to assay an ore is

to conduct experiments on a sample to arrive at a tentative determination of the metal content, and thus value, of the lode.)" (Buckle, "British Sceptical Realism," 3–4). Buckle notes the equivalence of essay and assay in his discussion of Locke's title page, but does not examine its relation to Locke's discussion of gold. According to the *Oxford English Dictionary*, not only "assay," but also the noun and the verb "essay" refer to the trial of metals. One instance given in the *OED* derives from none other than John Locke. But the *OED* incorrectly sources the phrase to Locke's 1691 *Considerations of the Consequences of the Lowering of Interest*; in fact, it derives from John Locke, *Further Considerations Concerning Raising the Value of Money* (London, 1695), where Locke asks: "whether, whilst our Coin is not of value above Standard Buillion, Goldsmiths and others, who have need of Standard Silver, will not rather take what is by the *Free* labour of the Mint ready essaid and adjusted to their use, and melt that down, rather than be at the trouble of melting mixing and essaying of Silver for the uses they have?" (101).

26. Accepting Locke's assessment of childhood as a time rife with improper association of words and significations, Leibniz expresses surprise that children learn languages as well as they do. (See *NE* 341.)

27. It is no wonder that Rousseau later argued so passionately for physical education and against reading in early childhood. The more children are occasioned to have simple ideas from contact with things, and the less children are occasioned to have complex ideas from contact with words, the better. Recall that Rousseau would not have his child even hear the name of God until he is an adolescent. See Rousseau, *Emile*, trans. Bloom, 254.

28. "Creatures known as 'changelings,' substituted for human children by fairies, trolls, witches, demons, or devils, appear frequently in the compilations of world folklore that have been a widespread genre for nearly two centuries. . . . For a period in early modern history, roughly from the creation of the Royal Society to the beginning of the nineteenth century, the same word also signified someone with an intellectual disability" (Goodey and Stainton, "Intellectual Disability," 223). Until Locke's time, changelings had been part of a theological discourse, providing palpable evidence of the existence of the devil (and therefore of God). "The association between child substitution and monstrosity only became established in the later seventeenth century . . . this was when the monstrosity provoking [the] most anxiety began to be intellectual rather than physical" (234).

29. Thus I dispute what seems to be a commonplace of Locke scholarship, which simply identifies the changeling with the imbecile or idiot. Yolton correctly notes that the term changeling sometimes "refers to the notion of a child supposedly left by fairies, perhaps as a substitute child," but goes on to state confidently that "other times—and this was the sense in which Locke used this term—it refers to a half-witted person, an idiot or imbecile, perhaps misshapen and lacking in reason" (Yolton, *Locke Dictionary*, 36). See also Christopher Hughes Conn, *Locke on Essence and Identity* (Dordrecht: Kluwer, 2003), who states more tentatively that "by 'changeling' Locke seems to mean a mentally retarded or severely deformed human being" (44). I submit that Yolton and Conn are mistaken in identifying the changeling as either a "person" or a "human being." According to Locke's criteria, the changeling is neither one. Jonathan Bennett's abridgement of the *Essay* (available at http://www.earlymoderntexts.com) gives this note at the first mention of changelings: "In Locke's time 'changeling' was a label for anyone whose congenital deficits include a level of intelligence too low for speech to be learned" (203). I submit

that such explanations fail to explain why Locke was so concerned with species boundaries when discussing changelings. It seems there remains a bit of early modern "superstition" in Locke, against the "enlightened" view that some contemporary commentators
attribute to him. Two very recent studies of Locke are more careful in their assessment
of changelings. See William Uzgalis, *Locke's* Essay Concerning Human Understanding.
A Reader's Guide (London: Continuum, 2007). As Uzgalis explains, Locke in chapter 4.4
uses the changeling to show the inadequacy of Aristotelian essentialism, which cannot
explain hybrids or interstitial beings. Thus Locke "asks rhetorically whether a
changeling, that is a man without reason, is not a new species, one that would be as distinct from the already existing species of 'man' and 'beast' as the idea of 'an ass with reason' would be. And if asked what are these things between man and beast, Locke would
answer changelings!" (108). See also Margaret Atherton, "Locke on Essences and Classification," in *The Cambridge Companion to Locke's "Essay Concerning Human Understanding,"*
ed. Lex Newman (Cambridge: Cambridge University Press, 2007), 258–85. Atherton
sounds a note of caution: "[Locke] is not, as some have imagined, arguing that the existence of monsters indicates that natural species don't have fixed boundaries. It is therefore not a refutation of Locke's claim to point out, as does Jolley, that the problem can
be overcome by labeling monsters (e.g., physically deformed humans) and changelings
(reason-impaired humans) members of new species" (273). In Atherton's view, Locke is
concerned not with species boundaries per se, but rather with discourse on species
boundaries: "when we pay attention to the way in which Locke deploys these examples,
they are in service of his theory of language rather than his ontology" (ibid.). I find this
latter conclusion suggestive, if not conclusive.

30. Walker suggests that Locke's catachresis (his inappropriate naming the human
species according to one gender) is part of Locke's attempt to describe general concept
formation in the "history of male consciousness" (Walker, "Locke Minding Women,"
257). Accordingly, the forgetting of particulars in the process of abstraction amounts to
a forgetting of the initially female caretakers in the process of forming the concept Man.
Walker regards Locke ambivalently on this score: on the one hand, Locke's notes represent a laudable recuperation of forgotten childhood knowledge. On the other, Locke's
own text demonstrates the very amnesia that it seems to want to overcome. Thus "what
is peculiar about this history of the general idea of and term for humanity is how reference to the nurse and the mother drops out. . . . Indeed, the first part of the passage may
lead us to expect that the general concept the child is formulating will be not that of humanity in general, but that of the woman or female since that is the more specific common ground of the particulars first described" (255). Walker's analysis of the "fade of the
female" (255) and "female vanishings" (256) shows how gender is both ostensibly omitted in the child's formation of the concept of humanity and perversely included in the
term used to name that concept (Man). But given Locke's double use of the terms
man/men, it is unclear to me what criteria would allow us to decide where Locke means
male and where he means *human*. In describing Locke's passage as sketching a history of
male consciousness, Walker's implicit assumption seems to be that the female mind, as it
forms general concepts, is untouched by the androcentrism that molds the male mind.
Patriarchal thinking is certainly evident in Locke's passage on "Man," but I think it more
likely that Locke is guilty of it, than that he tries to diagnose it. In brief, I find that Locke
can be read through gender theory, but that it is a stretch to suggest that Locke was
much of a gender theorist.

31. It may be coincidental (though a few pages before he had been discussing Locke), but when Rousseau wrote about how children acquire religious faith, he used similar names: "When a child says that he believes in God, it is not in God that he believes, it is in Peter or James [*à Pierre ou à Jaques*] who tell him that there is something called God." See Rousseau, *Emile*, trans. Bloom, 258; see also Rousseau, *Œuvres complètes*, vol. 4, 555. In any case, Rousseau's point comports precisely with Locke's notes on principling children.

32. Against Locke, Leibniz writes this beautiful passage on the definition of man: "In place of saying that man is a 'reasonable animal' we could, if language permitted, say that man is an 'animable rational,' that is a rational substance endowed with an animal nature, as contrasted with Spirits which are rational substances whose nature is not animal, i.e. not shared with the beasts" (*NE* 292). This neologism is emblematic of Leibniz's belief, not shared by Locke, that man has a substance knowable by man, and that this substance is rationality.

33. On Locke and the cassowary, see Walmsley, *Locke's* Essay, 13–16, 41–47, and 55.

34. Thanks to Adriana Benzaquén for identifying the querechinchio/quirquincho.

35. "The changeling was someone whose will and opinions could be easily altered" (Goodey and Stainton, "Intellectual Disability," 235).

36. In this passage, Locke asks us "to consider how the changeling or idiot fits into none of our nominal categories, but seems to fall between the stools of man and beast. . . . Our absolute distinctions are muddied as Locke's unrelenting hand twists the features of the changeling before our eyes. . . . The lolling changeling, ostensibly human and yet devoid of reason, leads him along the treacherous verges of his subject" (Walmsley, *Locke's* Essay, 128–29).

37. On the ostensible need for syllogism, Locke continues the visual metaphor: "Some Eyes want Spectacles to see things clearly and distinctly; but let not those that use them therefore say, no body can see clearly without them" (4.17.4).

Chapter 4. Leibniz

1. *Pascal's* Pensées, trans. H. F. Stewart (New York: Random House, 1967), 150–53.

2. *Augustinus*, the final work of Cornelius Jansen, for whom the movement was named, concerned Augustine's notion of grace. Important Jansenists included Arnauld, Nicole, Pascal, and Pasquier Quesnel.

3. G. W. Leibniz, *Theodicy*, ed. Austin Farrer, trans. E. M. Huggard (Chicago: Open Court, 1985). Subsequent references to Leibniz's three "Essays on the Justice of God and the Freedom of Man in the Origin of Evil" are cited parenthetically in the text with the abbreviation "*T*" and section number. References to Leibniz's "Preliminary Dissertation on the Conformity of Faith with Reason" or other materials are given by the abbreviation "*Theodicy*" and page number in Farrer's edition.

4. Evidence for the wide acceptance in the seventeenth century of the belief that infants dying unbaptized are damned is provided by the popularity of Michael Wigglesworth's theological poem, "The Day of Doom," which contains a passage explaining that original sin justifies the seemingly cruel fate. See Elmar J. Kremer, "Leibniz and the 'Disciples of Saint Augustine' on the Fate of Infants Who Die Unbaptized," in *The Problem of Evil in Early Modern Philosophy*, ed. Elmar J. Kremer and Michael J. Latzer (Toronto: University of Toronto Press, 2001), 119–37; here 119–20. In the American colonies, not only baptism but also conversion were seen as necessary to escape the

flames of hell. The doctrine may not have been calmly accepted, but accepted it was: "according to Puritan doctrine, infants who died unconverted were doomed to eternal torment in hell. Although parents were supposed to accept these deaths with resignation, many could barely contain their grief." See Steven Mintz, *Huck's Raft: A History of American Childhood* (Cambridge, MA: Belknap Press, 2004), 15.

5. The term *limbo*, signifying a temporary waiting place for the souls of adults awaiting entrance into heaven (*limbus patrum*) and an eternal location for the souls of unbaptized infants (*limbus infantium*), was once used to refer to the border or hem of a garment. (See Kremer, "Leibniz on the Fate of Infants," 136, note 32). An antique source, Virgil's *limen* (the threshold to Hades across the Styx, where infants weep), may have served as a model for the development of the Christian concept. See Joseph Horrell, "Milton, Limbo, and Suicide," *The Review of English Studies* 18 (1942): 413–27; here 417.

6. In a personal communication, John Fitzgerald has informed me that the origins of infant baptism are the subject of considerable debate, but that it is likely a second-century phenomenon. The earliest explicit reference to infant baptism is in Tertullian, *On Baptism*, a treatise not written until ca. 200. Tertullian opposed the practice, explicitly referring to childhood as an "innocens aetas [innocent age]." See *Tertullian's Homily on Baptism*, trans. Ernest Evans (London: S.P.C.K., 1964), 38. A generation later, Origen and Cyprian argued in favor of infant baptism, the former stating that there must be something in infants requiring forgiveness and pardon, the latter specifying that something as being Adam's sins. Once the practice of infant baptism was linked with the developing doctrine of original sin, the two would become inseparable; the only issue that remained was the fate of infants who died with inherited Adamic sin not removed through the grace of baptism. See Hans Herter, "Das unschuldige Kind," *Jahrbuch für Antike und Christentum* 4 (1962): 146–62. See also E. Glenn Hinson, "Infant Baptism," in *Encyclopedia of Early Christianity*, vol 1, ed. Everett Ferguson (New York: Garland, 1997), 571–73. My thanks to John Fitzgerald for these references.

7. Although it is difficult to precisely ascertain Pelagius's actual views, since much of what we know of Pelagius comes from citations in Augustine, rather than from original sources, an excellent reconstruction of Pelagius's theology is provided by Robert F. Evans, *Pelagius: Inquiries and Reappraisals* (New York: Seabury Press, 1968). Also helpful is John Ferguson, *Pelagius: A Historical and Theological Study* (Cambridge: Heffer & Sons, 1956).

8. Interestingly, Pelagius himself defended infant baptism, although there was no logic for it given his premises. On infant baptism as a serious self-contradiction in Pelagius's thought, see ibid., 113–19.

9. An excellent summary of the debate between Pelagius and Augustine is given by J. N. L. Myres, "Pelagius and the End of Roman Rule in Britain," *The Journal of Roman Studies* 50 (1960): 21–36; see esp. 21–23. See also William J. Collinge's introductions in *Saint Augustine: Four Anti-Pelagian Writings*, trans. John A. Mourant and William J. Collinge (Washington, DC: Catholic University of America Press, 1992), 3–21 and 93–110.

10. Luther asked "why shouldn't faith and spirit come into the child through Christ's words and baptism [warum *solt nicht auch der glawbe und geist durch sein reden und teuffen . . . ynn das kind komen*]" (Luther, *Werke* 18: 784–85, my translation). My thanks to Horst Lange for this reference and for helping me gain some clarity on baby faith in Lutheranism.

11. See Jane E. Strohl, "The Child in Luther's Theology," in *The Child in Christian Thought*, ed. Bunge, 134–59.

12. See *A Golden Chaine of Divine Aphorismes Written by John Gerhard Doctor of Divinitie and Superintendent of Heldburg*, trans. Ralph Winterton (1632), 277–78. Available through Early English Books Online: http://eebo.chadwyck.com/home. Thanks to Ulrich Rosenhagen for this reference.

13. On various pre- and post-Augustinian views of limbo, see *New Advent Catholic Encyclopedia*, art. "limbo": http://www.newadvent.org/cathen/09256a.htm.

14. "To please a prince, to refute a rival philosopher, or to escape the censures of a theologian, he would take any pains." Bertrand Russell, *The Philosophy of Leibniz* (London: Routledge, 1997), 1. If one recalls the consequences that could follow theological censure in Europe around 1700, one might entertain a more generous explanation of why the *Causa Dei*, a Latin summary of his text, appears much more orthodox than does the *Theodicy* itself. Leibniz's actual beliefs are, I suggest, better expressed in the longer French text, sometimes explicitly and sometimes implicitly.

Leroy E. Loemker argues that for Leibniz and many of his contemporaries, nothing less than "the hope of European order seemed to rest upon [confessional agreement]," first among the Protestants and then between Protestants and Catholics. See Leroy E. Loemker, "Introduction," in *Philosophical Papers and Letters* by G. W. Leibniz (Dordrecht: D. Reidel, 1970), 50.

15. Ernst Cassirer, *The Philosophy of the Enlightenment* (Princeton, NJ: Princeton University Press, 1968), 139. *Die Philosophie der Aufklärung* (Hamburg: Meiner, 1998), 185.

16. For a discussion of original sin in the seventeenth and eighteenth centuries, see Cassirer, *Philosophy of Enlightenment*, 137–60.

17. "It must be remembered that Leibniz was a Lutheran. During his lifetime various incentives for converting to Catholicism were presented to him: there was no conversion." Robert C. Sleigh, Jr., "Introduction," in *Confessio philosophi* by G. W. Leibniz (New Haven, CT: Yale University Press, 2005), xx. Ariew reports that "Leibniz could have become a full member of the Académie [des Sciences de Paris], with pension. . . . Apparently, the only condition on his membership was a conversion to Catholicism, which he rejected." Roger Ariew, "G. W. Leibniz, Life and Works," in *The Cambridge Companion to Leibniz*, ed. Nicholas Jolley (Cambridge: Cambridge University Press, 1995), 26.

18. Kremer, "Leibniz on the Fate of Infants," 127.

19. Bayle's extended discussion of King's thought is in chapters 74–92 of *RQP*, but the *Dictionary* provided Bayle a forum to continue thinking through the problem of evil. See D. Anthony Larivière and Thomas M. Lennon, "Bayle on the Moral Problem of Evil," in *The Problem of Evil*, ed. Kremer and Latzer, 101–18.

20. Pierre Bayle, *Historical and Critical Dictionary: Selections*, trans. Richard H. Popkin (Indianapolis, IN: Bobbs-Merrill, 1965).

21. In 1695, Leibniz published the article "New System of Nature . . ." in the *Journal des Scavants*. Foucher wrote a rebuttal, to which Leibniz replied twice. Pierre Bayle referred to these four texts when he composed an entry on Rorarius for his *Dictionary*. In footnote H, Bayle gave a fair enough account of Leibniz's new doctrine and posed several questions and difficulties. Leibniz replied to this, leading Bayle to add footnote L in his entry Rorarius for the second edition of the *Dictionary*.

22. Bayle did not reply to Leibniz's letter, and he died before Leibniz completed this his second book. But it seems the courts as well as the academies were quite eager to see

how Leibniz would reply to Bayle. This may explain why Leibniz chose to publish *Theodicy* even after Bayle had died, whereas he had omitted publication of his previous book manuscript after Locke's death.

23. The religious persecutions in France, following the revocation of the Edict of Nantes, touched Bayle's life by ending those of his father and brother; the latter, Jacob, died in prison, presumably tortured to death in Pierre's place. For brief discussions of Bayle's life, see Richard H. Popkin, "Introduction," in Bayle, *Dictionary*, xiv–xxii and Thomas M. Lennon, *Reading Bayle* (Toronto: University of Toronto Press, 1999), 3–8. For an extensive discussion of Bayle's life, see Elisabeth Labrousse, *Pierre Bayle*, 2 vols. (The Hague: Nijhoff, 1963–64).

24. This argument, attributed to Epicurus, was discussed as early as the fourth century C. E. by Lactantius in *De Ira Dei*. See Lactantius, *Minor Works*, trans. Mart Francis McDonald (Washington, DC: Catholic University of America Press, 1965), 91–93.

25. Jonathan Israel depicts a "triangular disagreement" (Israel, *Radical Enlightenment*, 333) that has remained unresolved since Bayle's time: was he a devout Christian, albeit heterodox, whose ideas could be excused? Was he a devout Christian whose ideas nevertheless were dangerous? Or was he a crypto-radical thinker worthy of the likes of La Mettrie and Diderot? Israel proposes this specification in treating the Bayle paradox: "Contrary to what is often said, Bayle is strictly speaking neither a sceptic nor a 'fideist'. His position is that philosophical reason is the only tool we have to separate truth from falsehood . . . and that, consequently, by its nature religious faith can never be based on reason. . . . But the ultimate paradox in Bayle is not that faith can never be explained or justified by reason, but that what is chiefly opposed to reason in his philosophy, namely 'superstition', is indistinguishable from faith" (338). However, as most scholars do, Israel resolves the Bayle enigma, as follows: "Bayle deploys Pyrrhonism as a tactical device to push readers towards a conclusion opposed to the fideist position he pretends to adopt" (339). I find this resolution attractive, but cannot help wondering how much of Bayle's pretense was based on conviction. It seems Bayle is one of those writers about whose views one must simply decide what to believe in the face of contradictory evidence.

26. Bayle, *Dictionary*, 149–50. Art. Manicheans, rem. D.

27. Susan Neiman, *Evil in Modern Thought: An Alternative History of Philosophy* (Princeton, NJ: Princeton University Press, 2002), 20.

28. Bayle, *Dictionary*, 175–78. Art. Paulicians, rem. E.

29. Neiman comments on the same passages in Bayle: "Traditional belief is said to play on childhood fantasy. We want a world ordered by wise and loving parents. . . . Bayle moved from children's dreams of safe landing to their most dreadful apparitions. Supposing God were not a sage and nurturing father, but one who let you fall to the bottom for his own narcissistic needs? Supposing God were not a protective and loving mother, but one who allowed you to ruin yourself forever—perhaps out of envy? Does any attempt to maintain God's benevolence by claiming He was only trying to offer us presents provide a better picture?" (Neiman, *Evil in Modern Thought*, 123).

30. In "Preliminary Dissertation," section 39, which cites Nicole (via Bayle, *RQP*) on the triumph of authority over human reason, Leibniz's text correctly refers to Bayle's chapter 177, but Huggard's translation incorrectly refers to "p. 120" (*Theodicy*, 96) in Bayle's *RQP*. The correct reference is to p. 1201.

31. On the distinction between doctrines above and those against reason, see *Theodicy*, 88; G 6:64. For a discussion on Leibniz not being very clear on the boundary between these two, see George MacDonald Ross, "The Demarcation Between Metaphysics and Other Disciplines in the Thought of Leibniz," in *Metaphysics and Philosophy of Science in the Seventeenth and Eighteenth Centuries*, ed. R. S. Woolhouse (Dordrecht: Kluwer, 1988), 133–63.

32. The passage in "Preliminary Dissertation," section 87, that Leibniz renders: "Ita quomodo hoc justum sit, ut immeritos damnet, incomprehensibile est modo" (*Theodicy*, 122) appears to be a paraphrase, rather than a citation, of the final pages of Luther's *De servo arbitrio* (*On the Bondage of the Will*). For the relevant passages, see *Luther's Works*, vol. 33, ed. Philip S. Watson (Philadelphia, PA: Fortress Press, 1972), 289–92 and Luther, *Werke* 18:784–85.

33. However, Voltaire clearly did read the opening "Preliminary Dissertation," which concludes with two quotes, the first one from Virgil's fifth eclogue: "Daphnis, in radiant beauty [*Candidus*], marvels at Heaven's [*Olympi*] unfamiliar threshold [*limen*]." See Virgil, *Eclogues: Georgics, Aeneid I–VI*, trans. H. Rushton Fairclough (Cambridge, MA: Harvard University Press, 1999), 58–59. (Cf. *Theodicy*, 122). This passage could well have inspired Voltaire to name the hero of his anti-Leibnizian novel *Candide*.

34. Pierre Bayle, *Reponse aux Questions d'un Provincial*, 4 vols. (Rotterdam, 1704–1707). Subsequent references to vol. 3 (1706) of this work are cited parenthetically in the text with the abbreviation "*RQP*" and page numbers.

35. Isaac Jaquelot is one of Bayle's recurring targets. In chapter 144 of *RQP*, Bayle discusses seven theological and nineteen philosophical propositions; where Jaquelot had wanted to harmonize them, Bayle emphasized their incompatibility. (Leibniz responds to these same propositions in *T* 109–34.)

36. The background to the debate reviewed by Bayle began with Pierre Nicole, *Prejugez legitimes contre les calvinistes* (Paris, 1671), which was answered by Jean Claude, *La defense de la Reformation* (n. p., 1673) and *Considerations sur les lettres circulaires* (The Hague, 1683), both of which were criticized in Pierre Nicole, *Les pretendus reformez* (Paris, 1684), which in turn was criticized in Pierre Jurieu, *Le vray systeme de l'Eglise & la veritable analyse de la foy* (Dordrecht, 1686). Bayle's review covers rejoinders by Pierre Nicole, *De l'unité de l'église, ou, Réfutation du nouveau systeme de M. Jurieu* (Paris, 1687), and responses by Jurieu, *Traité de l'unité d'Eglise et des points fondamentaux: contre Monsieur Nicole* (Rotterdam, 1688).

37. Bayle's troubled relationship with Jurieu is often mentioned in biographical and scholarly work on both writers. For a helpful discussion linking this relationship to religious controversies surrounding Socinianism and Origenism, see Barbara Sher Tinsley, *Pierre Bayle's Reformation. Conscience and Criticism on the Eve of the Enlightenment* (Selinsgrove: Susquehanna University Press, 2001), 314–20.

38. I have been unable to access the first edition of Nicole's work. In the second edition, Pierre Nicole, *De L'unité de L'eglise, ou Refutation du nouveau systême de M. Jurieu: Nouvelle Edition* (Lille, 1709), Bayle's quote corresponds to 257–58.

39. On Socinianism, and Bayle's discussion thereof, see Tinsley, *Pierre Bayle's Reformation*, 302–20.

40. Cf. Nicole, *De L'unite de L'eglise*, 260.

41. Cf. ibid., 263.

42. Cf. ibid., 263–64.

43. Cf. ibid., 261–62. Bayle here elides several interesting passages from Nicole, including two scriptural quotes of great importance to our topic: John 3:5 and 2 Corinthians 7:14.

44. The biblical source for this phrase is Matthew 23:24.

45. "'What will become of original sin?' they shouted at him. 'Let it become what it may,' said Leibniz and his friends; but in public he wrote that original sin necessarily was a part of the best of worlds." Voltaire, *Philosophical Dictionary*, vol. 1, trans. Peter Gay (New York: Basic Books, 1962), 116–17.

46. A comparison between Leibniz and Descartes on sin and the intellect is instructive. Descartes's fourth meditation may be seen as a theodicy in brief: despite its supposedly philosophical concern with epistemological clarity and distinctness, the latter depend upon God's grace. And because the mind is potentially infallible, Descartes concludes that not restricting one's will to the bounds of one's intellect amounts to a moral lapse. Error in judgment amounts to sin. For a discussion (and defense) of Descartes's position, see Michael J. Latzer, "Descartes's Theodicy of Error," in *The Problem of Evil*, ed. Kremer and Latzer, 35–48.

47. Huggard translates "une punition de leurs progéniteurs" as "punishment of their progenitors." I believe "punishment *from* their progenitors" to be a better translation in this context. Although original sin may be a punishment of us all, the punishment does not come from God (as a penalty of law would), but rather from our parents, in the form of inherited feebleness.

48. In a November 1697 letter to a friend, Leibniz claims not to share Sfondrati's views, but offers a reasonable agreement to defend them from censure. After all, if one *could* choose between dying innocent and living to sin and repent, one could not actively choose sin and still merit heaven. The second half of this letter looks favorably upon the counter-reformation claim (of Diego Andrada de Payva) that the justice of God does not permit Him to damn men on the grounds that they lacked faith through a fault not their own. In another letter, Leibniz repeats that Sfondrati's views might be excused, though he adds that Sfondrati did not seem to establish his assertion satisfactorily. See G. W. Leibniz, *Opera Omnia*, vol. 1, ed. Louis Dutens (Geneva, 1768), 32–34. My thanks to Joshua Davies for rapid assistance in translating this text.

49. The Lisbon earthquake of 1755 is commonly noted as the event that made Leibniz's optimism useless to the modern world. It seems noteworthy, then, that Leibniz was still able to state in 1710 that the upheavals of the earth had "ceased at last, and the globe assumes the shape that we see" (*T* 245). After Lisbon, it would certainly be harder to argue convincingly in the face of so much seemingly undeserved death that "this small disorder is apparent only in the whole, and it is not even apparent when one considers the happiness of those who walk in the ways of order" (*T* 243).

50. Voltaire, *Philosophical Dictionary*, 117.

51. Leibniz concludes a discussion of Bayle on freedom and the notion of the indifference of will by underscoring Bayle's inconsistency. See *T* 319.

52. Leibniz extols Friedrich Spee's 1632 *Cautio Criminalis circa Processus contra Sagas*, written against the early seventeenth-century witch burnings in Franconia. It seems Spee's text led the Elector to put an end to these burnings, and most German principalities followed suit. This text has been recently translated: see Friedrich Spee, *Cautio crim-*

inalis, or, A book on witch trials, trans. Marcus Hellyer (Charlottesville: University of Virginia Press, 2003).

53. On Augustine's and the Jansenists' view of baptism as the normal requirement for entry into heaven, see Kremer, "Leibniz on the Fate of Infants," 122. On the Council of Trent, see ibid., 134, note 13.

54. Ibid., 129.

55. Ibid.

56. Ibid., 131.

57. Ibid., 129.

58. On the implausibility of theodicy after Lisbon, see Neiman, *Evil in Modern Thought*, 238–50. In the final pages of her study, Neiman associates the attempt to explain evil with the basic need of children to understand the world. She makes this historical descriptive claim: "The child emerged as a figure in philosophy at the moment when the demand for theodicy was loudest" (321) and this prescriptive one: "I believe we should use Enlightenment resources to develop a different picture of childhood needs from the one Freud offered. The child seeks sense as well as protection" (ibid.). The final sentence of her book concludes with the paradoxical affirmation of the desire to make sense of a world recognized to lack it: "Between the adult who knows she won't find reason in the world, and the child who refuses to stop seeking it, lies the difference between resignation and humility" (328). Neiman's book on various attempts to find reason in the world underscores the limitations of these attempts, but also attempts to understand them from within. It seems to follow that Neiman and her implied reader are neither "children" nor "adults," but rather both.

Chapter 5. Wolff

1. Walter Bruford summarized Wolff's philosophy as consisting of "Leibniz and water." See his *Theatre: Drama and Audience in Goethe's Germany* (London: Routledge and Kegan Paul, 1950), 42.

2. Lewis White Beck, ed., *Eighteenth-Century Philosophy* (New York: Free Press, 1966), 215.

3. On Wolff as an innovator in the German language, see Eric Blackall, *The Emergence of German as a Literary Language, 1700–1775* (Ithaca, NY: Cornell University Press, 1978), 26–48.

4. The very few studies that consider Wolff's understanding of childhood focus on his pedagogy and the history of education. The best study remains a dissertation by Thomas Link, *Die Pädagogik des Philosophen Christian Wolff (Halle) aus seinen Werken zusammengestellt und durch seine Philosophie erläutert* (Bamberg, 1906). Link provides an interesting reconstruction of Wolff's theory of education, referring primarily to the *Politics* but also occasionally to the *Ethics* and *Metaphysics*. However, Link's focus is generally on Wolff's educational goals rather than his understanding of the children who are supposed to strive toward them. The most recent study of relevance to my topic is provided by F. Andrew Brown, "On Education: John Locke, Christian Wolff and the 'Moral Weeklies,'" *University of California Publications in Modern Philology* 36.5 (1952): 149–72. Brown shows convincingly enough that Wolff must have known Locke's *Some Thoughts* and borrowed from it in his own writings. Brown also states that Locke's influence on

Wolff was passed on to the latter's students, many of whom went on to become schoolteachers, thus ensuring the spread of Locke's thoughts via Wolff and setting the stage for the later pedagogical reforms of Basedow, Pestalozzi, and others. Brown cites from the *Politics*, and to a lesser extent the *Ethics*, to point out almost ad nauseam the similarities between Wolff and Locke. Again, as with Link, Brown's focus is on Wolff's educational theory rather than his philosophy of childhood. A recent article by Peter R. Senn, "What is the Place of Christian Wolff in the History of the Social Sciences?" *European Journal of Law and Economics* 4 (1997): 147–232, provides an extremely useful overview of anglophone scholarship on Wolff but adds nothing new to our understanding of Wolff on childhood. Half of Senn's discussion of Wolff's importance for education (194–96) is devoted to higher education, and the other half relies completely on Brown's essay.

5. Christian Wolff, *Christian Wolffs eigene Lebensbeschreibung*, ed. Heinrich Wuttke (Leipzig, 1841). Also reprinted in E 1.10. All translations of Wolff into English in this chapter are mine.

6. Wolff, *Lebensbeschreibung*, 110–11.

7. Ibid., 112.

8. Ibid.

9. I am here explaining Wolff's cursory treatment of his childhood by referring to his philosophical concerns. One should also consider the generic status of his text: Wolff's was one of the first "scholar's autobiographies." See Gunter Niggl, *Geschichte der deutschen Autobiographie im 18. Jahrhundert* (Stuttgart: Metzler, 1977), 22–23. This genre concentrates on the success story of an academic career. Any attention to childhood is minimal; after all, the story concerns the scholar. This focus on the adult's career precluded consideration of what one was when one was not yet an adult, not yet a scholar. By contrast, a number of autobiographies written within two generations of Wolff trace precisely the *development* of the adult subject, that is, the subject's beginnings in childhood and its becoming something *different* through maturation.

10. Eric Watkins, "From Pre-established Harmony to Physical Influx: Leibniz's Reception in Eighteenth Century Germany," *Perspectives on Science* 6.1&2 (1998): 136–203; here 141.

11. Christian Wolff, *Vernünfftige Gedancken von GOTT, Der Welt und der Seele des Menschen, Auch allen Dingen überhaupt* (1751 ed.; Hildesheim: Georg Olms, 1983). Reprinted in E 1.2.1 and E 1.2.2. (I refer to this text as Wolff's *Metaphysics*.) In the editorial introduction (E 1.2.1:1–47), Charles A. Corr reports that Wolff's changes to the second (1722) and third (1725) editions amount primarily to expanding his explanations, while retaining the section numbers. Later editions (there were twelve in Wolff's lifetime) involve only minor editorial changes.

12. I follow Watkins, "From Pre-established Harmony," in referring to the theories of occasionalism, physical influx, and preestablished harmony as Occasionalism, Physical Influx, and Pre-established Harmony.

13. See Gottfried Wilhelm Leibniz, *Kleine Schriften zur Metaphysik*, ed. and trans. Hans Heinz Holz, *Philosophische Schriften*, vol. 1 (Frankfurt am Main: Suhrkamp, 1996), 438–83. (The following translations are mine.) Holz's inclusion of draft versions of the text allow us to observe Leibniz considering the role of change in the monads. A draft version of section 8 contains the following sentence: "However, there must be some *change* [*changement*] in the monads" (440, my emphasis). In the draft, this sentence is

crossed out and replaced by the following: "However, monads must have some *qualities and* some *changes* [quelques *qualités et* quelques *changements*]" (ibid., my emphases). But the final version begins: "However, monads must have some *qualities* [quelques *qualités*]" (ibid., my emphasis). Thus, in two steps, Leibniz redefines as a quality *of* the monad what could have been viewed as an alteration that happens *to* the monad. In section 10, Leibniz concedes that monads must indeed be subject to change: "I also take it as given that every created being is subject to change, and thus the created monad as well, and even that this change is continual in every one" (442). The concession is slight, however, since this change is entirely the product of an *inner* principle. Change is in fact the basic activity of the soul, which attends to perception after perception. Once again, the final version of section 21 subordinates change: "For the simple substance cannot perish; nor can it subsist without some *affection*, which is nothing other than its perception" (448, my emphasis). In the draft version of section 21, Leibniz had written "variation" instead of "affection." Change, then, initially a possible limitation upon the monad's autonomy, has been absorbed, transformed into one of the monad's qualities, namely its power to perceive. In Leibniz's final draft, change is an expression of the monad's autonomy.

14. Christian Wolff, *Ausführliche Nachricht von seinen eigenen Schrifften, die er in deutscher Sprache von den verschiedenen Theilen der Welt=Weißheit heraus gegeben* (1733 ed.; Hildesheim: Georg Olms, 1973). Reprinted in E 1.9.

15. It must be said, though, that Wolff also presumes a "regency" [*Regiment*] (E 1.2.1:328; sec. 539) of the soul over the body; this is his final word on the matter in the chapter on empirical psychology.

16. Compare Leibniz: "Thus, one can say that monads can only begin or end all at once, that is, they can only begin by creation and end by annihilation, whereas composites begin or end through their parts" (AG 213).

17. In addition to Pinto-Correia, *The Ovary of Eve*, a helpful overview of eighteenth-century embryology in Europe is provided by Helmut Müller-Sievers, *Self-Generation. Biology, Philosophy, and Literature Around 1800* (Stanford, CA: Stanford University Press, 1997), 26–47.

18. Christian Wolff, *Vernünfftige Gedancken von den Würckungen der Natur* (1723; Hildesheim: Georg Olms, 2003). Reprinted in E 1.6. See E 1.6:718–720; sec. 444.

19. This passage recalls Descartes's reply to Gassendi on the state of the soul as the body grows and declines. See CSM 2:245 and my chapter 1.

20. See Richard J. Blackwell, "Christian Wolff's Doctrine of the Soul," *Journal of the History of Ideas* 22.3 (1961): 339–54. See esp. 348–49.

21. Christian Wolff, *Vernünfftige Gedancken von der Menschen Thun und Lassen, zu Beförderung ihrer Glückseeligkeit* (1733 ed.; Hildesheim: Georg Olms, 1996). Reprinted in E 1.4. (I refer to this text as Wolff's *Ethics*.) The reprinted edition to which I refer is from 1752, but its title page gives the year as 1733. After the first (1720), second (1722), third (1728) and fourth (1733) editions, no further changes were made.

22. Wolff's statement that unreasonable people need rewards and punishments in order to be moved to do good, whereas reasonable people do good because it is good, and his comparison of the unreasonable ones to children and animals, who require beatings to be tractable, may be a source for Lessing's similar claims in his essay, "The Education of the Human Race," which regards the early Jews as children, the early Christians as adolescents, and contemporary Enlightenment philosophers as the mature adults who can offer a much better education than that provided by the Bible. See Gott-

hold Ephraim Lessing, *Philosophical and Theological Writings*, ed. and trans. H. B. Nisbet (Cambridge: Cambridge University Press, 2005), 217–40.

23. For instances of these phrases, see E 1.4:173, 178, 222, 251, 258, 259, 314, 362, 364, 370, 395; secs. 269, 277, 337, 377, 387, 389, 465, 532, 535, 545, 578.

24. Later, in his *Politics*, Wolff supplements his view of children's religious education: "as long as the use of reason does not show itself in them, [parents should] mainly use the observation of nature to this end" (E 1.5:89–90; sec. 116). He does append a note that Christianity also has "other means" of making children godly, but for his part, he is speaking "as a philosopher." Three sections before, he had just praised the Chinese for their ethics. Here it seems useful to recall Hans Werner Arndt's observation that while Wolff's *Ethics* affirmed the compatibility of rational moral philosophy and Christian revelation, his *Politics* was more concerned with demonstrating the compatibility of rational political philosophy and Confucian thought. (See E 1.5:x.)

25. Locke, *Some Thoughts*, 10; sec. 1.

26. Ibid., 75–76; sec. 101.

27. Christian Wolff, *Vernünfftige Gedancken von dem gesellschaftlichen Leben der Menschen und insonderheit dem gemeinen Wesen* (1736 ed.; Hildesheim: Georg Olms, 1996). Reprinted in E 1.5. (I refer to this text as Wolff's *Politics*.) There were five editions (1721, 1725, 1732, 1736, 1740) in Wolff's lifetime. Only the second edition adds several passages. This reprint is based on the fourth edition.

28. G. W. Leibniz, "Vom Naturrecht," in *Deutsche Schriften*, vol. 1, ed. G. E. Guhrauer (Berlin, 1838), 414–19. (My translation.)

29. Ibid., 414–16.

30. Arndt also identifies Grotius, Pufendorf, and Thomasius as possible sources for Wolff's *Politics*. See E 1.5:xiiff.

31. Wolff does not regard even marriage as a legitimate forum for experiencing sensual pleasure. As one might expect, bestiality, male homosexual behavior (which he calls pederasty), prostitution, adultery, and intercourse with pregnant women are also proscribed (see E 1.5:16–18; secs. 24–27). Female homosexual behavior would also have made the list, had Wolff thought to mention it. Chastity may be difficult, but for Wolff it is a virtue. It is a matter of nothing less than removing oneself "from slavery into freedom" (E 1.5:21; sec. 37), which is why one should practice it "from youth on" (ibid.). Children, by the way, are not allowed to marry because they cannot physically beget children (see E 1.5:15; sec. 22). Evidently, children do not experience sexual desire as youths and adults do. In attempting to refute arguments for polyamory and polygamy, Wolff gives reasons for preferring a traditional marriage, but finally concedes that certain behaviors are simply not allowed: "If women and men, or humans in general, were angels, that is, if in all of their actions they oriented themselves only according to reason, and never gave room to evil desires and affects, then many things would be possible that are not now allowed, given the imperfection of humans" (E 1.5:31; sec. 42). Wolff's marginal note to this section refers to "the ruined nature of humans" (ibid.). Thus, it seems Wolff straddles a line between a Pelagian position (by practicing chastity, we are capable of moving ourselves from slavery into freedom) and an Augustinian one (we give in to evil desires due to our ruined human nature).

32. Wolff does write that children imitate others precisely because they operate only according to the senses and imagination, rather than according to rational consideration. This is the reason children should not be shown indecent things until they have devel-

oped the use of reason. (See E 1.5:75–76; sec. 101). Wolff adds that some adults can be considered children in this manner, if they live according to senses and the imagination, and have no experience with or habit in the good. His example here is young people who live without supervision at universities. It seems that fraternal society is inferior to paternal society. This judgment corresponds to Wolff's preference for monarchy over republics.

33. Rousseau formulates his method of negative education paradoxically, as gaining time by losing it: "Dare I expose the greatest, the most important, the most useful rule of all education? It is not to gain time but to lose it. Common readers, pardon me my paradoxes. When one reflects, they are necessary" (Rousseau, *Emile*, trans. Bloom, 93).

34. Slaves do not enjoy the good of self-rule. Wolff's chapter on master/servant relations is important for my topic only insofar as it considers slaves human beings who become part of a society without agreeing to do so per contract. (In this respect, children and slaves are in a similar category.) Wolff says that there are conditions in which it is not only allowed to make someone a slave, it is actually the right thing to do. And slaves are bound, as are children, to do all that their masters ask, as long as it does not contradict natural law. The class of slaves forms an exception in a chapter that focuses on servants, people who have contracted their labor with their masters.

35. Ingeborg Weber-Kellermann has shown that the idea of a special room in the house for children took root around 1800, with social reality catching up within a few decades. This development was part of the shift in middle-class Europe from the whole house to the nuclear family as the dominant model for domestic organization. See Ingeborg Weber-Kellermann, *Die Kinderstube* (Insel: Frankfurt am Main/Leipzig, 1991), 15–109. On the working classes, who had no such room, see 110–19.

CHAPTER 6. BAUMGARTEN

1. *Reflections on Poetry: Alexander Gottlieb Baumgarten's Meditationes philosophicae de nonnullis ad poema pertinentibus*, trans. Karl Aschenbrenner and William B. Holther (Berkeley: University of California Press, 1954).

2. Ibid., 35–36.

3. For an excellent discussion of Baumgarten's project, see Leonard P. Wessell, Jr., "Alexander Baumgarten's Contribution to the Development of Aesthetics," *The Journal of Aesthetics and Art Criticism* 30.3 (1972): 333–42. Benedetto Croce found that rationalism's reliance upon laws of continuity tended to inhibit the development of aesthetics as an autonomous realm. Thus Croce contests Baumgarten's position as the founder of philosophical aesthetics. Wessell agrees that Baumgarten's continualist metaphysics precludes a nonreductive treatment of "the *qua talis* of aesthetics against the *lex continui* of rationalism" (334), but finds precisely this *qua talis* in Baumgarten's psychology. Thus Wessel asserts Baumgarten's position as the legitimate founder of aesthetics, but finds this achievement inconsistent with his rationalist metaphysics.

4. Baumgarten names his discipline in the penultimate section 116. The intrinsic difficulty of clearly recognizing Baumgarten's object has been compounded for the English reader, for Aschenbrenner and Holter translate the following crucial passage: "graeci iam philosophi & patres inter *aistheta* & *noeta* sedulo semper distinxerunt, satisque apparet *aistheta* iis non solis aequipollere sensualibus, quum absentia etiam sensa (ergo

phantasmata) hoc nomine honorentur" (Baumgarten, *Reflections*, 39) as follows: "The Greek philosophers and the Church fathers have already carefully distinguished between *things perceived* [*aistheta*] and *things known* [*noeta*]. It is entirely evident that they did not equate *things known* [sic!] with things of sense, since they honored with this name things also removed from sense (therefore, images)" (ibid., 78). The latter sentence should of course have begun thus: "It is entirely evident that they did not equate *things perceived* with things of sense." The remainder of the paragraph is translated correctly: "Therefore, *things known* are to be known by the superior faculty as the object of logic; *things perceived* [are to be known by the inferior faculty, as the object] of the science of perception, or **aesthetic**" (ibid.).

5. Wessell, "Baumgarten's Contribution," 337.

6. Ibid., 340.

7. Ibid., 337.

8. On the connection between animal psychology and Baumgarten's use of the term, see Ursula Franke, "Analogon rationis," in *Historisches Wörterbuch der Philosophie*, vol. 1, ed. Joachim Ritter (Darmstadt: Wissenschaftliche Buchgesellschaft, 1971), 229–30, and Ursula Franke, *Kunst als Erkenntnis: Die Rolle der Sinnlichkeit in der Ästhetik des Alexander Gottlieb Baumgarten* (Steiner: Wiesbaden, 1972), 51–52.

9. For a clear overview of Baumgarten's inclusion of the obscure, the senses, and the body in the human whole, see Hans Adler, "La lucidité de l'obscur: la fondation polémique de l'esthétique au siècle des lumières," in *Signs of Humanity/L'homme et ses signes*, ed. Michel Balat and Janice Deledalle-Rhodes (Berlin: de Gruyter, 1992), 221–28. See also Steffen W. Gross, "The Neglected Programme of Aesthetics," *British Journal of Aesthetics* 42.4 (2002): 403–14. Following Ernst Cassirer, Gross insists that Baumgarten's aesthetics was not primarily a philosophy of art, but rather an anthropological philosophy of the whole person: "His *felix aestheticus* is by no means merely the artist or poet: instead he is the whole man" (404). See as well Steffen W. Groß, *Felix Aestheticus: Die Ästhetik als Lehre vom Menschen* (Würzburg: Königshausen & Neumann, 2001).

10. Aristotle, *Poetics*, ed. and trans. Stephen Halliwell (Cambridge: Harvard University Press, 1995), 1448b. To facilitate reference to other editions, I cite by Bekker number rather than page number.

11. I quote the original Latin from a reprint of the first edition: Alexander Gottlieb Baumgarten, *Aesthetica* (1750/58; Hildesheim: Georg Olms, 1986). Subsequent references to this work are cited parenthetically in the text with the abbreviation "*A*" and what I have referred to in previous chapters as section numbers. In this chapter, I refer to the latter as *paragraphs*, in order to maintain Baumgarten's designation of *Section* as a grouping of numbered paragraphs. I have also profited from Hans Rudolf Schweizer's edition and parallel partial translation: Alexander Gottlieb Baumgarten, *Theoretische Ästhetik. Die grundlegenden Abschnitte aus der "Aesthetica" (1750/58)*, ed. and trans. Hans Rudolf Schweizer (Hamburg: Meiner, 1983). There are slight differences between these editions, as Schweizer made several corrections, modernized the spelling, and simplified the punctuation. (See xvii.) A full translation into German, with parallel Latin text, was published after I completed this study. See Alexander Gottlieb Baumgarten, *Ästhetik*, 2 vols., ed. and trans. Dagmar Mirbach (Hamburg: Meiner, 2007).

12. "Pulchre cogitare" is a nonconceptual, sensate form of cognition. It should be distinguished from sensate cognition in general, which perceives confusion. The anony-

mous notes taken from Baumgarten's lectures, compiled in Bernhard Poppe, *Alexander Gottlieb Baumgarten: Seine Bedeutung und Stellung in der Leibniz-Wolffischen Philosophie und seine Beziehungen zu Kant; Nebst Veröffentlichung einer bisher unbekannten Handschrift der Äs- thetik Baumgartens* (Leipzig, 1907), clarify that the reason for having an *ars* for sensate cognition is to show "how confused representations should become beautiful" (81, my translation). Aesthetics shows "how I can bring forth beauty, how I can think more richly, purely, truly" (ibid., 106). On some of the difficulties occasioned by Baumgarten's term, *ars pulcre cogitandi*, see Franke, *Kunst als Erkenntnis*, 76–87.

13. Aristotle, *Poetics*, 1448b.

14. Ibid., 1449a.

15. Ibid.

16. On Baumgarten's role in the exploration of sensate knowing, see Hans Rudolf Schweizer, *Ästhetik als Philosophie der sinnlichen Erkenntnis* (Basel: Schwabe, 1973), 9–103. Friedrich Solms, *Disciplina Aesthetica* (Stuttgart: Klett, 1990), 115–61 regards Baumgarten's "rehabilitation of sensuality" (7, my translation) as seminal for the devel- opment of later eighteenth-century anthropological thought, especially Herder's. On Herder's reception of Baumgarten, see Hans Adler, *Die Prägnanz des Dunklen. Gnoseolo- gie—Ästhetik—Geschichtsphilosophie bei Johann Gottfried Herder* (Hamburg: Meiner, 1990), 63–87.

17. Baumgarten's 1739 *Metaphysica* shares a Wolffian reticence to discuss develop- ment. On the innovations of *Metaphysica* with respect to Wolff, see Alexander Gottlieb Baumgarten, *Texte zur Grundlegung der Ästhetik*, ed. and trans. Hans Rudolf Schweizer (Hamburg: Meiner, 1983), x–xv. On Baumgarten's gnoseological understanding of sen- sation as a crucial innovation in Wolffian metaphysics, see Franke, *Kunst als Erkenntnis*, 37–50. Space precludes discussion here of the continuities and discontinuities between Baumgarten's texts; I would like to just note that Baumgarten's psychology is "presen- tist" in *Metaphysica*, which is replete with sentences like: "Conscius sum status mei [I am conscious of my status]" (Baumgarten, *Metaphysica*, § 557, my translation). In *Aesthetica*, by contrast, Baumgarten considers the mind in formation, such that prior states of life (i.e., infancy and childhood) enter into discussion.

18. The notion of avoiding paradox by temporalizing the terms of an initial distinc- tion is articulated in Niklas Luhmann, "Die Paradoxie der Form," in *Kalkül der Form*, ed. Dirk Baecker (Frankfurt am Main: Suhrkamp, 1993), 197–212.

19. Herder's sole reservation with Baumgarten's aesthetics (upon which he otherwise lavishes praise) concerns the gradual transition Baumgarten traced between nature and art: such a transition leaves the difference between the opposed terms indistinct. In his 1769 *Viertes Kritisches Wäldchen*, Herder insists upon this difference: "Baumgarten, it is known, has a natural and an artificial aesthetics, which appear not to differ from one an- other except by degree, but which are perhaps completely different, even though they presuppose one another." Johann Gottfried Herder, *Schriften zur Ästhetik und Literatur, 1767–1781*, ed. Gunter E. Grimm (Frankfurt am Main: Deutscher Klassiker Verlag, 1993), 268 (my translation). What Baumgarten attempted to link, Herder sees as prop- erly separate: "what two ends of the human spirit! They nearly cancel each other out in the moment of energy" (ibid., 269). But these separate ends are, after all, conceived by Herder as ends of the same human spirit. When one posits the unity of the human being beneath opposed terms, one must somehow mediate these opposed terms or "ends." But in this discussion of Baumgarten, Herder appears to be stuck with a static opposition be-

tween nature and culture. On Herder's 1784–85 attempt to articulate a dynamic opposition between nature and culture, in parts one and two of *Ideen zur Philosophie der Geschichte der Menschheit*, see W. Ch. Zimmerli, "Evolution or Development?" in *Herder Today*, ed. Kurt Mueller-Vollmer (Berlin: de Gruyter, 1990), 1–16.

20. David E. Wellbery, *Lessing's* Laocoon: *Semiotics and Aesthetics in the Age of Reason* (Cambridge: Cambridge University Press, 1984), 21.

21. Rousseau, *Emile*, trans. Bloom, 93.

22. When he writes of children, Baumgarten uses the masculine term *puer* or *boy*. My own discussion occasionally combines ungendered nouns such as *child* with pronouns such as *he*. Translating in this manner allows me to expose Baumgarten's use of false universal terms while underscoring his age-specific distinctions, which are my primary interest here.

23. For an extensive discussion of Baumgarten's Prolegomena, see Michael Jäger, *Kommentierende Einführung in Baumgartens "Aesthetica:" Zur entstehenden wissenschaftlichen Ästhetik des 18. Jahrhunderts in Deutschland* (Hildesheim: Olms, 1980).

24. One can also identify aesthetic exercise as the "acquired" aesthetic nature described in paragraph 2.

25. Section 2 additionally considers the superior faculties, intellect and reason (*A* 38), and how they may interact with the inferior faculties in beautiful knowing (*A* 39–43), concluding with a brief discussion of innate aesthetic temperament (*A* 44–46).

26. On the episteme of continuity, see Arthur Lovejoy, *The Great Chain of Being* (Cambridge: Harvard University Press, 1974). Lovejoy identifies plenitude, continuity, and gradation as central to the conception of the universe as a chain of being. This understanding derives from ancient Greek thought but "attained [its] widest diffusion and acceptance" (183) in the eighteenth century.

27. Baumgarten cites Horace, *Epistles* 2.1.126. See Horace, *Satires, Epistles and Ars Poetica*, trans. H. Rushton Fairclough (New York: Putnam's Sons, 1929), 406–7.

28. Compare Baumgarten's description of aesthetic exercises to Wilhelm Meister's getting his friends together to play at theater, which led them to attempt to mount a production of Tasso's *Gerusalemme Liberata*. This passage is from *Wilhelm Meisters Lehrjahre*, book 1, chapter 7: "The distractions of youth began to take their toll of the solitary pleasures, especially when the circle of my friends grew larger. I was huntsman, foot-soldier, cavalryman, as our games demanded; but I always had a slight edge over the others, because I could provide the necessary properties for these occasions: The swords were mostly from my workshop, it was I who decorated and gilded the sleds, and some curious instinct made me transform our whole militia into Romans. We made helmets and topped them with paper plumes; we made shields, even suits of armor, and many a needle was broken by those of our servants who knew how to sew or make clothes. Some of my young comrades were now well armed, the rest were gradually, though not quite so elaborately, equipped, and soon we were a respectable army. We marched into courtyards and gardens, knocking against each others's shields and heads." Johann Wolfgang von Goethe, *Wilhelm Meister's Apprenticeship*, trans. Eric A. Blackall and Victor Lange (Princeton, NJ: Princeton University Press, 1989), 11.

29. See *A Greek-English Lexicon*, comp. Henry George Liddell et al. (Oxford: Clarendon Press, 1996). Liddell states that *skhedia*, a raft or float, is probably the feminine form of *skhedios*, "something knocked up off-hand" (1744). Compare this to the definition of *autoskhediasma* as "work done offhand, impromptu, improvisation" (283).

30. According to the *Oxford Latin Dictionary*, ed. P. G. W. Glare (Oxford: Clarendon Press, 1982), *cortex* is bark or "a piece of cork used as a float by swimmers" (451). Baumgarten here alludes to Horace, *Satires* 1.4.120: "When years have brought strength to body and mind, you will swim without the cork [*nabis sine cortice*]." See Horace, *Satires, Epistles and Ars Poetica*, 58–59.

31. See Glare, *Oxford Latin Dictionary*, 1158.

32. On Aristotle's view of children as biologically, ethically, and politically unfinished human beings, see Daryl McGowan Tress, "Aristotle's Children," in *Philosopher's Child*, ed. Turner and Matthews, 19–44.

33. Aristotle, *Poetics*, 1449a.

34. Terry Eagleton, *The Ideology of the Aesthetic* (Oxford: Blackwell, 1990), 15.

35. Ibid., 16.

36. A gendered critique of *Aesthetica* might begin by noting that aesthetics and logic, represented as younger and older sister, and nature, referred to as "Lady Nature [*domina natura*]" (*A* 58), are marked as feminine, whereas all aestheticians are marked as masculine.

AFTERWORD

1. Rousseau, *Œuvres complètes*, vol. 4, 241.

2. Rousseau, *Emile*, trans. Bloom, 33.

3. Rousseau, *Émile*, trans. Foxley, 1.

4. For a discussion of Pufendorf's moral epistemology, including a number of statements on maturation, see T. J. Hochstrasser, *Natural Law Theories in the Early Enlightenment* (Cambridge: Cambridge University Press, 2000), 86–95.

5. For an interesting note on the role of play in Gadamer's magnum opus, *Wahrheit und Methode* [*Truth and Method*], see David Ellison, "Camus and the Rhetoric of Dizziness: La Chute," *Contemporary Literature* 24.3 (1983): 322–48; here 334–35.

6. On "the human race in its childhood," see Johann Gottfried Herder, *Schriften zu Philosophie, Literatur, Kunst, und Altertum, 1774–1787*, ed. Jürgen Brummack and Martin Bollacher (Frankfurt am Main: Deutscher Klassiker, 1994), 16. On "the child-age of history," see Georg Wilhelm Friedrich Hegel, *Vorlesungen über die Philosophie der Geschichte* (Frankfurt am Main: Suhrkamp, 1986), 135.

APPENDIX

1. See above, p. 195. [Bayle here refers to *RQP* vol. 2, chapter 87, where he first mentions the debate between Jurieu and Nicole.]

2. Ibid, p. 197.

3. Nicole, *Unity*, book 2, ch. 2, p. 325 (Paris, 1687). [Pp. 257–58 in second ed.]

4. Jurieu, p. 141.

5. [Ibid.,] 79.

6. [Ibid.,] 92.

7. See above, p. 195.

8. Nicole, see above, pp. 326–27. [P. 259 in second ed.]

9. Ibid., pp. 327–28. [P. 260 in second ed.]

10. Here is a passage that Mr. Jaquelot should consider well.

11. Gal. 5:20

12. Ibid., pp. 329–30. [Pp. 261–62 in second ed. Bayle incompletely cites four paragraphs of Nicole. In the passages Bayle elides, Nicole paraphrases and cites from John 3:5 ("unless one is born of water and the Spirit he cannot enter into the kingdom of God") and 1 Corinthians 7:14 ("For the unbelieving husband is sanctified through his wife, and the unbelieving wife is sanctified through her believing husband; for otherwise your children are unclean, but now they are holy"); in Nicole, the passage is incorrectly identified as 2 Corinthians 7:14.]

13. See above, p. 331. [P. 263 in second ed.]

14. See above, p. 332. [P. 263 in second ed.]

15. Another passage that Mr. Jaquelot should consider.

16. Ibid. [Pp. 263–64 in second ed.]

17. Ibid., p. 333. [P. 264 in second ed.]

18. Ibid., p. 334. [P. 265 in second ed.]

19. Ibid., p. 336. [Pp. 266–67 in second ed.]

20. Gal. 5:21.

21. Ibid., p. 339.

22. Ibid., p. 340. [P. 270 in second ed.]

23. Jurieu, *On the Unity of the Church*, pp. 369–70.

24. Another passage on which Mr. Jaquelot should reflect.

25. Ibid., p. 373.

26. Ibid., pp. 374–75.

27. Ibid., pp. 376–77.

28. Ibid., pp. 378–79.

29. 1 Cor. 6:10 [Some Bibles, including the Latin Vulgate, distribute the list across 1 Cor. 6: 9 10. I do not know which Bible Bayle used here, but note 65 (below) refers to a 1665 Geneva Bible. This edition would likely have been based on the 1535 translation of Robert Olivetan (a cousin of John Calvin). The terms in Bayle's list, and their attribution to 1 Cor. 6:10 alone, are nearly identical to David Martin's revision of the Olivetan translation. Only Bayle's "those who live with males [*ceux qui habitent avec les mâles*]" is rendered differently by Martin, as "those who commit crimes against nature [*ceux qui commettent des péchés contre nature*]." This term (for what it is worth: *masculorum concubitores* in the Latin Vulgate, *die bij mannen liggen* in a 1618–19 Dutch translation) is the subject of much debate and various translation choices. See D. F. Wright, "Translating *arsenokoitai* (1 Cor. 6:9; 1 Tim. 1:10)," *Vigiliae Christianae* 41 (1987): 396–98.]

30. Gal. 5:19–21.

31. The poets do not speak at all of stones, but of a very large boulder, *saxum* [Latin for boulder], that Sisyphus must carry to the top of a mountain from which it falls down again every time he rolls it up, etc.

32. Jurieu, ibid., pp. 379–80.

33. Ibid., pp. 381–82.

34. Ibid., p. 383.

35. Ibid., p. 384.

36. One finds a trace of the same accusation in a sermon by Mr. de Langle, Minister of Rouen, given on 1 Jan 1655 on 1 Corinthians 10:32, printed the same year: see there pp. 57–58.

37. This is the system of the Church according to Mr. Jurieu.

38. See above, p. 1223.

39. See above, p. 1206.

40. Jurieu, see above, p. 377.

41. See above, p. 821, note 11.

42. That is, according to the force of reason alone: even the Jesuits regard it as invincible in this sense, because they contend that man has need of sufficient grace in order to do good.

43. The Macedonians among others. See Quinte Curce book 6, chapter 11 and the notes of Freinshemius.

44. See in Pierre Mattheiu's discourse on the death of Henry IV, p. 101, that which concerns the pain of Ravaillac's family.

45. "By this will (*eternal and omnipotent*), (*God*) willed and ordered the sin of Adam, so that in him all would sin and in sin be conceived, and accordingly all would be rendered subject to eternal death. Whence, indeed, has it come about that all men have in Adam become liable to sin and death, without remedy: except that God has so willed it? This has not come about naturally, namely that the fault of one man would exclude so many thousands of men from salvation. Thus it has come about by the will of God." *Zanchius, Observations on the divine attributes, book 5, chapter 2, cited in Wittich, On God's providence*, p.189. [My translation, Bayle's italics and parentheses. In the English translation of Zanchius I consulted, this passage is absent. See Jerom Zanchius, *The Doctrine of Absolute Predestination*, trans. Augustus M. Toplady (Grand Rapids, MI: Baker Book House, 1977). I have not been able to access a copy of Christoph Wittich's text to determine the source of the passage Bayle cites here.]

46. See above, p. 1200.

47. See above, p. 1209.

48. See above, p. 1210.

49. See above, p. 195.

50. Ibid., p. 197.

51. Jurieu, p. 379.

52. In the sixth book of the Aeneid.

53. This, as everyone sees, includes just about all men, whether infidels or Christians: the exception is almost negligible, not only among those whom one calls decent people according to the world, but also among the predestined.

54. See above, p. 187f.

55. See that which was said above, p. 190. But note that one must not understand this as a rigid universal truth. There are cases where the people approve that certain criminals are burned at the stake, as when François I thus executed several persons accused of heresy according to the famous public notices of 1534. No one had any pity for Ravaillac who was tormented in several horrible manners. See le Mercure François book 1, folio m. 455f. See also Pierre Matthieu in his history of the death of Henri IV and don't forget that which he says on p. m. 99 touching on what the judges discussed regarding the torture of this parricide.

56. Apply here the words of Pliny the Younger, *Letter* 22, book 8: "Let us always remember what was so often said by Thrasea, whose gift of sympathy made him the great man he was: 'Anyone who hates faults hates mankind.'" [Pliny, *Letters and Panegyricus*, vol. 2, trans. Betty Radice (Cambridge, MA: Harvard University Press, 1976), 69.]

57. Plutarch, in Solone, p. 87. I use Mr. Dacier's translation, p. 440, ed. in Holland. See also Horace satire 3, book 1, and Mr. Dacier's commentary. [Plutarch, *The Lives of the Noble Grecians and Romans*, vol. 1, trans. John Dryden, ed. and rev. Arthur Hugh Clough (New York: Modern Library, 1992), 117.]

58. See above, p. 1210.

59. See above, p. 1210.

60. See above, p. 1224.

61. As torture on the wheel was employed in France under François I against the brigands due to the crimes they committed. See Varillas in the history of François I, book 2, p. 246 (Holland, 1690) from the year 1535.

62. See above, p. 980 and la Bibliotheque choisie 10.7, p. 305f.

63. Jurieu, see above, p. 379.

64. That is to say that if God wished it, he would change the malice of their heart and grant them an ardent love of virtue.

65. Liturgy of the Last Supper. I use the edition of Geneva 1665 at the end of the Bible printed by Pierre Chouët in 4 [quarto]. See also article 26 of the Confession of faith of the Reformed Churches.

66. He said in ten rejoinders that the Protestant States have a full right to establish penal laws against sects, but that the Papist States do not have any such right.

67. See his depiction of Socinianism, p. 82. I have cited something from this above, p. 698.

68. If they are not formally Socinians, one sees well by their writings that at least they regard the Socinian heresy as a very minor thing, and the Socinians as people with whom it is not necessary to break communication. I confess that being this way and being Socinian, for me this is just about the same thing. Jurieu, preface to the *Treatise on Nature and Grace*. [Pierre Jurieu, *Traité sur la nature et la grâce* (Utrecht, 1688).]

69. The Anabaptists have had martyrs of which trial reports supply a great volume: and there have been Arminian ministers who have withstood exile, prison, etc., with constancy.

70. See above, p. 698.

71. As he wrote against the philosophical commentary [Pierre Bayle, *Commentaire philosophique sur ces paroles de Jésus-Christ : "Contrains-les d'entrer"* (1688, n.p.)]. And note that all Ministers who have written against the same commentary, whether in passing or expressly, deny that the good faith of the heretics exculpates them.

72. [Bayle alludes here to Matthew 23:24: "You blind guides, who strain out a gnat and swallow a camel!"]

73. Entitled *Janua Coelorum reserata*. [Pierre Bayle, *Janua Coelorum reserata cunctis religionibus a celebri admodum viro domino Petro Jurieu* (Rotterdam, 1692).]

Bibliography

Aarsleff, Hans. *From Locke to Saussure: Essays on the Study of Language and Intellectual History*. Minneapolis: University of Minnesota Press, 1982.

Adelung, Johann Christoph. *Versuch eines vollständigen grammatisch-kritischen Wörterbuches der hochdeutschen Mundart, mit beständiger Vergleichung der übrigen Mundarten, besonders aber der oberdeutschen*. Vol. 2. Leipzig, 1775.

Adler, Hans. "La lucidité de l'obscur: la fondation polémique de l'esthétique au siècle des lumières." In *Signs of Humanity/L'homme et ses signes*, ed. Michel Balat and Janice Deledalle-Rhodes, 221–28. Berlin: de Gruyter, 1992.

— — —. *Die Prägnanz des Dunklen: Gnoseologie—Ästhetik—Geschichtsphilosophie bei Johann Gottfried Herder*. Hamburg: Meiner, 1990.

Almond, Ian. "Leibniz, Historicism, and the 'Plague of Islam.'" *Eighteenth-Century Studies* 39.4 (2006): 463–83.

Archard, David. *Children: Rights and Childhood*. Oxon: Routledge, 2004.

— — —. "John Locke's Children." In *The Philosopher's Child: Critical Essays in the Western Tradition*, ed. Susan M. Turner and Gareth B. Matthews, 85–103. University of Rochester Press, 1998.

Ariès, Philippe. *Centuries of Childhood: A Social History of Family Life*. Trans. Robert Baldick. New York: Vintage, 1962.

Ariew, Roger. "G. W. Leibniz, Life and Works." In *The Cambridge Companion to Leibniz*, ed. Nicholas Jolley, 18–42. Cambridge: Cambridge University Press, 1995.

Aristotle. *Poetics*. Ed. and trans. Stephen Halliwell. Cambridge, MA: Harvard University Press, 1995.

Arnauld, Antoine, and Pierre Nicole. *Logic or the Art of Thinking*. Ed. Jill Vance Buroker. Cambridge: Cambridge University Press, 1996.

Atherton, Margaret. "Locke on Essences and Classification." In *The Cambridge Companion to Locke's "Essay Concerning Human Understanding"*, ed. Lex Newman, 258–85. Cambridge: Cambridge University Press, 2007.

Augustine. *On the Trinity: Books 8–15*. Ed. Gareth B. Matthews. Trans. Stephen McKenna. Cambridge: Cambridge University Press, 2002.

— — —. *Saint Augustine: Four Anti-Pelagian Writings*. Trans. John A. Mourant and William J. Collinge. Washington, DC: Catholic University of America Press, 1992.

Baumgarten, Alexander Gottlieb. *Aesthetica*. Hildesheim: Georg Olms, 1986.

— — —. *Ästhetik*. 2 vols. Ed. and trans. Dagmar Mirbach. Hamburg: Meiner, 2007.

———. *Reflections on Poetry: Alexander Gottlieb Baumgarten's Meditationes philosophicae de nonnullis ad poema pertinentibus.* Trans. Karl Aschenbrenner and William B. Holther. Berkeley: University of California Press, 1954.

———. *Texte zur Grundlegung der Ästhetik.* Ed. and trans. Hans Rudolf Schweizer. Hamburg: Meiner, 1983.

———. *Theoretische Ästhetik: Die grundlegenden Abschnitte aus der "Aesthetica" (1750/58).* Ed. and trans. Hans Rudolf Schweizer. Hamburg: Meiner, 1983.

Bayle, Pierre. *Historical and Critical Dictionary: Selections.* Trans. Richard H. Popkin. Indianapolis, IN: Bobbs-Merrill, 1965.

———. *Reponse aux Questions d'un Provincial.* 4 vols. Rotterdam, 1704–7.

Beck, Lewis White, ed. *Eighteenth-Century Philosophy.* New York: Free Press, 1966.

Bennett, Jonathan. *Early Modern Texts.* http://www.earlymoderntexts.com.

Blackall, Eric. *The Emergence of German as a Literary Language, 1700–1775.* Ithaca, NY: Cornell University Press, 1978.

Blackwell, Richard J. "Christian Wolff's Doctrine of the Soul." *Journal of the History of Ideas* 22.3 (1961): 339–54.

Boas, George. *The Cult of Childhood.* Dallas, TX: Spring, 1990.

Brown, F. Andrew. "On Education: John Locke, Christian Wolff and the 'Moral Weeklies.'" *University of California Publications in Modern Philology* 36.5 (1952): 149–72.

Brown, Saskia. "The Childhood of Reason: Pedagogical Strategies in Descartes's *La recherche de la vérité par la lumière naturelle.*" *Romanic Review* 87.4 (1996): 465–80.

Bruford, Walter. *Theatre: Drama and Audience in Goethe's Germany.* London: Routledge and Kegan Paul, 1950.

Buckle, Stephen. "British Sceptical Realism: A Fresh Look at the British Tradition." *European Journal of Philosophy* 7.1 (1999): 1–29.

Bunge, Marcia J., ed. *The Child in Christian Thought.* Grand Rapids, MI: Eerdmans, 2001.

Cassirer, Ernst. *Die Philosophie der Aufklärung.* Hamburg: Meiner, 1998.

———. *The Philosophy of the Enlightenment.* Princeton, NJ: Princeton University Press, 1968.

Clarke, Desmond M. *Descartes: A Biography.* Cambridge: Cambridge University Press, 2006.

Cleverley, John, and D. C. Phillips. *Visions of Childhood: Influential Models from Locke to Spock.* New York: Teachers College Press, 1986.

Conn, Christopher Hughes. *Locke on Essence and Identity.* Dordrecht: Kluwer, 2003.

Cottingham, John. "Cartesian Trialism." *Mind* 94 (1985): 218–30.

Cunningham, Hugh. *Children and Childhood in Western Society Since 1500.* Harlow: Pearson Education Limited, 2005.

De Grazia, Margreta. "Imprints: Shakespeare, Gutenberg, and Descartes." In *Printing and Parenting in Early Modern England*, ed. Douglas A. Brooks, 29–58. Hampshire: Ashgate, 2005.

De Man, Paul. "The Epistemology of Metaphor." *Critical Inquiry* 5.1 (1978): 13–30.

De Mause, Lloyd. "The Childhood Origins of the Holocaust." Lecture, Klagenfurt University, 2005. http://www.psychohistory.com/htm/childhoodHolocaust.html.

———. "The Evolution of Childhood." In *The History of Childhood*, 1–73. New York: Harper, 1974.

Descartes, René. *Œuvres de Descartes*. 11 vols. Ed. C. Adam and P. Tannery. Paris: Vrin, 1964–76.

———. *The Philosophical Writings of Descartes*. 2 vols. Ed. and trans. John Cottingham, Robert Stoothoff, and Dugald Murdoch. Cambridge: University of Cambridge Press, 1984–85.

———. *The Philosophical Writings of Descartes*. Vol. 3. Ed. and trans. John Cottingham, Robert, Stoothoff, Dugald Murdoch, and Anthony Kenny. Cambridge: University of Cambridge Press, 1991.

Diderot, Denis, and Jean LeRond D'Alembert. *L'encylopédie ou dictionnaire raisonné des sciences des arts et des métiers*. Vol. 1. 1760. New York: Readex, 1969.

Dunn, Kevin. "'A Great City is a Great Solitude': Descartes's Urban Pastoral." *Yale French Studies* 80 (1991): 93–107.

Eagleton, Terry. *The Ideology of the Aesthetic*. Oxford: Blackwell, 1990.

Early English Books Online. http://ets.umdl.umich.edu/e/eebo/.

Ellenberger, Henri. *The Discovery of the Unconscious: The History and Evolution of Dynamic Psychiatry*. N.p.: Basic, 1970.

Ellison, David. "Camus and the Rhetoric of Dizziness: *La Chute*." *Contemporary Literature* 24.3 (1983): 322–48.

Evans, Robert F. *Pelagius: Inquiries and Reappraisals*. New York: Seabury Press, 1968.

Ewers, Hans-Heino. *Kindheit als poetische Daseinsform. Studien zur Entstehung der romantischen Kindheitsutopie im 18. Jahrhundert: Herder, Jean Paul, Novalis und Tieck*. München: Fink, 1989.

Ferguson, John. *Pelagius: A Historical and Theological Study*. Cambridge: Heffer & Sons, 1956.

Franke, Ursula. "Analogon rationis." In *Historisches Wörterbuch der Philosophie*, ed. Joachim Ritter, vol. 1, 229–30. Darmstadt: Wissenschaftliche Buchgesellschaft, 1971.

———. *Kunst als Erkenntnis: Die Rolle der Sinnlichkeit in der Ästhetik des Alexander Gottlieb Baumgarten*. Steiner: Wiesbaden, 1972.

Furetière, Antoine. *Le Dictionnaire universel*. Ed. Alain Rey. Vol. 2. 1690. Paris: Le Robert, 1978.

Garber, Daniel. *Descartes Embodied: Reading Cartesian Philosophy through Cartesian Science*. Cambridge: Cambridge University Press, 2001.

Gerhard, Johann. *A Golden Chaine of Divine Aphorismes Written by John Gerhard Doctor of Divinitie and Superintendent of Heldburg*. Trans. Ralph Winterton. N.p. 1632.

Goethe, Johann Wolfgang. *Wilhelm Meister's Apprenticeship*. Trans. Eric A. Blackall and Victor Lange. Princeton, NJ: Princeton University Press, 1989.

Goodey, C. F., and Tim Stainton. "Intellectual Disability and the Myth of the Changeling Myth." *Journal of the History of Behavioral Sciences* 37.3 (2001): 223–40.

Gouhier, Henri. *La pensée métaphysique de Descartes*, 4th ed. Paris: Librairie philosophique J. Vrin, 1999.

Grayling, A. C. *Descartes: The Life and Times of a Genius*. New York: Walker, 2005.

A Greek-English Lexicon. Comp. Henry George Liddell, et al. Oxford: Clarendon Press, 1996.

Greenlee, Douglas. "Locke and the Controversy over Innate Ideas." *Journal of the History of Ideas* 33.2 (1972): 251–64.

246

Groß, Steffen W. *Felix Aestheticus. Die Ästhetik als Lehre vom Menschen.* Würzburg: Königshausen & Neumann, 2001.

———. "The Neglected Programme of Aesthetics." *British Journal of Aesthetics* 42.4 (2002): 403–14.

Haack, Susan. "'Dry Truth and Real Knowledge': Epistemologies of Metaphor and Metaphors of Epistemology." In *Manifesto of a Passionate Moderate: Unfashionable Essays*, 69–89. Chicago: University of Chicago Press, 1998.

Hegel, Georg Wilhelm Friedrich. *Vorlesungen über die Philosophie der Geschichte.* Frankfurt am Main: Suhrkamp, 1986.

Herder, Johann Gottfried. *Schriften zu Philosophie, Literatur, Kunst, und Altertum, 1774–1787.* Ed. Jürgen Brummack and Martin Bollacher. Frankfurt am Main: Deutscher Klassiker, 1994.

———. *Schriften zur Ästhetik und Literatur, 1767–1781.* Ed. Gunter E. Grimm. Frankfurt am Main: Deutscher Klassiker, 1993.

Herter, Hans. "Das unschuldige Kind." *Jahrbuch für Antike und Christentum* 4 (1962): 146–62.

Hertz, Neil. "Dr. Johnson's Forgetfulness, Descartes' Piece of Wax." *Eighteenth Century Life* 16.3 (1992): 167–81.

Heyndels, Ralph. "*Camera obscura* de la mémoire: Descartes." *Biblio* 17 (1993): 259–66.

Heyse, Johann Christian, and Karl Wilhelm Ludwig Heyse. *Handwörterbuch der deutschen Sprache.* Vol. 1. Magdeburg, 1833.

Heywood, Colin. *A History of Childhood: Children and Childhood in the West from Medieval to Modern Times.* Cambridge: Polity Press, 2001.

Higham, John. "American Intellectual History: A Critical Appraisal." *American Quarterly* 13.2.2 (1961): 219–33.

Hinson, E. Glenn. "Infant Baptism." In *Encyclopedia of Early Christianity*, ed. Everett Ferguson, vol 1, 571–73. New York: Garland, 1997.

Hirschmann, Nancy J., and Kirstie M. McClure. *Feminist Interpretations of John Locke.* University Park: Pennsylvania State University Press, 2007.

Hochstrasser, T. J. *Natural Law Theories in the Early Enlightenment.* Cambridge: Cambridge University Press, 2000.

Horace. *Satires, Epistles and Ars Poetica.* Trans. H. Rushton Fairclough. New York: Putnam's Sons, 1929.

Horrell, Joseph. "Milton, Limbo, and Suicide." *The Review of English Studies* 18 (1942): 413–27.

Israel, Jonathan I. *Radical Enlightenment: Philosophy and the Making of Modernity, 1650–1750.* Oxford: Oxford University Press, 2002.

Jaeger, Siegfried. "The Origin of the Diary Method in Developmental Psychology." In *Contributions to a History of Developmental Psychology*, ed. Georg Eckardt, et al., 63–74. Berlin: Mouton, 1985.

Jäger, Michael. *Kommentierende Einführung in Baumgartens "Aesthetica:" Zur entstehenden wissenschaftlichen Ästhetik des 18. Jahrhunderts in Deutschland.* Hildesheim: Olms, 1980.

Jolley, Nicholas. *Leibniz and Locke: A Study of the* New Essays on Human Understanding. Oxford: Clarendon Press, 1984.

— — —. *Locke: His Philosophical Thought.* Oxford: Oxford University Press, 1999.

Kant, Immanuel. *Critique of Pure Reason.* Trans. Norman Kemp Smith. New York: St. Martin's Press, 1965.

Kittler, Friedrich. *Discourse Networks 1800/1900.* Stanford, CA: Stanford University Press, 1990.

Kremer, Elmar J. "Arnauld's Interpretation of Descartes as a Christian philosopher." In *Interpreting Arnauld*, ed. Elmar J. Kremer, 76–90. Toronto: University of Toronto Press, 1996.

— — —. "Leibniz and the 'Disciples of Saint Augustine' on the Fate of Infants Who Die Unbaptized." In *The Problem of Evil in Early Modern Philosophy*, ed. Kremer and Latzer, 119–37. Toronto: University of Toronto Press, 2001.

Labrousse, Elisabeth. *Pierre Bayle.* 2 vols. The Hague: Nijhoff, 1963–64.

Lactantius. *Minor Works.* Trans. Mary Francis McDonald. Washington, DC: Catholic University of America Press, 1965.

Landgraf, Edgar. "The Education of Humankind: Perfectibility and Discipline in Kant's Lectures *Über Pädagogik*." *Goethe Yearbook* 14 (2007): 39–60.

Larivière, D. Anthony, and Thomas M. Lennon, "Bayle on the Moral Problem of Evil." In *The Problem of Evil in Early Modern Philosophy*, ed. Elmar J. Kremer and Michael J. Latzer, 101–18. Toronto: University of Toronto Press, 2001.

Latzer, Michael J. "Descartes's Theodicy of Error." In *The Problem of Evil in Early Modern Philosophy*, ed. Elmar J. Kremer and Michael J. Latzer, 35–48. Toronto: University of Toronto Press, 2001.

Leibniz, G. W. *G. W. Leibniz's Monadology: An Edition for Students.* Ed. Nicholas Rescher. Pittsburgh: University of Pittsburgh Press, 1991.

— — —. *Kleine Schriften zur Metaphysik.* In *Philosophische Schriften*, ed. and trans. Hans Heinz Holz, vol. 1. Frankfurt am Main: Suhrkamp, 1996.

— — —. *New Essays on Human Understanding.* Ed. and trans. Peter Remnant and Jonathan Bennett. Cambridge: Cambridge University Press, 1996.

— — —. *Opera Omnia*, vol. 1. Ed. Louis Dutens. Geneva, 1768.

— — —. *Philosophical Essays.* Ed. and trans. Roger Ariew and Daniel Garber. Indianapolis, IN: Hackett, 1989.

— — —. *Die philosophischen Schriften von Gottfried Wilhelm Leibniz.* 7 vols. Ed. C. J. Gerhardt. 1885; Hildesheim: Olms, 1961.

— — —. *Theodicy.* Ed. Austin Farrer. Trans. E. M. Huggard. Chicago: Open Court, 1985.

— — —. "Vom Naturrecht." In *Deutsche Schriften*, ed. G. E. Guhrauer, vol 1, 414–19. Berlin, 1838.

Lekschas, Jan. *Alexander Gottlieb Baumgarten.* http://www.jan.lekschas.de/.

Lennon, Thomas M. *Reading Bayle.* Toronto: University of Toronto Press, 1999.

Lessing, Gotthold Ephraim. *Philosophical and Theological Writings.* Ed. and trans. H. B. Nisbet. Cambridge: Cambridge University Press, 2005.

Link, Thomas. *Die Pädagogik des Philosophen Christian Wolff (Halle) aus seinen Werken zusammengestellt und durch seine Philosophie erläutert.* Bamberg, 1906.

Locke, John. *An Essay concerning Human Understanding.* Ed. Peter H. Nidditch. Oxford: Clarendon Press, 1975.

— — —. *Further Considerations Concerning Raising the Value of Money*. London, 1695.

— — —. *The Reasonableness of Christianity*. Ed. George W. Ewing. Washington: Regnery, 1997.

— — —. *Some Thoughts Concerning Education* and *Of the Conduct of the Understanding*. Ed. Ruth W. Grant and Nathan Tarcov. Indianapolis, IN: Hackett, 1996.

— — —. *Two Treatises of Government and A Letter Concerning Toleration*. Ed. Ian Shapiro. New Haven, CT: Yale University Press, 2003.

Loemker, Leroy E. "Introduction." *Philosophical Papers and Letters* by G. W. Leibniz. Dordrecht: D. Reidel, 1970.

Lovejoy, Arthur. *The Great Chain of Being*. Cambridge, MA: Harvard University Press, 1974.

— — —, and George Boas. *Primitivism and Related Ideas in Antiquity*. Baltimore, MD: Johns Hopkins University Press, 1935.

Luhmann, Niklas. "Die Paradoxie der Form." In *Kalkül der Form*, ed. Dirk Baecker, 197–212. Frankfurt am Main: Suhrkamp, 1993.

Luther, Martin. *Luther's Works*. Vol. 33. Ed. Philip S. Watson. Philadelphia: Fortress Press, 1972.

— — —. *Werke: Kritische Gesamtausgabe*. 120 vols. to date. Weimar: Böhlhaus, 1883–.

Martin, Raymond, and John Barresi. *Naturalization of the Soul: Self and Personal Identity in the Eighteenth Century*. London: Routledge, 2000.

Matthews, Gareth. "Socrates's Children." In *The Philosopher's Child: Critical Essays in the Western Tradition*, ed. Susan M. Turner and Gareth B. Matthews, 11–18. Rochester, NY: University of Rochester Press, 1998.

McCann, Edwin. "Locke's Philosophy of Body." In *The Cambridge Companion to Locke*, ed. Vere Chappell, 56–88. Cambridge: Cambridge University Press, 1994.

Meier, Georg Friedrich. *Alexander Gottlieb Baumgartens Leben*. Halle, 1763.

Mintz, Steven. *Huck's Raft: A History of American Childhood*. Cambridge, MA: Harvard University Press, 2004.

Müller, Anja, ed. *Fashioning Childhood in the Eighteenth Century: Age and Identity*. Aldershot: Ashgate, 2006.

Müller-Sievers, Helmut. *Self-Generation: Biology, Philosophy, and Literature Around 1800*. Stanford, CA: Stanford University Press, 1997.

Myres, J. N. L. "Pelagius and the End of Roman Rule in Britain." *The Journal of Roman Studies* 50 (1960): 21–36.

Nadler, Steven. *Arnauld and the Cartesian Philosophy of Ideas*. Princeton, NJ: Princeton University Press, 1989.

Ndiaye, Aloyse-Raymond. "The Status of Eternal Truths." In *Interpreting Arnauld*, ed. Elmar J. Kremer, 64–75. Toronto: University of Toronto Press, 1996.

Neiman, Susan. *Evil in Modern Thought: An Alternative History of Philosophy*. Princeton, NJ: Princeton University Press, 2002.

Nelson, Alan. "The Falsity in Sensory Ideas." In *Interpreting Arnauld*, ed. Elmar J. Kremer, 13–32. Toronto: University of Toronto Press, 1996.

New Advent Catholic Encyclopedia. http://www.newadvent.org/cathen/14210a.htm.

Nicole, Pierre. *De L'unité de L'eglise, ou Refutation du nouveau système de M. Jurieu: Nouvelle Edition*. Lille, 1709.

Niermeyer, J. F., and C. van de Kieft. *Mediae Latinitatis Lexicon Minus: A–L*. Leiden: Brill, 2002.

Niggl, Gunter. *Geschichte der deutschen Autobiographie im 18. Jahrhundert*. Stuttgart: Metzler, 1977.

Noonan, Harold W. *Personal Identity*. London: Routledge, 1989.

Oxford English Dictionary. www.oed.com.

Oxford Latin Dictionary. Ed. P. G. W. Glare. Oxford: Clarendon Press, 1982.

Parfit, Derek. "Personal Identity." *The Philosophical Review* (1971): 34–47.

———. *Reasons and Persons*. Oxford: Clarendon Press, 1984.

Pascal, Blaise. *Pascal's Pensées*. Trans. H. F. Stewart. New York: Random House, 1967.

Pinto-Correia, Clara. *The Ovary of Eve: Egg and Sperm and Preformation*. Chicago: University of Chicago Press, 1997.

Pliny. *Letters and Panegyricus*. Vol. 2. Trans. Betty Radice. Cambridge: Harvard University Press, 1976.

Plutarch. *The Lives of the Noble Grecians and Romans*. Vol. 1. Trans. John Dryden. Ed. and rev. Arthur Hugh Clough. New York: Modern Library, 1992.

Poppe, Bernhard. *Alexander Gottlieb Baumgarten: Seine Bedeutung und Stellung in der Leibniz-Wolffischen Philosophie und seine Beziehungen zu Kant; Nebst Veröffentlichung einer bisher unbekannten Handschrift der Ästhetik Baumgartens*. Leipzig, 1907.

Pritchard, Michael. "Philosophy for Children." *Stanford Encyclopedia of Philosophy*. http://plato.stanford.edu/entries/children/.

Ready, Kathryn J. "Damaris Cudworth Masham, Catharine Trotter Cockburn, and the Feminist Legacy of Locke's Theory of Personal Identity." *Eighteenth-Century Studies* 35.4 (2002): 563–76.

Reiss, Timothy J. "Denying the Body? Memory and the Dilemmas of History in Descartes." *Journal of the History of Ideas* 57.4 (1996): 587–607.

Ricoeur, Paul. *Freud and Philosophy: An Essay on Interpretation*. Trans. Denis Savage. New Haven, CT: Yale University Press, 1970.

Rodis-Lewis, Geneviève. *Descartes: Biographie*. N.p.: Calmann-Lévy, 1995.

———. *Descartes: His Life and Thought*. Trans. Jane Marie Todd. Ithaca, NY: Cornell University Press, 1999.

Ronell, Avital. "On the Unrelenting Creepiness of Childhood: Lyotard, Kid-Tested." Lecture, The European Graduate School, New York, 2001. www.egs.edu/faculty/ronell/ronell-unrelenting-creepiness-of-childhood-2001.html.

———. *Stupidity*. Urbana: University of Illinois Press, 2002.

Ross, George MacDonald. "The Demarcation Between Metaphysics and Other Disciplines in the Thought of Leibniz." In *Metaphysics and Philosophy of Science in the Seventeenth and Eighteenth Centuries*, ed. R. S. Woolhouse, 133–63. Dordrecht: Kluwer, 1988.

Rousseau, Jean-Jacques. *Emile or On Education*. Trans. Allan Bloom. N.p.: Basic, 1979.

———. *Œuvres complètes*. Ed. Bernard Gagnerin and Marcel Raymond. Vol. 4. N.p.: Gallimard, 1969.

— — —. *Émile.* Trans. Barbara Foxley. London: Everyman, 1993.

Rubidge, Bradley. "Descartes's *Meditations* and Devotional Meditiations." *Journal of the History of Ideas* 51.1 (1990): 27–49.

Russell, Bertrand. *The Philosophy of Leibniz.* London: Routledge, 1997.

Schindler, Stephan. *Das Subjekt als Kind: die Erfindung der Kindheit im Roman des 18. Jahrhunderts.* Berlin: Schmidt, 1994.

Schneewind, J. B. "Locke's Moral Philosophy." In *The Cambridge Companion to Locke*, ed. Vere Chappell, 199–225. Cambridge: Cambridge University Press, 1994.

Schouls, Peter A. "Arnauld and the Modern Mind." In *Interpreting Arnauld*, ed. Elmar J. Kremer, 33–50. Toronto: University of Toronto Press, 1996.

— — —. *Reasoned Freedom: John Locke and the Enlightenment.* Ithaca, NY: Cornell University Press, 1992.

Schultz, James A. *The Knowledge of Childhood in the German Middle Ages, 1100–1350.* Philadelphia: University of Pennsylvania Press, 1995.

Schweizer, Hans Rudolf. *Ästhetik als Philosophie der sinnlichen Erkenntnis.* Basel: Schwabe, 1973.

Senn, Peter R. "What is the Place of Christian Wolff in the History of the Social Sciences?" *European Journal of Law and Economics* 4 (1997): 147–232.

Simonis, Annette. *Kindheit in Romanen um 1800.* Bielefeld: Aisthesis, 1993.

Sleigh, Robert C. Jr. "Introduction." In *Confessio philosophi* by G. W. Leibniz, xix–xli. New Haven, CT: Yale University Press, 2005.

Solms, Friedrich. *Disciplina Aesthetica.* Stuttgart: Klett, 1990.

Sommerville, C. John. *The Rise and Fall of Childhood.* Beverly Hills, CA: Sage, 1982.

Spellman, W. M. *John Locke and the Problem of Depravity.* Oxford: Clarendon Press, 1988.

Strohl, Jane E. "The Child in Luther's Theology." In *The Child in Christian Thought*, ed. Marcia J. Bunge, 134–59. Grand Rapids, MI: Eerdmans, 2001.

Tertullian. *Tertullian's Homily on Baptism*, trans. Ernest Evans. London: S.P.C.K., 1964.

Tiedemann, Dietrich. "Beobachtungen über die Entwickelung der Seelenfähigkeiten bei Kindern." *Hessische Beiträge zur Gelehrsamkeit und Kunst* 2.2., 313–33, 486–502. Frankfurt am Main, 1787.

— — —. "Tiedemann's observations on the development of the mental faculties of children." Trans. Anon. *Pedagogical Seminary* 34 (1927): 205–60.

Tinsley, Barbara Sher. *Pierre Bayle's Reformation: Conscience and Criticism on the Eve of the Enlightenment.* Selinsgrove, PA: Susquehanna University Press, 2001.

Tress, Daryl McGowan. "Aristotle's Children." In *The Philosopher's Child: Critical Essays in the Western Tradition*, ed. Susan M. Turner and Gareth B. Matthews, 19–44. Rochester, NY: University of Rochester Press, 1998.

Turner, Susan M., and Gareth B. Matthews, eds. *The Philosopher's Child: Critical Essays in the Western Tradition.* Rochester, NY: University of Rochester Press, 1998.

The Unbound Bible. http://unbound.biola.edu/.

Uzgalis, W. L. "The Anti-Essential Locke and Natural Kinds." *The Philosophical Quarterly* 38.152 (July 1988): 330–39.

— — —. *Locke's* Essay Concerning Human Understanding: *A Reader's Guide.* London: Continuum, 2007.

Van Den Abbeele, Georges. *Travel as Metaphor: From Montaigne to Rousseau*. Minneapolis: University of Minnesota Press, 1992.

Van Den Berg, J. H. *The Changing Nature of Man: Introduction to a Historical Psychology*. New York: Norton, 1961.

Virgil. *Eclogues, Georgics; Aeneid I–VI*, trans. H. Rushton Fairclough. Cambridge, MA: Harvard University Press, 1999.

Voltaire. *Philosophical Dictionary*. Vol. 1. Trans. Peter Gay. New York: Basic Books, 1962.

Walch, Johann Georg. *Philosophisches Lexicon*. 1775 ed. 1726. Hildesheim: Georg Olms, 1968.

Walker, William. "Locke Minding Women: Literary History, Gender, and the *Essay*." *Eighteenth-Century Studies* 23.3 (1990): 245–68.

Walmsley, Peter. *Locke's* Essay *and the Rhetoric of Science*. Lewisburg, PA: Bucknell University Press, 2003.

Watkins, Eric. "From Pre-established Harmony to Physical Influx: Leibniz's Reception in Eighteenth Century Germany." *Perspectives on Science* 6.1&2 (1998): 136–203.

Watson, Richard. *Cogito, Ergo Sum: The Life of René Descartes*. Boston: Godine, 2002.

Weber-Kellermann, Ingeborg. *Die Kinderstube*. Insel: Frankfurt am Main/Leipzig, 1991.

Wellbery, David E. *Lessing's* Laocoon: *Semiotics and Aesthetics in the Age of Reason*. Cambridge: Cambridge University Press, 1984.

Wessel, Leonard P. Jr. "Alexander Baumgarten's Contribution to the Development of Aesthetics." *The Journal of Aesthetics and Art Criticism* 30.3 (1972): 333–42.

Wilson, Adrian. "The Infancy of the History of Childhood: an Appraisal of Philippe Ariès." *History and Theory* 19.2 (1980): 132–53.

Wolff, Christian. *Christian Wolffs eigene Lebensbeschreibung*. Ed. Heinrich Wuttke. Leipzig, 1841.

———. *Gesammelte Werke*. Ed. Jean Ecole, et al. 150 vols. to date. Hildesheim: Olms, 1962–.

Woolhouse, Roger. *Locke: A Biography*. Cambridge: Cambridge University Press, 2007.

Wright, D. F. "Translating *arsenokoitai* (1 Cor. 6:9; 1 Tim. 1:10)." *Vigiliae Christianae* 41 (1987): 396–98.

Yolton, John W. *A Locke Dictionary*. Cambridge: Blackwell, 1993.

Yousef, Nancy. *Isolated Cases: The Anxieties of Autonomy in Enlightenment Philosophy and Romantic Literature*. Ithaca, NY: Cornell University Press, 2004.

Zanchius, Jerom. *The Doctrine of Absolute Predestination*. Trans. Augustus M. Toplady. Grand Rapids, MI: Baker Book House, 1977.

Zedler, Johann Heinrich. *Grosses vollständiges Universal Lexicon aller Wissenschaften und Künste*, vol 15. 1744; Graz: Akademische Druck- und Verlagsanstalt, 1961.

Zimmerli, W. Ch. "Evolution or Development?" In *Herder Today*, ed. Kurt Mueller-Vollmer, 1-16. Berlin: de Gruyter, 1990.

Zweig, Arnulf. "Immanuel Kant's Children." In *The Philosopher's Child: Critical Essays in the Western Tradition*, ed. Susan M. Turner and Gareth B. Matthews, 121–35. Rochester, NY: University of Rochester Press, 1998.

Index